HOLD THE! BACK PAGE!

"FOOTBALL'S TABLOID TALES"

Harry Harris

HOLD THE! BACK PAGE!

"FOOTBALL'S TABLOID TALES"

Harry Harris

www.knowthescorebooks.com

First published in the United Kingdom
by Know The Score Books Limited, 2006

First published in the United Kingdom
by Know The Score Books Limited, 2006

Know The Score Books Limited
118 Alcester Road
Studley
Warwickshire
B80 7NT

www.knowthescorebooks.com

A CIP catalogue record is available for this book from the British Library
ISBN-10: 1-905449-91-7
ISBN-13: 978-1-905449-91-0

Jacket and book design by Lisa David

Jacket Photography by Thomas Skovsende

Printed and bound in Great Britain
By Cromwell Press, Trowbridge, Wiltshire

Photographs in this book reproduced by kind permission of Daily *Express*, EMPICS, Harry Harris

Jacket Photographs
Front cover; right hand side; clockwise from top left
- George Best captured the nation's hearts with his legendary antics
- Steve McClaren arrives at FA Headquarters to be appointed as England coach
- Alan Sugar adds 'Sir' to his list of achievements which included owning Spurs
- David Beckham regularly hit the headlines throughout his career both on the back and front pages
- Tony Blair, I can exclusively reveal, is not a liar
- Piers Morgan, my former editor at the *Mirror*, during some turbulent times
- Richard & Judy, appearing on their TV programme is one the great pleasures of my career
- Pelé, the greatest player the world has ever seen, who I interviewed at length researching my book about him

Front cover; left hand side; clockwise from left
- Ken Bates, took me to court twice – and won!
- Robert Maxwell, my former employer at the *Mirror*, whose story, I believe, is not yet over
- Sven-Göran Eriksson looks pensive during the 2006 World Cup

AUTHOR'S ACKNOWLEDGEMENTS

Special thanks to all those who have helped me throughout my career in journalism over the past thirty years, especially my current colleagues at the Express Group Newspapers. In particular, my *Daily Express* sports editor Bill Bradshaw, who has won awards himself as an on the road reporter, so knows how to deal with my welter of investigative material, and Scott Wilson, the Sports Editor of the *Sunday Express*. My thanks also to Editors Peter Hill and Martin Townsend for their very kind words at the beginning of this book.

Special mention to Denis Signy, who has been a great source of advice and help over those years, together with Vic Wakeling, the Leeds United chairman Ken Bates and the former Spurs chairman Irving Scholar.

I would like to thank Simon Lowe and his team at Know The Score Books, especially designer Lisa David who has done a wonderful job converting my life in newspapers into a beautiful design, for persuading me to write a book I thought would be best penned in another 20 years or so.

Perhaps there might be a second volume soon enough.

Harry Harris
October 2006

CONTENTS

TO LINDA

FOREWORD

I have known Harry for nearly 25 years. He was the first journalist I met after becoming Chairman of Chelsea and his opening phrases of "Woshapnin?" and "Wosnew?" are legendary. Harry is a fascinating mix of the occasional howler ("overlooking the Himalayas") and his steady stream of exclusives and exposés about the game. People will talk to him because he checks his facts and always respects confidences. We've had our differences, but they were resolved when our respective (now) wives knocked our heads together and we have been firm friends (despite the occasional spats) ever since.

Ken Bates
Chairman, Leeds United FC

Harry Harris has been Fleet Street's top football story-getter for more than 20 years and when he has a quarry in his sights, there is no escape. His favourite trick is to catch his man early – usually before they've had their first cough, still less a shower. When the phone rings with an especially piercing tone just after dawn, that'll be Harry. He is a telephone reporter par excellence; never takes no for an answer and invariably gets the answer he wants. When I joined the *Daily Express* as sports editor in 2002, I was delighted that after years of pitting myself against Harry – as fellow reporter or sports editor – I'd now have him on my team. And while the piercing ringing in my ear from Harry's calls can be just as jolting for me as for the subject of his inquiry, there is not a happier sports editor in national newspapers. To have him in my corner is the newspaper equivalent of a goal headstart for any football team. The remarkable lesson for any aspiring, would-be sports reporter is that Harry is as enthusiastic and unrelenting today as when I first met him in Newcastle more than a quarter of a century ago. He's certainly good for quite a few years – and awards – yet.

Bill Bradshaw
Sports Editor, *The Daily Express*

A journalist is only as good as his contacts book, so it is said in Fleet Street. Harry Harris has one of the most comprehensive lists of contacts in our profession. He has used it consistently over the years to provide this paper with exclusive football stories that have set a unique standard. Often copied, but never bettered. And he has set the agenda with a unique brand of investigative reporting that has won him an enviable reputation and some of the top awards the newspaper industry bestows upon its most distinguished writers.

Harry is never happier than when he is given the opportunity to expose just what goes on in our national game. His track record is unsurpassed in sports journalism.

Peter Hill
Editor, *The Daily Express*

Harry Harris, or 'Harry Harris-Exclusive' to give him his full title, has been a mate of mine for 15 years and an esteemed employee of the *Sunday Express* for five. He is, in my opinion, the true Voice Of Football because he never loses sight of the fact that, beyond the hype and the cash, the game belongs to the fans.

I admire his energy, his passion and his downright courage in standing outside the normal cosy clique of sports writers and rooting out the truths and stories which clubs and players would rather we didn't know.

In the end the game he – and we – love is always the winner.

I also admire his connections – does any football writer have a contacts book quite as wide-ranging as this bloke?

Most of all I admire him as a true friend.

All the best, Harry.

Martin Townsend
Editor, *Sunday Express*

I was Harry's Sports Editor on the old *London Evening News* back in the late 70s and his contact book then was among the best in the business. More important, when we needed back page leads for a first edition which went to bed at 7 am, he knew exactly who to call at what time. In the days before mobiles, he would rouse his contacts (including club directors, and some of the top managers of the era) as early as 6 am. He knew the early risers. The others, he'd spoken to after midnight.

Wherever they were, Harry knew where to find them. If Harry slept, I never worked out when. A few people (or their wives) did hang up on him, of course, but that never worried Harry. He'd give it five minutes, and call them again. Nine times out of ten, he got the story he wanted.

Vic Wakeling
Head of Sport, BSkyB

INTRODUCTION

Hold The Back Page was originally a Saturday night television programme on Sky TV, with four newspaper journalists sitting around a table debating the sporting events of the week and arguing about what was coming up. The show was devised after the first get-together which Sky hosted for the newspapers' top football writers to mark the start of the football season. The lunch has now become a very popular annual event.

Sky's Head of Sport, Vic Wakeling, listened and participated in the vociferous discussions as the wine flowed at that inaugural writers' lunch, and the debate continued long into the afternoon. It wasn't long before the format of that lunch was turned into a successful TV show.

I appeared on the Saturday night live programme on many occasions until, after several years, Vic decided that the programme had run its course and switched it to Sunday mornings and tweaked the format. It became *Jimmy Hill's Sunday Supplement,* set in Jimmy's mocked up kitchen to discuss the stories in the Sunday papers and develop the themes that were a regular part of *Hold The Back Page.*

Hold The Back Page often deteriorated into a slanging match between certain journalists who had their own agenda, and who wanted to hog the limelight and the microphone, attempting to dictate the conversation. Certainly it became more sedate when Jimmy got involved and it changed format.

But *Hold The Back Page* sums up my life in football journalism. My forte has been breaking big football stories and, as I told one of my many Sports Editors, of which Vic was one of the first, it always gave me great pleasure to shout '*Hold The Back Page!*' when I had picked up a belter of a back page 'lead'.

The book *Hold The Back Page*, delves behind those headlines, and tells you how the stories came about and also reveals, for the first time, the full truth behind some of the headlines and personalities, which have dominated football over the past thirty years.

As well as telling some of the secrets of the Movers and Shakers, the stars themselves, the managers and the administrators, the bungs and the blockbusters, it also gives an insight into how the job of being a football writer works.

The World Cup is a perfect example of the highs and the pitfalls of the job. I have covered World Cups since Mexico 1986 in the days of biros and note books, right through until the computer age, and laptops, mobile phones, and the internet. At the World Cup in Germany in 2006, came another first... travelling with the corporate hospitality sponsorship of Samsung Mobile, sitting in the plush seats just four rows behind Sven and the boys in Frankfurt and suffering and experiencing the heat at first hand along with the players and the coaching entourage. That provided me with another perspective of the opening game against Paraguay in Frankfurt.

World Cups are a rich source of stories, some bizarre, some intruiging, and this book will take you behind the scenes. For example, a national newspaper's Chief Football Writer trudged along the beautiful Sardinian beach in 1990, sweltering under the midday sun, booted and suited and struggling with his luggage. Along with the entire media corps of around 300 journalists, radio and TV crews, he had been sharing the gorgeous Forte Village resort, just three miles from the England team's base. We had been living in the lap of luxury for three weeks and the World Cup was still two weeks away from kick-off. Not too shabby!

But for this reporter the scenario was far from idyllic. He looked a bizarre sight as he plodded along, plunging his heavy size 10 brogues deeper into the golden sand, purposefully making his way towards my sun lounger. He wanted to thank me for all the help I had given him, compared to other writers who had made his life hell. He said he couldn't take any more and the pressure of filing 'live' during such a big tournament had taken its toll and he was going home. With that he turned and walked off as I squinted in the intense sun light until he disappeared. I have never set eyes on him since.

By no means is this an isolated incident. I've seen a football writer cowering under his bed, having called me out in the middle of the night declaring, 'someone is out to get me'. Other football writers have been mugged in the middle of nowhere as they took late night taxis in Eastern European footballing outposts. One returned from a late night on the tiles having been struck by an ash tray across his face. Another football writer was so upset with one of his rivals that he waited for his adversary to get out of a taxi one evening and punched him in the face.

Not all of these incidents took place in or around a World Cup, but they highlight the enormous tension that surrounds the coverage of major sporting events, the stress some journalists find themselves under, brought about by the pressure to get the big stories, exclusively, from their offices, who, of course, are removed from the intricacies of being there.

It might seem glamorous. And, yes, at times it is. First class travel, unless the bean counters are making the usual economies, five star accommodation, because you need to be near the action, and the team hotels are always in the best locations. Then there's the games themselves; the excitement, watching the players, listening to their interviews, studying the managers.

But there's a downside. The raised blood pressure when deadlines near, the palpitations if your main rivals come up with a big exclusive, the sometimes bizarre requests from the office to sneak into the England hotel and steal the team sheet!

So, with the life style comes the hassle. The two are never far apart. For Italia 90, England were based in Cagliari, the theory being it would be easier to contain the hooligans on an island (wrong). The Forte Village was the media centre, with sponsors laying on big screens to watch games, a free bar, and facilities you would only dream about. Bobby Robson was the England manager, noted for his eccentricities, and it typified the divide that existed between the England camp and the media.

After a Sunday newspaper exposé about a gorgeous, young, and single hostess and a couple of the England players, the training ground virtually became a no-go area for the press. The players had previous co-operated, and, however reluctantly, had been part of a rota system of interviews in the laborious build up to the games. Now, the players were on the coach and leaving the camp before Robson had finished his press conferences, which he was obliged to do by FIFA.

When a handful of the younger press brigade, fit enough to chase after the team bus, got within shouting distance of the players, a couple of reporters were spat on. No prizes for guessing that one of the charming players concerned was Gazza. It can be a delightful job at times!

I have covered five World Cups and the media has mushroomed beyond belief. At one time there was the Chief Football Writer from each British paper, and maybe the

No.2 who was the quotes man. Now there's the No.1, No.2, the columnist, the feature writer, the colour writer, the diarist, the news reporter, the blogger, the podcasters and two or three photographers.

When I travelled to Mexico with England in 1986, we were on the same plane as the team, and stayed in the same hotels, and there was a closer affiliation with the players, they often trusted certain journalists.

The FA didn't actually want the journalists with them, but the newspapers paid the travel bills, so the FA didn't have to cough up.

Glenn Hoddle's New England, with his alternative thinking and techniques, was partly responsible for calling a halt to the previous cosy co-existence. He argued that his players increased their fatigue by sitting on planes waiting sometimes up to an hour for the media to arrive for the charter flight. We were always as late as the last man, often a photographer struggling to wire the final picture.

Coverage is now dictated to by an FA communications department that has increased in volume almost as much as the media. The media are press conference obsessed. Every day, the manager, and one or two players are on press conference duty, while other nations usually have open house where the media can talk to just about the entire squad. The FA have also tried this method, but only use this rarely as the players don't really enjoy it. Paul Scholes, for example, was so shy he hardly ever gave an interview. And Paul Gascoigne, yes, him again, flatly refused to co-operate at times – little wonder when he was the target of some front page scandal, ranging from wife beating to kebab gorging.

The upshot is that nothing will keep the media at bay apart from results. Good results equals a good press and, effectively, good sales. Bad results lead to uncontrolled mayhem in the camp. Ultimately, the further the England team goes in a competition, the more newspapers are sold. The *Mirror* put up 250,000 extra copies a day when England reached the semi-final of Italia 90. Good news for England is good news for sales.

It's hard to gauge reaction 'back home' when you're out at a tournament, but every World Cup seems to create a siege mentality that grips the England camp once the adverse publicity kicks in. Graham 'Do I Not Like That' Taylor had a major a showdown with Rob Shepherd, a chief football writer at the time, who turned out for the manager's press conference looking as though he had just walked in from the night before – and no doubt he had.

Shepherd was a good footballer in his own right, at least for the England press team, was a great enthusiast for the game, and knew as much about the game as most managers. He had queried Taylor's team selection and Taylor turned on him. 'I don't want people here with a face like yours, Rob.' Shep bit back and told Taylor it was no surprise he looked like he did because he had no faith in his team and he turned out to be right. Taylor hired a personal PR to try to protect him from the hacks, but there is no shield from bad results when you are the England manager.

Hoddle himself was undone partly for writing a World Cup diary. He was savaged by a media that preaches freedom of speech, yet believed that the England manager should not be divulging secrets of the dressing room.

I have covered all the World Cups since 1986 in person, except for the one in Japan & Korea in 2002. the *Express'* Sports Editor, Bill Bradshaw, and I felt that, with the time difference, I would be better positioned over here making calls to find out what was going on behind the scenes. Immediately before the tournament began, I got a tip from an agent who told me that one of his clients inside the Irish camp had phoned him to say that just before he left the bar at midnight, Roy Keane had come up and said he was leaving the next morning after having an unholy row with manager Mick McCarthy, so if he didn't see him again 'goodbye'.

It was a great story. I remembered being in the Dutch camp to hear Ruud Gullit's farewell press conference when he walked out of the 1994 World Cup over racial divisions within the squad. But I had never heard of anything like this involving a British team.

So, as the huge media entourage actually at the event slept, or partied, I checked out this incredible story.

Keane's agent was the highly respected lawyer Michael Kennedy. I called his London offices. 'Not true', he told me with great authority. Of course, he pointed out, if all I had said about a row with McCarthy over training facilities, and a threatened walk out the next morning was true, surely he would know about it. And he didn't.

As it was pretty late here in England before they woke up in Japan, I really needed to be 100% sure of my facts to go with this story in our first edition, which went to the presses at around 8.00-9.00pm.

I went back to my source, who told me that the player concerned was a sober type and had not been excessively drinking that evening, was highly intelligent and would have related the conversation with Roy with incredible accuracy. That was good enough, I felt, to go with the story, and Bill backed me up – as usual.

Bill's vast experience as an on-the-road journalist gave him an astute insight into how these kind of stories can never be guaranteed, and on occasion you have to go with your hunch.

As a back up, I began making calls to the Irish team hotel at the crack of dawn. I rang and asked to speak to Mick McCarthy. He declined to come to the phone, but dispatched his assistant to speak to me. I put the facts to him, and although he didn't deny them, he wouldn't confirm them either, but pointed out that meetings were on-going, and they hoped to persuade Roy to stay. Fine, so trying to convince him to stay, meant that he had threatened to walk out. That was confirmation in my book. We were already running the story as the back page 'splash' and added the comment for the later editions.

Our rivals first got wind of the story when they saw our first edition, and then the Irish team hotel was bombarded with calls. Roy was persuaded to stay, albeit for just a couple more days, before he eventually packed his bags – just as we said he would do. From the day of our story, for weeks, months and even a year later, that story set the sports pages agenda. The whole episode has even been transformed into a West End play and earned the *Express* and myself the Sports Writers Association Sports Story of the Year 2002.

Before I hang up my note book and pen, my PC, and *Hold The Back Page* podcasts, my greatest wish is to see England win the World Cup again. Sadly the events of the summer of 2006 in Germany mean I will have to wait at least another four years. Who knows what stories they will bring.

Harry Harris
September 2006

ROMAN ABRAMOVICH, TONY ADAMS, SAM AND CRAIG ALLARDYCE, JEROME ANDERSON, OSSIE ARDILES, JIMMY ARMFIELD, GERRY ARMSTRONG, JARVIS ASTAIRE, RON ATKINSON

THE ABRAMOVICH EFFECT

ROMAN ABRAMOVICH
Billionaire Owner of Chelsea Football Club

The Russian owner of Chelsea shies away from the media to such an extent that he has never given an in-depth interview, but I managed to get pretty close to him when I was a guest of the club's sponsors Samsung Mobile in one of those plush £10m executive boxes at Stamford Bridge.

In fact we were in the box virtually next to his.

The security checks were intense when we arrived at the West Stand entrance to be admitted to the most expensive boxes in football, ready to be wined and dined in style in the up-market boxes that carry a £1m a year price tag with a minimum ten year lease. There were airport-style scanning machines, body searches, and scrutiny of accreditation.

There was no sign of Mr Abramovich in the corridors pre-match or even during the game as he kept his usual low profile.

Chelsea demolished Sunderland in the second half, and after plenty of celebratory champagne to wash down the earlier glass or two of champers, the Samsung Mobile box was the last to empty.

As we strode, or should I say, stumbled along the corridor, accompanied by a couple of Roman's minders, who had been instructed to help us find our way out of the establishment, we passed by the open door to the governor's box.

There stood the teetotaller, pretty bemused by the sight of so-called executives waving their drunken farewells to him!

That's as close as any journalist has ever got to the multi-billionaire.

Of course I penned a detailed account of Abramovich's first season as the owner of Chelsea, and I must say his aides were extremely helpful with a supply of information, and I even sent a copy of the manuscript to them to ensure there were no inaccuracies. Special mention should go to Roman's man in Moscow, John Mann, a highly approachable and very personable young American public relations point of contact.

ADAMS IS A "DONKEY"

TONY ADAMS
Reborn Arsenal and England centre-half

Arsenal fans have never quite forgiven me for Tony Adams being nicknamed 'The Donkey'.

As the one time England captain became synonymous with donkey chants over the years, Gunners supporters used to sarcastically mock my labelling of the centre-half – but in fact it is something that I cannot claim as my own. Believe it or not, I am the innocent party, and I have explained how it happened to Tony himself.

I was at an away game, which I was covering for the *Daily Mirror* at the time, when I heard some of the donkey chants coming from a small section of Arsenal fans behind one of the goals. Tony had a poor game, and the chants got a touch louder. And naturally, as they emanated from his own fans, I made reference to the chants in my match report, suggesting how unfair it was to taunt such an influential defender who'd had an off night.

Back at the old *Mirror* offices in Holborn on the third floor, the paper's sports editor Keith Fisher was hard at work putting to 'bed' that night's edition.

Now Keith was quite a colourful character in his own right. He was also a totally committed, hard-nosed, Gooner.

The usual procedure is for the writer on the spot to check in with his sports desk, and in my case as the chief football reporter, usually I would check in with Keith himself. I did so that night and stood in the freezing cold press box chatting away to Keith on the phone. As I did so, I sensed he was taking a more than passing interest in the donkey chants aimed at Adams. You tend to have a sixth sense about these kind of 'chats' and I pondered whether Keith had perhaps made this the main issue of my match report, and when I questioned him about it, he said he was just bringing it further to the fore.

However, when I picked up the paper the next morning over breakfast, there it was.... Adams Is A Donkey – my story complete with a mocked up picture of Tony Adams dominated the whole *Mirror* back page, his face superimposed on a huge pair of donkey's ears. I just prayed Tony had a sense of humour.

He didn't.

He was on the phone first thing that morning, shouting and swearing at me. At this point in his career, he was still one of the game's big boozers, although the level of his drinking habit was not really known and had certainly not been made public. Now he is a far more considered personality, calm and quietly spoken.

Not back then.

He was a pretty aggressive adversary, as most centre-forwards discovered, whether he was sober or not. However, I am sure there was a degree of mutual respect, sufficient for him to listen to my argument as I explained precisely what had happened. I told him I would speak to the Sports Editor and come back to him.

Whether it was the usual Keith Fisher bravado, or genuine sympathy for Adams, the Sports Editor invited the towering defender to meet him on the editorial floor of the *Mirror*, whereupon Keith would show him his backside and invite him to kick it!

I related this unusual 'apology' to Tony. He thought about it for a moment, then politely declined. Well, not politely, actually. He swore and told me to pass on his sentiments to the Sports Editor.

Keith Fisher was often extreme. However, he was intensely loyal to me for many years, promoting my work, calling me every morning every evening, and pushing me for more work, and the more I gave him, the bigger the headlines, the bigger the pictures and the best use of colour at the outset of the colour presses.

But just like Adams, he also had a drink problem. He couldn't get enough.

Sometimes he would call all his senior executives and a few hand-picked writers to a mid-morning conference – in the local pub. We would stay there for lunch, a liquid one in the main, and most of the afternoon, with the odd executive going back to the office to put into motion some of the more bizarre ideas that cropped up during these 'think-tank' sessions. As someone who couldn't keep up the drinking pace, I would always volunteer to return to my desk to write a few words to go with the headline grabbing ideas!

There was the odd occasion where I never quite made it back.

Once Keith invited virtually the entire sports staff to a cocktail bar in the Strand, where he was hosting a 'meeting' with Ian Botham and his agent on the pretext of sealing a new contract for the England cricketer to continue to write a column. Some excuse for binge drinking! By early evening, as we all stayed there from the mid-morning start, there must have been a dozen champagne cocktails lined up ahead of me on the bar, I was so far behind the rest.

I made a routine visit to the loo, but fell asleep there at around 6pm.

Everyone must have returned to the office eventually, but no-one seemed to notice I hadn't returned, until a colleague on another newspaper inquired about my whereabouts. Then, they realised I must still be back at the bar – somewhere.

Eventually I was carried out of the loo, and back to the office where they spread me out in Keith's office on his sofa until I came round enough to go home.

Keith eventually moved to the *Sunday Mirror* as Sports Editor, but, following a series of internal rows, his meteoric rise within *Mirror* Group newspapers was on the wane. After being squeezed out, he turned out in a wine bar with a white suit for talks about starting up a national sports daily paper... It never got the funding to get off the ground.

SAM AND CRAIG ALLARDYCE
Father & Son, manager & agent at the centre of the BBC *Panorama* 'bung' programme

Around February 2006, the FA were gearing up for a series of interviews for those who made the shortlist to succeed Sven-Göran Eriksson. One of my many FA insiders told me that Big Sam, manager of Bolton Wanderers, would be a contender, and that he would have strong credentials. The only issue was a lingering question mark over his connections to his own son Craig, who, as an agent, was involved in a number transactions for players joining Bolton Wanderers. There was clear potential for conflict of interest, possibly worse, which would not look good for Sam if he wanted the England job. I resolved to get to the bottom of this.

I deepened my investigation into the links between Craig and Sam, something I had been doing for some time. A year earlier I had received my one and only call from Big Sam. He was on tour with his club in the States and had got to hear about one of my articles in the *Express* exposing the links between himself and Craig. Big Sam was most polite during the conversation, but also indignant. But I assured him that there was no hidden agenda, that I had nothing against him or his son, and would not be deterred from presenting any evidence should I come across it. Big Sam reassured me that there was nothing to find.

Fast forward to the FA's convoluted headhunting process to find Sven's successor, and the issue of the potential conflict of interest was high on my agenda once again. I felt that Sam had a good chance of being offered the job if his veracity could be proved.

Then, during a conversation with my FA insider, a solution to the Big Sam conundrum was hatched. The idea was that I would attempt to persuade Craig to quit as an agent to give his father the best chance possible of fulfilling his lifetime ambition to become England manager.

I contacted Big Sam's agent Mark Curtis, and told him that I knew his client had every chance of becoming the next England coach, but he would fall at the final hurdle unless he could resolve the issue with his son Craig. Mark was instantly onside, confiding that he had tried on several occasions to persuade Craig to opt out of the agency business for his father's sake, if nothing else. Mark contacted Craig on my behalf, and supplied his mobile phone number.

Craig seemed to want to co-operate. I prepared a hard hitting back page 'splash' story of Craig's decision to quit. I had promised Craig that I would supply him with a copy of the article to satisfy his lawyer, who was extremely nervous of the tone of my interview. To reassure Craig of my best intentions I agreed to allow him sight of the article, something that I almost never do. However, that proved to be a big mistake for all concerned. Whether it was the lawyer who was reluctant or whether Craig got cold feet, he wanted to tone down the interview and suggest he would quit as an agent, only if his dad actually did become the new England coach.

I was livid. That was not what I had in mind and let Craig know it. Sheepishly he tried to wriggle, suggesting he only ever meant to quit if his father was appointed as England coach.

Quite rightly, the article was dropped from the back and made just a couple of paragraphs inside the sports pages.

And Sam's big chance to become England coach had gone.

The Bolton manager did well enough in his interview along with the other candidates. In fact, he was impressive. His Bolton chairman Phil Gartside is on the FA Board, and had given the FA the go-ahead to conduct their interview with his manager. Gartside had chosen to take the honourable course and wouldn't stand in his manager's way, a reward for Big Sam's immense achievements at Bolton. Gartside had also privately reassured fellow Board members that the FA had nothing to worry about concerning Big Sam's relationship with Crag and other agents.

It might have been enough, but in the *Express* I was producing fresh evidence of Craig's suspect dealings with unlicensed agents, much to the annoyance of Gartside, who called me to rant his anger. Gartside threatened legal action, warning me off. The conversation deteriorated into a slanging match, but nothing was going to deter me from writing the truth – and I told Gartside that.

I also reminded Gartside that he had told me that when Craig worked for Mark Curtis, the Bolton chairman had insisted that a clause was inserted in Craig's contract that he could not deal with any players coming in or going out of Bolton. Yet, here was Gartside trying to condone Craig using an unlicensed agent in a transaction involving – yes, Bolton. Relationships with him have been frosty ever since, but the hypocrisy is clear.

As the FA moved close to making their decision on who should be the next England coach, all the candidates were asked, during their interviews, whether they had any skeletons in their cupboards. You can see why the FA might want to ask it, but it was naive to expect anyone to own up. The FA wanted to have the moral high ground, in case anything came out of the woodwork, then they would be able to act as if they had been lied to.

Big Sam tried to reassure the selection committee that he had nothing to hide from his associations with agents. However, the FA had, just days before, been reading my exposé of how Craig had cut an Israeli agent out of a deal to bring an Israeli player, Idan Tal, to Bolton, and instead had used an unlicensed agent in his plot to snap up a tidy commission on the free transfer signing.

The ramifications were enormous. The Lord Stevens Quest enquiry was just up and running and clearly interested in my exposé. Little did I know though, that the producers of the BBC's hard-hitting investigative show *Panorama*, were just as interested. They were in the middle of their covert undercover operation to try to snare agents into admitting they offered bungs and tapped up players. *Panorama* turned their attentions to Craig. As we all now know *Panorama* had targeted Big Sam through Craig and did a fabulous journalistic job on Craig, filming him boasting about being able to influence his father's choice of player. But it fell short of actually finding damning evidence to nail Big Sam – and one has to question, whether after such a thorough investigation, there is any to find. Even so *Panorama* broadcast the accusations against Big Sam in their programme on 19 September 2006, who in turn threatened a law suit.

Prior to *Panorama*'s broadcast, I had got wind that they would attempt to link Craig and his father with bungs and I spoke to Craig, who said he would talk to me after the programme had been shown to give me his reaction to it. But the morning after the programme had aired, it was impossible to contact him. I've no doubt that he would have received thousands of calls.

I spoke to Mark Curtis, who told me just how 'pissed off' Sam had been and there was now absolutely no doubt in everyone's mind that Craig had cost his father the opportunity to become England coach. In fact I believe that *Panorama*'s programme ensured that Big Sam could never again be even a candidate.

But the BBC programme didn't reveal any new evidence which hadn't already been published in the *Express*. Here's how we reacted to that now infamous *Panorama* show.

"The main plank of the *Panorama* accusations that Sam takes bungs revolved around his relationship with Craig – and that was uncovered by the *Express* SEVEN MONTHS earlier. In fact *Panorama* actually showed two of the many hard hitting headlines from the *Express*, and one tame response in *The Sun* where Big Sam completely refuted our findings of conflict of interest between manager and agent son.

Here is how, in the *Express*, I broke the Big Sam-Little Craig story.

10 March 2006
    Back page: "Big Sam, His Son An Amazing Transfer."
    Inside pages: "*Express* Investigation: Craig in spotlight... Sam And Son In Tal Deal Row."

11 March 2006
    Back page: "Inquiry Set to Look into Bolton deal... Inquiry set to probe the Reebok."

At the time of this book going to press, Sam and Craig were still in the dock, with their future uncertain, threats of legal action being tossed around like confetti and the stench of illegal payments still surrounding football prior to the publication of the result of the Lord Stevens enquiry.

JEROME ANDERSON
Football Agent to the stars

Jerome heads Sport, Entertainment and Media Group and is one of football's ground-breakers. He was the first FIFA licensed agent based in the UK and represents high profile clients such as Thierry Henry and Rio Ferdinand. He also engineered Ian Wright's move from Arsenal goalscoring legend to prime time Saturday night TV presenter (see Ian Wright) and boasts rising stars John Obi Mikel and Micah Richards amongst his stable.

Jerome personally pioneered many of the changes which have shaped football in the last decade. By bringing into the country world class players who made a difference, such as Dennis Bergkamp, who transformed the image not only of Arsenal but the entire Premier League, Jerome can be credited with the vision of the much-heralded 'foreign invasion' (see Dennis Bergkamp).

The spin-off of Bergkamp's arrival as the first truly world class player to appear in the Premier League who was not coming to end of his career was that outsiders were able to see the potential in England, which had been a European pariah for so long since the events of Heysel and the resulting ban from English clubs competing in Europe. A number of top players followed and the value of the Premiership rose to become greatest in world football, taking over from Italy's Serie A.

I first met Jerome as I was strolling along the Avenell Road heading toward the press entrance at Highbury, when he stopped me to introduce himself. His top client at the time was Charlie Nicholas. Jerome and Charlie have remained firm friends to this day, and Jerome, as well as being hugely likeable, is an agent with whom I know I can get a straight answer to any of my difficult questions. That doesn't mean Jerome is indiscrete. If there is something that is confidential, he will simply tell me so and explain that he is unable to discuss it. Precisely how I like it. It's my job to find out what is going on, and once in possession of such information, I would then expect people to confirm it, and not deny something that I know to be the truth. There are many more unscrupulous football agents who do not have the integrity of Jerome.

One of his closest friends was David Rocastle. 'Rocky' had lost own father at four and used to call Jerome 'Dad'. Charlie Nicholas had brought Rocastle into Jerome's office as an outstanding 15-year-old talent and said, "this is a very special kid with a very special talent and I want you to look after him like you do me." Jerome kept his word as Rocky became a multiple Arsenal trophy winner and England international (see David Rocastle).

Just before Rocky sadly died in March 2001, Jerome made him made another promise: that he would look after his wife and kids. To do so he set up the David Rocastle Charitable Trust, which was recognised by Arsenal in their last season at Highbury as their headline charity. It was a highly successful partnership and, as well as taking care of David's family, the money raised has benefited a mix of charities, including cancer research and hospitals. It only goes to show that not all agents should be tarred with the same spiteful brush.

OSSIE ARDILES
Argentinian World Cup winner and former Tottenham manager

When he was still plain old Alan, and owner of Spurs, Sir Alan Sugar had the good sense to consult the 'professionals' when it came to some of his major decisions, such as managerial appointments. With Ossie, however, it was a question of the manager not taking the advice.

Ossie was one of my footballing heroes as a winner of a World Cup with Argentina in 1978. His arrival at White Hart Lane with compatriot Ricky Villa was a landmark in English football history. It is often credited with opening the floodgates for foreign footballing imports.

Ossie and Ricky were one of the main reasons for a change of direction for me, as their arrival convinced me I needed to return to London to cover this momentous event, rather than remain in the north-east with the *Newcastle Journal*, my first 'proper' newspaper.

A switch to the *London Evening Standard* was the start of my journey through some of the major tabloid newspapers in Fleet Street, the street synonymous with national newspapers, as it was there that the majority of the offices were situated, until the late 80s exodus to Wapping, Canary Wharf and elsewhere.

At the end of their playing careers, Ricky returned to his homeland to buy a ranch, while Ossie moved into management. After a successful stint with Swindon, followed by spells at Newcastle and West Brom, he was welcomed 'home' as manager of Spurs. He took on a challenge that Glenn Hoddle, at that time, shied away from. Hoddle had opted to join up with Ken Bates at Chelsea, but a phone call from Alan Sugar nearly scuppered Hod's planned management move to Stamford Bridge.

I contacted Glenn and asked him whether he would consider Spurs. He thought about it overnight, and told me that he was heading for Chelsea, and didn't feel the time was right to become Spurs boss, no matter how tempting. He felt it was far too 'political' to be the one to replace Terry Venables, with the fans siding with the ousted Chief Executive who had crossed swords with Sugar. In my view, Hoddle made the right judgment call.

But Ardiles took up the baton, and was well equipped to take on the political fallout from the Venables regime, and he won the hearts of the Spurs fans with a cavalier style, that became known as the Famous Five.

With Jürgen Klinsmann, and an array of attacking talent, Spurs were often a joy to watch going forward, but defensively they became a nightmare, and, for all of their attacking flair, there were large gaps at the back for opponents to exploit.

Determined to help Ossie as the sack rapidly approached in 1994, I convinced Alan that all that was required was a strong-minded defensive coach to organise a way of halting the leakage of goals. I suggested former England assistant coach Don Howe, and the chairman was persuaded by me, but Alan told me that he couldn't just pull in someone without consulting Ossie and that it would have to be Ossie's decision to go ahead. I contacted Don, whom I had known for many years, and had come to respect, not just for his extraordinary prowess as a coach, but for his honesty and integrity. Typically, Don showed all of those characteristics, and agreed with me that he would like to become the Spurs defensive mastermind, on the proviso that Ossie himself made the request. He, like the chairman, was uncomfortable to press ahead otherwise, and wanted the manager to call him.

I spoke with Ossie about the advantages, and he said he would think about it overnight.

But the next day he said a firm 'no'. Ossie had teamed up with playing pal and coach Steve Perryman, and he felt it would be an insult to Steve, who had played a record number of times for Spurs as a midfield star, or at times at full-back, and had sufficient experience to organise the defence. Ossie passed by the opportunity to recruit Don and results took a turn for the worse. Spurs were dumped out of the FA Cup at Notts County and Ossie was headed for the sack.

Alan told me at the time that it was one of the toughest decisions he has ever had to make in football because he liked Ossie so much, and there was always a nagging feeling at the back of his mind that Ossie could have succeeded at his beloved "Tott-ing-ham'.

Despite the hurt of being sacked at Spurs, Ossie continued to strive to be successful in management, even though he was forced to leave the country to try his luck in Japan.

Ossie and I have remained firm friends, and only recently I received a series of emails from him from Spain...

From: "Osvaldo Ardiles". To: harry.harris. Subject: Hello.
Date: Mon, Mar 20, 2006, 11:56 AM
    Dear Harry, Are you here? Kind regards. Ossie.

From: "harry harris" To: Osvaldo Ardiles Subject: Re: Hello
Date: Mon, 20 Mar 2006 13:14:26 +0000.
    Hi Ossie. Miss you very much. It would be great to see you again. Are you going to the Spurs reunion evening at the Dorchester next Sunday – I do hope so. Love to all the family. How are they doing? hh

From: "Osvaldo Ardiles". To: harry.harris. Subject: Hello.
Date: Mon, Mar 20, 2006, 09:23 PM
    Dear Harry, You are alive! Alleluia! I am in Marbella, Spain. What happens next Sunday in The Dorchester? Whatever it is, you did not invite me. I am going to England for Easter and for the Spurs '81 team dinner the 26th of April. I would give my son, Pablo, your email address. He wants to contact you and explain. You would have to do something with me (Interview, I think). Living these days more in Spain than in England. However, this could change if I get a job over there. GET ME A JOB! Hope everything is fine. Kind regards. Ossie.

From: "harry harris" To: Osvaldo Ardiles Subject: Re: Hello
Date: Tue, 21 Mar 2006 08:33:31 +0000.
    Hi Ossie....great to hear from you. Yes, the Spurs '81 team dinner is at the Dorchester on the 26th – see you there and yes, let's get you a job back in England – we miss you....and please do give Pablo my email address. Love hh

From: "Osvaldo Ardiles" To: harry.harris Subject: Re: Hello
Date: Tue, Mar 21, 2006, 1:25 PM.
    I will pass your email to Pablo and he will contact you. Thanks and see you the 26th if not before. Kind regards. Oss

From: "harry harris" To: Osvaldo Ardiles Subject: Re: Hello
Date: Tue, 21 Mar 2006 14:21:40 +0000.
    lovely

From: "Osvaldo Ardiles" To: harry.harris Subject: Re: Hello
Date: Tue, Mar 21, 2006, 14:35 PM.
    Not fxxxxxx 'lovely', get me a fxxxxxx job!!!

JIMMY ARMFIELD
Former England captain and FiveLive's top co-commentator

Uncle Jim is one of the great Gentleman of football, and when he became a key figure behind the scenes at the FA after being entrusted with the task of recommending a coach to succeed Graham Taylor in charge of England, he would always be on hand to provide advice if ever I was running a story. If he had confidential information, he would stick rigidly to the principle that he would never break a confidence. But if I had something that I ran by him which was incorrect, he would make sure that I was aware of it. Also, he would always take the time to ask about my family and show a great deal of interest. If ever I had a personal problem, he was someone you could trust to discuss it with.

GERRY ARMSTRONG
Former Northern Ireland centre-forward and Spanish football pundit

Now a specialist on Spanish football after his spell playing in the country for Real Mallorca, Gerry's services are much sought after on TV and radio, while he is also the Assistant Manager to the Northern Ireland team under Lawrie Sanchez.

I first met Gerry when he signed for Spurs as a raw centre-forward from Irish football. We seemed to hit it off immediately. Once you've struck a friendship with Gerry, there is no-one more loyal.

From time to time 'offending' journalists are placed in a manager's sin bin, banned from press conferences, out of the loop of any inside information, and generally treated like shit. The crime might be minor; being ultra critical of the team, a mis-quote, an over the top headline… sometimes it doesn't take an awful lot to trigger a fit of pique from a manager, particularly one under pressure, and the majority are always under some sort of pressure or other.

I was relatively new to the job of football reporting, still working on the *North London Weekly Herald* group of newspapers, in the Tottenham branch office about 500 yards from the White Hart Lane ground in 1978. My beat was everything and anything related to Tottenham. I travelled to every one of their games, home, away, aboard, friendlies, even covered reserved and youth team games, so being on the bad side of the manager was not good.

For some reason around that time Spurs boss Keith Burkinshaw had got the hump with me about something, and I was being shunned by him. In fact he even told me that he would not cooperate with me for a full month, as that was to be my punishment.

Of course being so close to the club as the local paper, it was soon the talk of the entire football club.

Players at any club like nothing better than to 'wind-up' their manager if they can, and at this time the Tottenham stars enjoyed winding up Keith, a blunt Yorkshireman, who didn't see the funny side of their many practical jokes.

Several players were in the treatment room, and Gerry decided he would use me as a means of winding up the manager. He kept look out at the door awaiting the manager's arrival to check out the injured players prior to the weekend's game. When Gerry spotted

Keith, he rushed over to the phone, and pretended to be having a conversation with me, pretending not to have noticed Keith entering the medical room.

"Sure Harry, no problem, we'll let you have the team for Saturday. We've got a few injuries, so the team will be Jennings..."

Keith went bright red, screaming and shouting at Gerry, who told him that the players always gave this particular journalist the team every week. That made Keith even madder. And so it went on. Gerry never letting on the Keith that he hadn't been talking to me at all.

The real funny aspect of it all was that the players often did tell me their team! And it was mostly Gerry.

JARVIS ASTAIRE
Showbiz Entrepreneur

There are not many people as well connected in so many spheres of entertainment, from showbiz to sport, as 'gentleman' Jarvis Astaire. Jarvis is a big Arsenal fan, and he is well connected at the North London club. He is also a big boxing man, and has promoted some major fights. In the main, he is an entertainment entrepreneur, and someone I have grown to admire and respect over a long association. I have also enjoyed the occasional social function with Jarvis, and thoroughly enjoyed being his guest at a lunch at a highly fashionable restaurant in New York.

He is also one of the most influential people within the Variety Club of Great Britain, and I received one of the most welcome telephone calls from him not so long ago, when he informed me that I had won the Variety Club's Contribution to Sports Journalism award. It was one of the cherished moments of my career, to receive the handsome Silver Heart Variety club trophy from TV executive-interviewer Gary Newbon during a lavish lunch at the London Hilton on Wednesday 2 June 2004, and I must thank my *Express* sports editor Bill Bradshaw for the highly flattering page advert that he placed in the glossy colour programme.

Claudio Ranieri might have just been sacked by Chelsea owner Roman Abramovich in favour of Jose Mourinho, but the Italian was awarded his own Silver Heart for the dignified manner in which he accepted his inevitable departure from the Premiership club.

RON ATKINSON
'Mr Bojangles', the nation's favourite football manager until 'that' remark

Bravo TV recently acquired the TV rights for Serie A football in Italy to revive British TV coverage of Calcio after Channel 4 dumped their highly successful *Gazzetta Football Italia* from its Saturday morning slot. Bravo took the brave decision to hire Ron Atkinson as a summariser for one of the biggest games in the Italian calendar; the Milan derby.

It was a bold move by Bravo to utilise Big Ron, who has been ostracised by the main-stream television networks and also lost his column in the *Guardian* after his racist comment aimed at Marcel Desailly. Big Ron thought the microphone was switched off during a break in ITV's transmission of a Champions League game in 2004 and his indis-creet aside, referring to Desailly as a 'nigger', was, unfortunately for Ron, picked up in the Middle East. The resulting furore over here cost him his lucrative TV and media career.

Ron, of course, was one of the nation's best-loved commentators on the game after a long career in management, and coined numerous of his own terms which have become known as 'Ronglish'. Among my favourites are:

- **lollipop:** a trick performed by a player, often a winger, consisting of passing the foot over the ball in an attempt to fool an opposition defender (from the rhyming slang "lollipop stick" – "trick")
- **reducer:** a firm tackle made early in the game to reduce a skilled player's contribution
- **Hollywood ball:** an overambitious, showy pass

Getting involved in Bravo's Serie A coverage was Ron's first route back into foot-ball in what has become something of a rehabilitation, led by Bravo's commissioning editor Johnny Webb.

I was fortunate enough to be able to witness the rebirth of Ron at close quarters. As a guest of Bravo, I was invited to make the delightful trip to Milan, for an entertaining lunch sitting opposite Big Ron before watching him do his stuff at the San Siro that evening for the Milan derby. The co-summariser for the game was Lee Sharpe, fresh from his exploits with Abi Titmuss on the first series of *Celebrity Love Island*. Also reinvented as a TV personality, Sharpe was hired by Bravo to kick-start his career in football once again. But, unlike Ron, whose renaissance has come on apace in shows such as *Excuse My French* on BBC2 and *Big Ron Manager* on Sky One, Sharpe failed to make the early morning flight and missed the lunch, just about making it to Milan in time to be whisked to the game.

I spent the match in the TV gantry close to Big Ron and Lee to watch them in action for a column for the *Express*.

Ideally Big Ron wants to re-establish his credibility as a football pundit. But it's tough going. Bravo, though, were not impressed, that, after taking such a huge gamble in giving him his TV comeback, he went off to work for Sky One to make the documentary *Big Ron Manager,* about his involvement with Peterborough United FC during the tail end of the 2005/6 season.

Bravo decided, in any case, that they would "prefer to use other talent – like Gazza" for their continued coverage of Italian football. What a come down for Big Ron!

As for 'Lovely' Lee, the real reason he missed his flight was that "he was out drinking the night before." But give Lee credit, he made it to the ground on time, even if he missed the lunch, and, although up most of the night before, and arriving a touch dishevelled, his contribution to the footie debate was spot on and he still looked gorgeous! So, he will most definitely be called up again by Bravo; as the TV station made it clear: "yes, he is signed up to be a pundit this season."

B

EDDIE BAILY, ALAN BALL, GORDON BANKS, TONY BANKS MP, JOHN BARNES, JONATHAN BARNETT, JOHN BARNWELL, BRIAN BARWICK, MARTIN BASHIR, KEN BATES, GRAHAM BEAN, DAVID BECKHAM, DENNIS BERGKAMP, GEORGE BEST, TONY BLAIR, DANNY BLANCHFLOWER, DAVID BLOOMFIELD, JIMMY BLOOMFIELD, LIAM BRADY, RICHARD BRANSON, ALAN BRAZIL, SIR TREVOR BROOKING, KEITH BURKINSHAW, TERRY BUTCHER

EDDIE BAILY
Former Spurs and England forward and Spurs Assistant Manager

The players used to unkindly call Bill Nicholson's assistant 'Strawberry nose', but Bill liked Eddie and so did I. I remember as a young football reporter going into the back office that Bill used to share with Eddie at White Hart Lane, and I was always guaranteed a warm welcome.

I co-wrote Bill's autobiography and in it Bill described Eddie as one of the many jokers within the club that helped to keep spirits up. But Eddie had his own unique style. By all accounts he could produce some colourful language, particularly for back in the 60s and 70s. According to Bill, Eddie just couldn't get on with some players. Graeme Souness was one. Souness was at Spurs in the very early days of his career and even then was a spiky presence around the place. He was one of those players who made Eddie throw his coat across the dressing room and curse, much as he has done fans at clubs such as Liverpool and Newcastle during his managerial career.

BALL WAS BETTER THAN BECKHAM

ALAN BALL
The most effervescent of England's 1966 World Cup winners

Ballie is as bubbly a character off the field as he used to be on it. I've been in his company many times socially, and he has always been willing to answer any of my questions, within reason, whenever I have contacted him for an interview. Alan was actually Man of the Match when England won the World Cup in 1966, not hat-trick hero Geoff Hurst, and when I wrote the book 'This Time', published by John Blake, as a prelude to the 2006 World Cup Finals, there were those in the '66 team who told me they considered Ball to be a more valuable player than captain David Beckham in the 2006 England team.

GORDON BANKS
The greatest goalkeeper the world has ever seen

Gordon Banks and a few of the other Boys of '66 came along to help launch my World Cup book, 'This Time'. We all met up at first at W'Sens, a really trendy French restaurant, quite close to the main event at the Sports Cafe in the Haymarket. One of the key elements of the book was the '66 players analysing their opposite numbers in the 2006 England World Cup team.

When I rang Gordon about the book, he was most reluctant to discuss the merits of Paul Robinson or any of the other England goalkeepers. His inference was clear – that he was uncertain about their qualities and would rather not be negative.

However, four months later, when we met up for the launch of 'This Time' and I reminded Gordon of his refusal to be quoted at any great length in the book, he told me how much he thought Robinson had improved, and he felt more comfortable discussing the Spurs and England goalkeeper's qualities.

Gordon was by now reasonably complimentary about England's current No.1, as he observed on the eve of the Finals in Germany, "He is consistent, and has improved over the last two years. Sven well make him the No.1 for all the games."

But Banks was deeply depressed about the quality in depth of English goal-keepers and extremely worried that there are only a handful of keepers available for selection to Sven-Göran Eriksson playing in a Premiership which is now dominated by foreign keepers.

"Oh God, what will we do if Paul is injured?" the legendary Banks gasped...

Put it this way, his comments on David James were not very complimentary, to say the least.

TONY BANKS MP
Former Minister of Sport and raconteur

Over the years I had come into contact a lot with this Labour MP with a love of football and Chelsea in particular. He organised for me a House of Commons book launch for one of my first of many Chelsea tomes, on Ruud Gullit and his first season as a manager, when the club ended 26 years without a trophy and won the FA Cup.

It was one of the experiences of a life-time to have a private room in the House dedicated to one of my books, and there was a formidable turn out of some of Chelsea's legends, and even the grand old FA Cup turned up as well. Needless to say we all had our picture taken with the Cup.

When Radio FiveLive's outstanding commentator Alan Green and myself set up an internet site called 'Voice Of Football" I approached Tony to become one of the chief pundits. He was always outspoken and the fans responded to his views. I am sure Tony felt he could compete with David Mellor in the role of chief political football pundit.

Tony was also one of Tony Blair's many Ministers of Sport, succeeding Kate Hoey, and was certainly one of the most outspoken. He even advocated that any player earning his living in England should be able to play for the England team.

He also led the highly flawed campaign for England to host the 2006 World Cup finals. It was a vast waste of resources, both financial, and in terms of time and effort on behalf of the Government and the FA. There had been a deal hatched in the football corridors of power whereby the FA had agreed to support Germany's candidacy for 2006 in return for the Germans backing the FA's bid for the European Championships in 1996, which England of course won. At least that is what both English and German FAs thought had happened. But FA Chairman Sir Bert Millichip had a memory lapse. It was claimed that he had fallen asleep when the 'deal' was hatched. Whatever the real circumstances, behind closed doors UEFA were loathe to endorse England's bid for 2006 – but the FA went ahead in any case.

Although from time to time Banks and his team thought they were gaining pledges from FIFA delegates, it all went pear-shaped as most experts had forecast. I too was a sceptic, based on inside knowledge of the 'deal' with the Germans. However, the FA and Banks went on a charm offensive taking a selected group of senior football writers, myself included, to Zurich when they delivered their lavishly produced book which was their submission to FIFA. We all trooped along to FIFA HQ, then to a wonderful lunch in a smart restaurant on the banks of the river, before being flown back again; all first class at enormous expense to the tax payer and the FA. And there was my series of revelations in the *Mirror* that the FA had been trying their luck at an old custom, usually reserved for other nations, in offering all sorts of 'inducements' to the countries where there were votes on the FIFA executive to smooth the way to becoming the 2006 hosts. Coaching schemes, even part paying for one of the countries' national coaches, just about every little 'trick' permitted, or at least on the borderline of acceptability, was used, but all to no avail.

Just before Tony died in January 2006, there had been representation made to me that he would like me to help him write a book about the 2006 bid in which he would reveal some startling information. He was bitter, and threatened to blow the lid, but could never quite bring himself to do it. Whatever he really wanted to tell me in the form of a book, we shall never now know.

BARNES IS FAT, SLOW AND LAZY

JOHN BARNES
Dazzling Liverpool and England left-winger and double Footballer of the Year

Despite my run-in with John over the Pelé articles (see Pelé) and the great man's belief that John was carrying too much weight to maximise his true potential, it has not dampened my admiration for him as a player and a persona, but I do have my reservations about his prowess as an anchor man on his Five TV show. Five's highly accomplished PR Gary Double, who had plenty of experience of reporters from his time on the *Sunday Mirror* news desk, had the tricky task of announcing how Barnes was taking on a new role within Five's TV coverage. Although I was sceptical at first, Barnes does appear much more comfortable out in the field assessing the game, then sitting in the studio trying to present. He is no Gary Lineker.

JONATHAN BARNETT
Controversial Football Agent

"The football authorities claimed to have struck a serious blow against malpractice yesterday when England left-back Ashley Cole's agent was banned for 18 months, half of it suspended, for touting the defender to Chelsea. The Football Association is hoping that the tough sanctions imposed on Jonathan Barnett will act as a deterrent."...so reported *The Times* the day after Jonathan felt the full force of the FA verdict on his involvement in the soap opera which surrounded how his client Ashley Cole came to meet with José Mourinho and Peter Kenyon in a central London hotel to spark one of the biggest tapping up cases of all time and a story which ran for well over a year before coming to a head with Cole's last minute, deadline day move to Chelsea in August 2006.

The chairman of Stellar Group, whose company represents up to 300 footballers, immediately announced his intention to appeal against an "excessive and disproportionate" penalty, which included a £100,000 fine.

Not that the six figure penalty in itself will concern the man that Ashley Cole, in his book My Defence, describes as being chauffeur-driven in a Bentley.

But Ashley's agent did feel it unfair that he ended up being penalised more than the £75,000 Cole and José Mourinho were fined by the FA Premier League for attending the infamous meeting at the Royal Park Hotel in 2005.

The suspension of Barnett's licence had a serious effect on a guy I have known for many years, and whom I would consider a friend as well as a contact in the game. The verdict was spun as the FA getting tough, the penalty acting as a deterrent to others who might have thoughts of 'tapping up' players, but the timing was important, the case was heard a week after the BBC's Panorama programme that delved into tapping up and bungs. The atmosphere contrived against Jonathan as the sport's business practices were under intense scrutiny.

After a hearing lasting a day and a half, a four-man commission chaired by an independent QC concluded that Barnett had been "a prime mover" in setting up the meeting attended by Barnett, Cole, Mourinho, Peter Kenyon, the Chelsea Chief Executive, and Pini Zahavi, the agent. "We consider this a most serious case of its kind, involving, as it did, a leading English international player contracted to one of England's premier clubs... and also involving the Chief Executive and manager of another leading English premier club," a statement read.

Barnett's failure to accept any blame (he and Cole have argued that they had no idea that Mourinho and Kenyon would be at the hotel) also counted against him.

"There having been no acceptance by Mr Barnett of his guilt on these charges, there is no scope for additional mitigation in that respect," the statement continued. "We are wholly satisfied that there is need in this case for an element of deterrence."

It was the first time an agent had had his licence revoked for any period of time by the FA in connection with illegal approaches for players. The FA passed its files to both FIFA and the Israeli FA, but no charges were brought against Zahavi, who was beyond the English governing body's jurisdiction because he is not registered in this country.

The Barnett case brought to a conclusion an epic saga. As well as the fines suffered by Cole and Mourinho, Chelsea FC had to pay £300,000 for negotiating Cole's transfer over tea and biscuits rather than in the Arsenal boardroom and were handed a suspended three-point deduction. In his book My Defence, which was instantly savaged by reviewers on publication in September 2006, "Cashley Cole", as he was dubbed by the media, launched a fierce attack on his former employers at Arsenal and the Premier League for pursuing a tapping up case against him.

But Barnett's suspension from involvement in the game was not absolute. He was still able to conduct commercial transactions such as sponsorship deals for his clients, while other directors at Stellar would be able to take up their clients' contract and transfer negotiations,.

So why is tapping up so bad? It is acknowledged that it is a daily feature of the game, routine almost, but, it must be said, rarely conducted in a hotel room so conspicuously open to being found out. Being caught doing it so brazenly is one of the real mysteries of this case. How could anyone have been so naive?

Well, knowing Jonathan as well as I do, I find it very strange. I am still convinced there is more in it, that everyone is still protecting themselves or someone else.

Jonathan, though, has kept his counsel since the verdict. However he did confide in one member of the media he can trust. Yours truly.

He told me a month before the hearing that he knew he would be banned. In fact he suspected he would be made a scapegoat for all of footballs ills, and the fact that the FA were failing to get a grip on the continuing travails of the financial scandals surrounding the English game which Steve McClaren's agent Colin Gordon branded the 'dirty man of Europe'.

The day after his sentence Jonathan told me "They were out to get me, and they got me. It was a disgrace, so grossly unfair, a kangaroo court, just as I told you a month ago, just as I suspected it would be. What really pissed me off was that the Arsenal vice-chairman David Dein gave his evidence and then sat at the back of the 'court' to listen to everything. He was the only one who seemed to be afforded such privilege. But then again he is on the FA Board! And, quite appropriately he was made very welcome, everyone saying 'nice to see you' etc. Sounds to me like a fair hearing – doesn't it! I don't know, of course, whether David Dein's presence at the back of the room was putting undue influence on the proceedings, but how can one not think that?"

However, one leading figure believed that Barnett's reputation had been significantly damaged. Simon Jordan, the Crystal Palace chairman, an outspoken critic of agents, said: "He's been named and shamed. He's been vilified. He's been whacked in the pocket, which none of them like. From the point of view of his personal credibility, it's in the toilet."

Jonathan's reputation had taken an enormous battering and wasn't conducive for him staying on the Board of the newly constituted Association of Football Agents with his co-founders such as Jon Smith, Jerome Anderson and Mel Stein. Could the backlash against agents have begun with this case, or was it just FA posturing, as Barnett contends, to punish one man heavily and sweep everything else under the carpet?

Barnett put on a brave face, saying "The company will carry on. Much of our work is not related to football in any case, but I might just bugger off and spend a lot of time on my yacht."

JOHN BARNWELL
Chief Executive of the League Managers Association

As the Chief Executive of the Managers' Union, the LMA, John Barnwell is among the game's administrators I come into contact with on a regular basis. He always tells me that there's no such thing as an off the record conversation with journalists. By using such a premise, he is careful about what he says to reporters, but appreciates that everything he does say will be quoted. That way he knows precisely where he stands. Very wise.

BRIAN BARWICK
Former Head of Sport at BBC & ITV, and current FA Chief Executive

Brian's appointment as FA Chief Executive was an interesting one as I have known Brian in his capacity as a top TV sports executive for some time, usually bumping into him at airports around the world and always finding him approachable and interested in his football.

I wish him the best of luck in his post – he will need it – especially if the handling of the Scolari situation (see 'Big Phil' Scolari) during the hunt for Eriksson's replacement as England coach is anything to go by. The last three Chief Executives have all come a cropper in a relatively short space of time.

MARTIN BASHIR
TV Journalist, Interviewer of Lady Diana and Michael Jackson

As an interesting diversion from pure football, it was fascinating to be involved in every aspect of an entire TV documentary when I was employed as a consultant by Roy Ackerman at Diverse TV to make a documentary on Terry Venables for Channel 4's 'Dispatches' strand.

After a couple of months, it became apparent that Dispatches were in a race to screen the Venables story ahead of *Panorama*, where Martin Bashir was also working on the same exposé. Dispatches came out a week before *Panorama*, but afterwards I became very close to Martin and got to know him well enough to call him a personal friend. We talked about collaborating on a number of other potential football-related exposés, but never quite found the right subject.

Martin was working as a freelance for the BBC at this time, and was very ambitious and, of course, his documentaries with Princess Di and then Michael Jackson brought him to a global prominence which eventually manifested itself into a lucrative contract to work in the States.

KEN BATES
The Ken Bates Only I Know

There are few more colourful characters in football than Ken Bates. He is loved and loathed in equal measures, and the division is clear. Friends of Ken love him – because they know him. His enemies detest him – because they do not. There is no grey area for Old Grey Beard.

It is often perceived that he has a lot of enemies in the media. That is probably because he has taken a handful of them to task with litigation. In reality he has an army of followers, and I have seen so many of them respond positively whenever he throws a media lunch or dinner. They all turn up. In fact, he has far more friends in the media than most people would imagine.

But there are some who love to take a pot shot and, to his credit, he doesn't mind, provided it is accurate and fair comment, and not merely personal, abusive… and, of course, libellous.

He hates being described as "Blaster", a common practise among the journalists who have never met him, as the alliterative clichés are so boring to him. He actually speaks quite softly unless provoked – and you do that at your peril.

Some journalists fall into the category of 'detesting' the former Oldham, Wigan, Chelsea and Patrick Thistle chairman/owner, who now is attempting to rescue Leeds United from the well-documented travails of its previous regime which saw the club saddled with around £100 million of debt.

Ever since one of Ken's off the cuff comments about journalists "going back to their council houses, while he resumes residence in his 500 acre country mansion," he has drawn the line between himself and the media. But you have to put that 'offensive' remark to journalists into context; Chelsea had just lost to Middlesbrough in a play-off and been relegated from the First Division. And yet still Ken sat down to talk to journalists for two hours about the club's future, despite his personal bitter hurt over what had happened both on the pitch, and in the stands where Chelsea's hooligan element had again disgraced the club. Tired and emotional, Ken happily played along with the usual banter about Chelsea's relegation which came his way and at the end of it all he closed the debate by saying, "I'm knackered, and I'm going off to my 500 acre farm and you can all bugger off to your council houses!" Everyone present laughed. However, that humour of the situation has got last in translation, especially when the remark was reported totally out of context by a member of the press who was not even present.

To say Ken doesn't care what is written about him would be entirely inaccurate. Ken is sensitive because he is like all of us – if it's fair comment he will accept what is said, as he will accept constructive criticism. Get it wrong, and you will be consulting your lawyers. He refuses not to act when he believes he has been libelled because he is concerned about what the fans think about his club, and he represents the club and those supporters. The bottom line is that Ken is actually a fan, he does love his football, he is committed to the game and he has put his neck on the line and his wad on the table more than any other Chairman in the country. He has also rarely taken a penny from any of the clubs he has been involved with – another myth which I can dispel.

With Bates seemingly always fighting on so many fronts, its not surprising that few journalists get close to him. I pride myself on being one of the Chosen Ones. There are precious few media people allowed into his life, his home, and into his innermost thoughts. Ken is a strange mixture. But aren't we all. He can be unbelievably kind, and most of the time wouldn't want anyone to know about it (see Bobby Moore). He gives willingly to charities, takes on some hopelessly lost causes out of the blue, has been known to respond to a letter from someone in need and will help them out for no particular reason other than he thinks he ought to.

In his professional life, Ken can be utterly ruthless as he himself admits. He is not in the business of being popular, he wants to do what is right and that is not always easy. It draws criticism from newspapers and reporters. But any newspaper which makes the mistake of getting basic facts wrong can expect a letter from one of the country leading libel lawyers. All major newspapers are insured against libel, and have in-house legal deportments to deal with these matters, but they are often so busy that they hire outside firms of lawyers to take on individual cases. The in-house legal team's primary function is to settle as best they can, usually an apology and costs, or an out of court settlement. Libel actions can drag on for ages, often up to a year before they reach the court, despite attempts to fast track certain serious cases.

The fact is that he actually bought Chelsea for £1, albeit only the football enterprise and not the ground, taking on the players wages, but not the £1.1m debt which was transferred into the company that continued to own the land. However, for the shorthand purposes of most journalists, they just say he bought Chelsea for £1. Ken worked for 22 years without ever once drawing a salary from the club. Ask any club director and chairman these days if they would do the same? I doubt whether they would. His lovely wife, Susannah, often joked that she was fed up with having new players for Christmas and birthdays, rather than a fur coat. She was actually only half-joking on many occasions as Ken poured his own money into developing Chelsea into a club and team able to take on the best.

When Ken first took over at Stamford Bridge, I was working on the *Daily Mail* and broke the story that the bulldozers were waiting to knock down the Bridge. Bates was the one who actually leaked the story to me, purposely to undermine what he perceived as a plot for the previous owners to cash in on the site and sell it to property developers. Bates fought a fierce battle for control of the Bridge, a much tougher assignment than eventually fighting off Matthew Harding's power coup.

At the outset of our relationship, Ken would regularly call the office to enquire "What's new?" He was great value for back page headlines, ranging from his decision to erect electrified fences to keep Chelsea's hooligan element amongst their fans at bay, to walking into the club on day one and sacking the first five people he came across who he caught out not actually doing their jobs or doing a job that was totally unnecessary. Ken demonstrated his ruthless streak, but was proved right in the end as he transformed a ramshackled ailing clichéd 'sleeping giant' into a European force and, after winning control of the land, fulfilled his vision of Chelsea Village. He kicked out all the freeloaders, and alienated the fawning media who had been so welcomed in the past by the Mears family, the previous owners of the club.

That put a few media noses out of joint. But my guess is that there is a undertone of respect for Bates. Wipe away some of the personal feeling, and I think that no-one will argue that he did everything in his power for the benefit of Chelsea.

Despite my inside knowledge of his methods, I then famously fell out with Ken and ended up banned from the Bridge. My exposure into dodgy payments ended up costing Chelsea, and Ken, a record Football League fine. That didn't aid our relationship, to say the least! It is a reporter's function to expose these things however, irrespective of personal loyalties.

Then, came two high profile libel actions, as Ken wreked his revenge. They were the only occasions I have ever had to appear in a High Court witness box. Believe me it is a nerve-wracking experience.

The first libel action arose from an unfortunate sequence of events inspired by my then employer at the *Mirror*, Robert Maxwell. Maxwell already owned Oxford United, and was bidding to buy Watford from Elton John. But the Football League management committee, of which Bates was a member at that time, blocked Maxwell from being the simultaneous owner of two clubs. It was the first issue of its kind of dual ownership and, quite rightly, the League adjudicated that it was unhealthy for the game for one man to control two clubs. For example, what would be the perception if those two clubs were drawn together in one of the domestic cup competitions, or played each other in the same division?

Maxwell was under the impression that Bates would support his quest to buy Watford as Ken had told him privately that he was providing a public service by keeping the ailing club alive, and was most miffed at the outcome of the League's Management Committee meeting.

He instructed the Editor, Sports Editor and myself to conduct a poll among all the chairman of every single football club to ask their view about whether Maxwell was entitled to be free to buy whichever club he wanted. He fully expected fellow chairman, many of whom he had already privately consulted, to back him. Of course what a chairman said to Maxwell face-to-face, might not necessarily have been their true feelings on the matter. Sometimes it was easier to agree with Maxwell rather than to challenge him with the expected torrent of abuse that might follow. Worse still, no-one really wanted to get into a conflict with the proprietor of the mighty *Mirror*, either. So, my function was to collate the views and votes of the chairman, as the sports department set about this arduous task.

Then, manna for Maxwell's heaven, the Wigan chairman gave an interview to our man in the region, stating quite categorically that Bates, in his role on the Management Committee, should have ensured that Maxwell could own two clubs, as he, Bates, was the present owner of both Wigan and Chelsea. Well, that was headline-grabbing stuff.

However, it was not quite as it seemed. Yes, Bates owned both Chelsea and Wigan alright, but he was trying to sell his Wigan shares. The Wigan chairman's stand was that Bates had been interfering with Wigan policy-making board room decisions, which he was miffed with. There was an obvious personal agenda there and, quite rightly, the night lawyer on the *Mirror* recommended caution. We did not have Bates' response to these allegations, we only had one man's word about it, and there was no tangible evidence. I wrote the story anyway and waited for a decision.

Unfortunately, I had made the mistake of alerting Maxwell to the joyful news of how there were allegations that his perceived adversary on the purchase of Watford, was now shown up to be a dual owner of clubs. As the hours ticked away before the print deadline, there was a constant debate going on between Sports Editor Keith Fisher and the lawyers. Editorially it was blockbuster story; legally it was a minefield. Should we go with it, shouldn't we?

Again, I made the wrong call, suggesting that if Maxwell was happy with it, then it was his newspaper and he could do what he liked with it. Eventually Keith took the executive decision, based on the lawyer's recommendation, even after we'd done more ground work, had gone back to the source and even got a signed statement. The item was dropped.

At around 11.00pm the first editions rolled off the presses. About ten minutes later, Maxwell rang down from his lofty Roman-styled marble-pillared apartment above the *Mirror's* Holborn offices to see the fruits of our work on his pet subject. I had been summoned.

To access Maxwell's lavish apartment one emerged from the private lift to his front door, where usually the butler would respond. On this occasion, however, Maxwell himself greeted me, wearing a grotesquely small T-shirt and pyjama bottoms. It was not a pretty sight. He seemed his usual jolly self when he saw me, but his mood changed dramatically when he searched the front page, then the back, then the few inside back pages, but could find no reference to the story he was eagerly looking forward to seeing.

"Where's the story on Ken Bates?" he bellowed, in the tone of voice that sent shivers down your spine. Generally Maxwell treated me with a huge degree of respect, bordering on kindness; it was rare to hear him bellow at me. This was one of those rare occasions. It wasn't pleasant.

I waited for the immediate impact to quell, and then tried to explain how the lawyer had killed the story recommending caution.

"What do you think?" he asked.

Now, this was my big downfall. I should have merely passed the buck, but it was always compelling to be in such a position to make such influential calls. I told him: "You are the proprietor. Surely what you say goes. We have a signed statement from the Wigan chairman, and he is entitled to express his views, in conjunction with everyone else. Are we men or mice?"

That kind of challenge you know Maxwell would rise to.

"Quite right," Maxwell responded with an air of total authority. He reached for the nearest telephone line. "Get me the lawyer."

There followed a deep conversation, as the lawyer warned Maxwell of the consequences of taking a risk now and failing to be in a position to prove it later – exactly the advice he had been providing for several hours down on the editorial floor.

While us mere mortals had heeded the lawyer's advice, in fact, couldn't really go against it, Maxwell made the definitive decision.

"I pay you so you do as I tell you – it goes in. If you don't like it, f*** off."

Down went the phone. In went the article.

Out came the writ the very next day.

Maxwell summoned me to his offices again. This time he was booted and suited. Thank God.

He was in an upbeat mood. He had hit back at Bates, as he saw it, through the article, and he had enjoyed it. As for the writ, he assured me, that Bates would not take the matter to court. We had a signed statement from the Wigan chairman, and under no circumstances were we to back down. "If need be we shall see him in court," he said grandiosely before making this pledge to me: "I will personally stand up and tell the court exactly what I think of Ken Bates."

I relayed the word of Maxwell to the lawyers and to the Sports Editor. There was to be no backing down. But Bates continued with the legal action.

About six months later, we had to submit a plea of justification, explaining our side of the matter, which we did. This was seemingly heading to the courts. Two months later a date was set down for a four day trial.

During the week proceeding the court case, I tried to contact Maxwell. Usually, he would take my calls without fail. This time, it was another matter. As each day brought the court case closer, I began to panic.

The day before the trial in the High court in the Strand I bombarded Maxwell's office and even threatened to march up to his apartment for an audience.

Eventually, Maxwell took my call.

"The court case is tomorrow," I reminded him, also pointing out about his promise right at the outset that he would attend. We had no other witnesses and the Wigan chairman had now changed his tune and withdrawn his statement claiming he had 'got it wrong'. "That's a coincidence," I thought at the time.

"If I go to the courts," Maxwell explained, "the jury might not like me and the damages might treble because they will see a very rich man."

Then he added: "I want you to go to the court, go down on your knees and beg them for mercy."

I did not know what to say. I was stunned. I am pretty sure I said very little, if anything, apart from goodbye as I put the phone down. For sure, I was not going to beg for mercy, but I was at a loss to know what to do.

I contacted Ken Bates. Surely, he would listen to reason under the circumstances. But as I reminded Bates of this story while in the process of writing this book, he recalled, "I had been bombarded with calls from Maxwell's office in the 48 hours before the case. Bob's secretary wanted to talk to me urgently. Finally the calls became more frantic the night before and the morning of the case. I sent a message back to Maxwell's secretary. 'He's had weeks and months to sort this out with me. Tell him I will speak to him, when I see him in the High Court at 10.30 in the morning."

Bates also tells me now, "The odd thing about all of this is that I actually supported him on the Football League Management Committee, I did not oppose his proposal to purchase Watford. I had been at the GMX Centre in Manchester for a 6-a-side tournament and Maxwell had rung me asking for my advice and I told him, "buy the club – and argue about it later." Bob had saved Oxford, he had saved Derby and he could also save Watford. The decision to block him was taken by Graham Kelly, who was Chief Executive of the Football League. It was not take by me or supported by me, so it was odd that we should all be heading to court on this issue."

But that was Maxwell for you, if he got a bee in his bonnet he pursued it to the bitter end. And now I had allowed myself to get in the firing line between Captain Bob and Bates.

The barrister heading up our legal team gave a pep talk to Keith Fisher, the Sports Editor, and myself, telling us the best course of action was to be short and sharp with our answers, tell the absolute truth and under no circumstances make matters worse by repeating any insinuations about Bates' dual ownership or make any other allegations about anything to do with Bates.

Of course, Bates' QC kept me in the witness box for cross examination for a day and a half of tough questioning. Eventually I cracked and let rip into Bates, telling the court exactly what I thought had been going on.

It didn't go down too well, I don't think. I could see Keith Fisher with his hands in front of his eyes. And, of course, we had no evidence

Needless to say we lost. The jury's verdict was that we had, indeed, libelled Bates and the judge awarded him costs as well as £75,000 damages. Bates has always said that he treated himself to a new Rolls Royce on the back of his winnings, and I have no doubt that he did.

But we were not finished. There would be a second libel trial to come just two years later.

Bates held a couple of media bashes while he was at Chelsea, usually one pre-season to announce his intentions for the new campaign and the second just before Christmas. Everyone enjoyed Ken's hospitality, which was always extremely generous. He always paid, so what was about to come was a complete shock to everyone. Needless to say, around this time I was not on his guest list, however, one of my colleagues, in fact, the No. 2 football writer at that time on the *Mirror*, Nigel Clarke, a life-long Chelsea supporter, had been invited along.

Nigel returned to the *Mirror* offices much, much later that day, the worse for drinking as you would expect at a Bates Christmas bash, regaling us with a tale of how Bates had made an announcement just after dessert that he had, regrettably, an unavoidable doctors appointment, and would be leaving the party a touch early. Bates was enjoying the lunch at Drones so much, he had forgotten how late it had got and, even though his doctor's appointment was at nearby Basil Street, he went off to the loo, waited around for Nigel and told him to pay the bill and he would sort it out tomorrow. Nigel was spitting blood that the dozen journalists present had been presented with the bill, which they'd been forced to pay equally between them.

Being invited to a Christmas lunch and then left to pay the bill turned from a laughing matter to a potential major story as the Sports Editor Keith Fisher began calling the Chelsea chairman 'Scrooge'. There was an opportunity for some revenge on the paper's part.

Before you knew it, Keith had suggested that I write a news item about it and the cartoonist was drawing up a caricature of Bates as the famous Dickens character. Fisher instructed Nigel to speak to a number of the journalists from the rival papers who had been present to make sure that there was absolutely no margin of error, and that everyone there was sure that they had been lumbered with the bill after being invited to the Xmas bash. Fisher also decided he would wait a few days before publishing the story in case Nigel was in fact reimbursed by Bates.

A few days later Nigel had still not been paid and he reassured us all that everyone was equally shocked at what had happened. The *Mirror* ran the story with the cartoon.

Next day, the writ arrived. But this time we were confident we were on firm ground.

We then discovered that hours before Bates' lawyers had issued the writ, each of the journalists at the lunch had received their money back.

Fisher called in Nigel to make sure that everyone was sticking to their original story.

One journalist was not. He had happily received his money and now wasn't quite so sure that Bates hadn't actually said, just before his departure, that he would settle up with everyone at a later date.

Nigel signed a witness statement, although when push came to shove, no-one else was prepared to help the *Mirror's* cause. Inter-paper rivalry was at play.

With another court case looming large Fisher made it plain to Nigel that, unless he put up a good show in the witness box, he need not bother to comeback to the office.

The case did go to court, and Bates was no doubt pre ordering yet another Rolls Royce, as the whole case hinged on his word against one journalist, plus a statement from the one other reporter who had now wavered, suggesting that Bates had probably suggested he would settle up eventually.

The case did not seem to be going all that well, at best it was 50-50. The main point in our favour was that Bates had not paid up until the article appeared, but the evidence that he was not going to eventually pay was flimsy to say the least. And, of course, had had eventually paid everyone back.

In order for him to attend the court case, Fisher had ordered Nigel back from his duties covering the Commonwealth Games in New Zealand, and told him in no uncertain terms that if he had fouled up about his account of the lunch, there was no alternative – he would have to lie! It put enormous pressure on Nigel's testimony. The realisation dawned on Fisher that he had got too excited by office chit chat, and ended up getting carried away with a story that never really stood up.

We were on the back foot in the High Court. Then, by pure chance, during a recess, Fisher and I were talking about the case in the loo, mentioning how we felt that it was about time Bates got what was coming to him. Afterwards, I noticed one of the jurors emerge from one of the cubicles in the gents toilets. I thought that if that juror had heard our conversation, he might have had a more sympathetic view of our case; one that our lawyers couldn't have possibly provided. I have no way of knowing, of course, whether that member of the jury took any of that chance banter on board or indeed passed any of it on to his jury colleagues.

Bates predictably won his case. Around this time judges had been advised to direct the juries not to award vast amounts of compensation in these matters. This new directive had followed the Jeffrey Archer case when *The Star* was ordered to pay a grotesquely large £600,000 in damages, which had caused a public furore.

Now it was up to the judge to guide the jury as to whether Bates deserved £1m (another new Roller) or perhaps an amount something more akin to an extravagant lunch out for Ken and a few of his friends.

The award was £2,500, probably closer to an extravagant lunch than a roller. Costs, though, tipped the balance back into Bates' favour. It had proved a costly, time-consuming mistake. But Fisher felt it was a moral victory for us, as at least the libel award was down to £2,500 and so didn't make too much of a splash in our rival papers.

I always tell Ken that we finished 1-1 in the courts, but he insists he won 2-0, and I can't really argue with him, because in reality he did win both cases.

Ken has a wicked sense of humour, which is a mixture of fun and the outrageous. He actually went to the trouble of having a sign specially commissioned in my honour. 'Harry's Bar,' in wonderfully graphic and large blue type. It was strategically placed on the door of the Stamford Bridge press room toilets!

But my lasting memories of Ken Bates, is not about the court case, nor about all the conflicts that I either gave him or supported him on. It is actually getting to know him, and finding a guy who is far removed from his public persona.

A mutual respect and liking between Ken's wife-to-be, Susannah, and my wife Linda was the catalyst to repair all the previous animosity, and after a period of time Ken and I became firm friends once again.

For the opening game of a new season at the Bridge, the club were at pains to know whether I planned to cover the match. I did. And, when I walked through the press room door, there was Ken, with a fair gathering of hacks. He made a short speech and then presented me with the plague that had been on that toilet door for a couple of years.

Once forgiven, that was it. No grudges held, and it was almost as though years of attrition and court room rows had disappeared in the blink of an eye. In fact, Ken was more friendly than ever and remains so to this day.

My memories are of lingering lunches, wonderful conversation and the day when I broke the news to Susannah and Ken that I planned to marry Linda. The Bates's whisked us off to the Cavier House in Mayfair for a wonderful meal to celebrate.

One wonderful lunch organised by the press prior to a Chelsea European tie in Marseilles ended up with French tennis legend Henri Leconte, who was on an adjoining table, challenging Ken and his English contingent to a sing-song. The tennis champion was an avid football fan and had long been an admirer of Ken's and Chelsea. In fact a long-standing friendship developed between them from that lunch. After about 30 songs in both French and English, everyone had run out of ideas, when the curtain finally came down as Susannah opted for Rain Drops Keep Falling On My Head.

Susannah never forgets our birthdays, my daughter Poppy's, Linda's or even mine.

We do have a very special relationship. I cannot pretend I agree with everything he says and does, but at least he allows me to contradict him.

Sometimes Ken was the under dog and I would come to his rescue. To prove it I backed him in his battle with Matthew Harding, the darling of the media. I am sure Ken appreciated it. Even my Editor at the *Mirror*, Piers Morgan, was a confirmed Harding fan, so it wasn't an easy stand to take.

Ken Bates is a good friend to have, and a very bad enemy. You have to admire the old bugger for not holding a grudge. I certainly didn't – even though he had put me through two libel cases.

Now he jokes that I should libel him again – so that we could split the profits.

At least I'm fairly sure he is joking.

SPIREITES 1 HARRY HARRIS 0

GRAHAM BEAN
Former Head of Compliance at the FA

Football agent Jon Smith introduced me to Graham at the launch of the ill-fated Football Hall of Fame, one of Gary Trowsdale's many well-intentioned projects that soon hit the buffers. Graham was the former policeman who headed up the FA's Compliance Unit before he fell out with some of the organisation's hierarchy, and left to set up his own company called Football Factors, which has acted for a number of clients who have been successfully defended against FA charges.

I helped Graham with some of his investigations and, in turn, he answered my questions on various issues openly and honestly. One of them, in the 2000/01 season, centred around the financial affairs of Chesterfield FC. UK Sports Group had bought the club as it suffered a traumatic relegation from Division Two in 1999/2000 and the following season, under their owner Darren Brown's chairmanship, hundreds of thousands of pounds disappeared from the club's accounts and Chesterfield were also docked nine league points for attempting to cheat Chester City FC out of a proper fee for striker Luke Beckett. Although those guilty were eventually brought to justice, many supporters, players and officials felt they had been subjected to a persistent campaign by me to cause their club to be destabilised and fall into administration, thus jeopardising their push for promotion from the Third Division.

During that season, Brown was hounded out and replaced by a Supporters Trust which still owns the club today. After the final game, a 3-0 win over Halifax which guaranteed the Derbyshire club a place in the Second Division despite that penalty, star striker David Reeves lifted his shirt up to reveal a T-shirt which read 'Spireltes 1 Harry Harris 0' – a rather uncomplimentary message directed at yours truly. I had never wished my investigation to cause the team problems, but Brown had behaved improperly, as a court of law recognised later by sentencing him to four years' imprisonment for fraud.

TO HARRY, LOVE, DAVID

DAVID BECKHAM
Former England captain and marketing machine

Pride of place on my office wall at home goes to an England No.7 shirt personally signed "To Harry, Love, David Beckham". The shirt fits in well alongside two Pelé shirts, both also personally signed to me, another from George Best, plus several further shirts I have picked up along my travels. That is most definitely one of the perks of doing my job out in the field and I'm honoured to have been considered a good enough friend for those legends of the game to have taken the time and trouble to sign memorabilia for me.

After David's shirt arrived, I thanked him for it next time I bumped into him, which just happened to be at the launch of his autobiography, *David Beckham – My Side*, in Madrid. I reassured him that I wouldn't be selling it on EBay, unless I could find someone called 'Harry'!

I have known David since he first arrived in the England camp with his autograph book searching for the signatures of his heroes like Alan Shearer, Paul Ince and David Seaman, and I have felt that, amidst all the hyperbole and headlines, he has retained that boyish enthusiasm and love for the game. As a football pundit I am asked numerous times to appear on documentaries to comment about David and the Beckhams, who have dominated the last decade in terms of media profile and been at the centre of moving football from the back to the front and often feature pages of newspapers, plus into magazines such as Time Out, Men's Health and GQ, instead of the usual Shoot, Match and FourFourTwo.

Here is one example......

From: "Esther Dere". Subject: Questions
Date: Fri, Sep 5, 2003, 5:30 PM
    Hi Harry,
    Thanks for agreeing to do this interview at such short notice. A car is booked for you to get you to the shoot (Babushka, Caledonia Road N1) for 4pm, but do give me a call on the mobile if you want one earlier. Please find attached an outline of the questions. If there is anything you are unhappy with or feel you don't know enough about to talk about do let me know, and also if you feel we have left anything out, please let me know also. Could you also let me know whether you will be happy for your on screen credit to read 'Sports Journalist'. I look forward to meeting you on Monday.
    Esther Dere. Associate Producer, THE BECKHAMS, SHINE

WHY BERGKAMP NEARLY SIGNED FOR SPURS

DENNIS BERGKAMP
Highbury's Dutch magician

Footballer writers are often used as middlemen in transfer transactions as a means of circumventing the rules on 'tapping up'. We can write the headlines agents want for their unsettled clients to be overtly 'unsettled', we can moot rumours and then write the inside story once a transfer has been completed allowing both sides to air their grievances. And there's usually a lot of muck to be raked over after one of these highly public deals, so it makes great copy and sells plenty of papers.

It doesn't always involve newspaper men though. There have been plenty of high profile tapping up cases which we merely revealed rather than helped broker, none more so than Ashley Cole's face to face meeting with Jose Mourinho and Peter Kenyon in a London hotel while still under contract to Arsenal.

Usually, third parties do all the tapping on the telephone. Agents are the perfect conduit for such tapping up. On occasions football writers might know a player or an agent, or might just help with a contact number.

I'd like to say here and now that I have never taken any money, or 'bungs' for my involvement in such dealings. My attitude has been simple. My 'payment' for any such assistance would be the exclusive rights on the story. And my 'tapping' process has often been tapped into by chairman, directors, managers and agents. They shall all remain nameless, for now.

As I say, I have never accepted, nor would accept any cash payments of any kind. That's not to say I haven't been offered a cut of the transfer action. But I would be insulted if anyone offered me money and I would soon put them right. From time to time there have been insinuations that I have taken back-handers. The *Sunday Times* made the mistake more than ten years ago of actually suggesting it in print.

It was at the time of the George Graham bung scandal and, even though the former Arsenal manager was attracting column after column inches, the *Sunday Times* produced a whole page and back page cross reference accusing me of taking a bung from the FA in order to promote the Premier League.

At that time, I was very friendly with Colin Gibson, who was then the chief football correspondent of the *Daily Telegraph,* Steve Curry, who was chief football writer for the *Daily Express,* and Stuart Jones, son of the late radio football reporter Bryan, and the Football Correspondent of *The Times* and we got dubbed 'The Morris Men'. We got the idea to write books for the Football Association. With publishers Random House, under the imprint Stanley Paul, we pulled together a book entitled *The FA Complete Guide to England Players since 1945.* This was also around the time that I had produced some hard hitting investigative reporting on Terry Venables.

An FA Council member who headed up the committee that dealt with such publications once approached me in an informal, social environment, to suggest there was something he had spotted in the FA accounts relating to the Morris Men. I told him to have another drink, that he must be mistaken. I was at pains to ensure that the Morris Men 'deal' involved payments from the publishers, and strictly only from the publishers, to make sure it was an arms length deal from the FA.

One Thursday afternoon I received a telephone call from a *Sunday Times* journalist informing me that they would be writing an exposé on me and my involvement in payments from the FA in relation to promoting the Premier League. I told the reporter I had no idea of what he was talking about, explained the mechanics of the publishing deal to write an FA book, and made it clear that no payments were made by the FA to me for anything, let alone promoting the Premier League. He said he would get back to me. He did on the Friday and again the Saturday morning, saying he had returned to his source and was sure of the facts. I warned him that the facts were wrong, and he said he would publish my comment, which he did right at the end of the huge article that dwarfed the story on George Graham.

The country's top libel firm Peter/Carter/Ruck were on the case that very Sunday the paper appeared when I contacted top lawyer Nigel Tait at home. By the end of the week the *Sunday Times* had realised their error and printed a very large apology and paid my lawyers their costs, which within that week already amounted to £20,000. I could have taken the *Sunday Times* to court and to the cleaners, but Piers Morgan, the *Mirror* Editor advised against it, and preferred to have it settled immediately. His argument was that it is never healthy for one newspaper journalist to be suing another, and the legal advice has always been you can never predict how a jury would react to such a court case, when in general they would suspect both newspapers and their reporters. The likelihood would be a victory – but minimal damages, and the worry how the judge would award costs, so I agreed to accept the apology and costs.

Very recently one prominent Premiership chairman had the audacity to infer to me that he had heard rumours of journalists taking bungs. I told him about the *Sunday Times* saga and that I would not hesitate to sue for slander if he repeated any such allegations. Of course, he backed down, insisting he meant he had heard of journalists taking bungs, but not me.

Why is this under heading of Dennis Bergkamp? Well, there is a connection because Bergkamp would have been a Tottenham player, not an Arsenal star, if my attempts to take him to White Hart Lane had succeeded. Technically a tapping up, but not really, as I will explain the circumstances.

A very close friend of mine, a journalist in Holland, rang me to say that Dennis wanted to quit Italy, where he had not been enjoying his football with Inter Milan and had not scored a goal in open play all season, having netted just once from the penalty spot. The journalist told me Dennis wanted to try his luck in England, had always been a Spurs fan because of his boyhood hero worship of Glenn Hoddle, and asked if Spurs would be interested?

I rang Alan Sugar. He was still plain Alan Sugar back then.

Would the Spurs chairman like the opportunity to sign Dennis Bergkamp?

"Dennis who?" replied Alan.

"Dennis Bergkamp. He's a fantastic footballer, can score goals, make them, brilliant signing for Spurs and reasonably priced, something like £3m, no higher than £5m."

Alan said he would make some enquiries with his manager, Gerry Francis, and come back to me. I didn't hear anything the next day, so I called back the day after. Alan told me that he was thankful for my help, but that I should tell whoever I was talking to that Spurs were not interested. Gerry Francis did not fancy him as he wanted an out and out striker and he felt that Bergkamp was more of a midfielder. Gerry went on to sign striker Chris Armstrong from Crystal Palace.

Mel Goldberg, who has been a very close friend over the years, is a sports lawyer. He then offered Bergkamp to Arsenal and was shocked how the price suddenly went up to £7.5m. But that's another story.

Of course, it didn't take long for the Dutchman to make his mark in English football at Highbury.

THE BEST I KNEW

GEORGE BEST
Simply The Best

It is still hard to believe that only last summer George and I were strolling along the Kings Road to determine an ideal location to sit down and chat about football. George opted for The Trafalgar, opposite Chelsea Town Hall. George had one glass of white wine and I had a mineral water, followed by a typically good pub lunch for that area. George paid for the wine, I paid for lunch.

On the agenda was the book I was ghost-writing for George entitled *Hard Tackles and Dirty Baths* for publishers Ebury. My pleasurable assignment was to aid George in penning a history of football in the 60s and 70s, when he was dubbed The Fifth Beatle and became the first of the real celebrity footballers, but it was more a broad sweeping picture of all facets of the game in that era, the players, managers and teams who were rivals to Manchester Untied as well as about the Red Devils themselves.

The chat with George lasted a few hours, but only about a third of it was spent talking about the golden era of the 60s and 70s, as so much time was spent by George unburdening himself about more distress and stress in his private life. "Just look at these text messages," he said. I suggested that they were too private, so he told me about them anyway. He was suffering through an acrimonious divorce from wife Alex, who made herself famous with her appearance in the jungle on ITV's *I'm A Celebrity... Get Me Out Of Here!*, and I had some empathy with him about that.

But he had also launched himself into a new relationship. He wanted to announce to the world that he had got engaged, and he wanted me to write the story for my paper, but it was later decided to be a touch more cautious.

I had also ventured down by train to Forest Mear near Liphook to visit George in his health spa, Champneys, until one drinking binge too many persuaded the owner to chuck him out. George had been living there free of charge courtesy of his friendship with the owner, but even he'd had enough. At the time I met up with George in the foyer, he had just come out of the gym. He was looking fit and trim, and there was a sparkle back in his eyes.

But when I made arrangements for George to visit me at my home to carry on work on the book, at 10am, when he was supposed to arrive, he did not show up. I called him on his mobile. "I'm on my way", he told me.

It was the same story at 12, 1pm and 3pm. He never showed up. I later discovered that he was back on the drink and his mind was once again in a confused state of crisis.

There is no doubt in my mind that George Best wanted a second chance with his new liver, he loved life, and he had vowed to himself to live to a ripe old age. But he could not cope with such a tumultuous, complex private life, and he went back to the drink to help him forget. But the George Best I knew was a bright, intelligent man, who looked a touch grizzly with that grey beard to still be pulling such gorgeous women at his age. But whenever he walked into a room people stopped and stared. He was a celebrity, even though he was off the TV screens and seemingly out of sight.

For me there was only one George Best, and I am proud to say that, for helping him to write the book, he presented me with a signed shirt, which is personally inscribed. That occurred when he did actually attend one of our appointments in the offices of his agent Phil Hughes, who looked after him like a son, a stone's throw from Stamford Bridge. It has pride of pace on my wall alongside signed shirts from many footballing icons.

Yes, it was a sad end to a football legend. Perhaps when he was 30, had somebody asked him if he could carry on with his lifestyle and live to 60 he would have taken that. Perhaps we should remember George Best in his prime – the flowing locks, the mazy dribble, the wondrous goals with feet and head. A sublime footballer, rightly hailed as the best British player of all time and not that far behind Pelé and Maradona.

Perhaps we should, but we won't.

25 November 2006 now marks the first anniversary of his death, and it's still hard to take in that he is no longer with us. I was in the privileged position of joining the 300 VIP guests inside the polished marble Parliament building of Stormont just outside Belfast, where there was a Who's Who of footballing legends present to say goodbye to George at his funeral.

I had been invited by George's agent, who gave me instructions to be on an early Belfast flight from Heathrow. Aboard that plane were several other VIPs, including Bobby Campbell, who I knew from way back, and he introduced me to George's doctors Professor Roger Williams and Dr Akeel Alisa. On arrival at Belfast airport we were requested to wait in our seats while the other passengers disembarked and then we were directed to a special room, where we were served with breakfast. From there a coach took us to a hotel and we were all thanked, on behalf of the Best family, for attending. It was hours before the funeral, yet there were already people lining the streets intent on gaining the ideal vantage point, ignoring the drizzle. We had a guided tour and we were shown the site of the cemetery, while it was pointed out to us where he used to live, and, as we sat there, the emotions were already building up with all the flags at half-mast.

At the hotel, I saw many familiar faces, such as Pat Jennings and Gerry Armstrong, whom I had known for many years. Inside the hotel, I chatted at length to Martin O'Neill over a cup of coffee and told him how much the media missed him and that we were all hopeful of a swift return for him to football.

It was raining heavily by the time we reached Stormont, and it was quite a walk up the 66 steps, it would be some haul for the coffin bearers.

Inside, England coach Sven-Göran Eriksson had arrived with an FA entourage that included Chief Executive Brian Barwick and Executive Director David Davies. I spotted Frank McLintock, and Derek Dougan, who sat alongside Sir Alex Ferguson who had flown in on a private jet before rushing back to be with his team at Old Trafford for another emotional occasion in honour of George.

I had been asked by the BBC to be their guest on their coverage throughout the funeral and, although I didn't ask, I can imagine there might have been a sizable fee to go with it. But I declined.

You just couldn't help yourself overdosing on emotion in an electrifying 'State' funeral, the music, the eulogies, it was impossible to stop the tears flowing relentlessly. As well as the grief there was also humour as, in Denis Law's speech, he said the bookies were taking odds of 7-1 on whether George would turn up for his own funeral.

Everyone I came across was only too willing to share their favourite George Best story. They were filled with enormous affection, not just for the player, but also the man. This was not a day, nor a place, for his detractors. For everyone who climbed those 66 steps to Stormont Castle did so to pay their homage to a legend.

Bobby Campbell told me a dozen tales of how he covered for George when he still was playing at Fulham, despite regularly failing to turn up for training after too many late nights. Bobby told me, "As the manager I had the key to his flat as well as George. I was the only other person to have a key, and we put him up in a nearby flat in Putney. I would go round there every morning at ten minutes past nine to get him out of bed, and sometimes it just wasn't possible. But when I used to turn the key in the latch I always knew what to expect. When I pulled the bedclothes up there would always be a beautiful woman underneath as well as George. But he was such a charming guy, he had such talent and charisma, I was prepared to make any excuse for him, put up with anything, to make sure he was in a fit condition to play. I would even lie to the press for him, and tell them that I had given him a day off when it was impossible for him to sober up in time to train. They probably didn't believe me, but they loved George too. Sometimes, though, I would take him to the ground and make him run and up and the terraces until the sweat was pouring off him and he could do it because he was a sublime athlete. When he played, even in the twilight of his career, he was still be best I've ever seen."

Back at the hotel, there was a lunch laid on for all the guests, Irish stew or curry, and there George's son Calum came over to our table to say "hello" and thank us for coming. Bobby recognised Best Wife No.1, Angie. 'I thought you were Calum's sister,' he exclaimed as the pair hugged.

Around 300,000 people had lined the streets to watch George's cortege pass by, and it was compared to the outpourings across the nation when Princess Di's funeral took place in 1997.

TONY BLAIR
Prime Minister and keen football fan

The Prime Minister was charming, inquired about the state of the game, and has a genuine affection for football as I discovered when my wife Linda and I were introduced to him at Sir Alan Sugar's 50th birthday bash.

As you would expect from the Sugars, it was a grand affair organised by his wife and family and Alan's trusted aid and PR guru, Nick Hewer, at the Reform Club, and although Tony Blair didn't stay for the dinner, he did put in an appearance during the lavish evening of festivities.

The Labour party leader has been savaged in the media for daring to suggest that he sat in the stands to watch Jackie Milburn, when, at that time, he would have had to have stood on the terraces. But I can reveal there were seats at St. James's Park then, and it is quite feasible that the young Blair did have an affection for the black and white stripes and the centre-forward whose goalscoring record has only just been surpassed by Alan Shearer.

DANNY BLANCHFLOWER
Captain of Spurs' 1961 Double winning side

In my early days at the *London Evening News,* I would leave home at 6am. My usual route was to take the Brighton line from East Croydon to Victoria and then the tube along the Embankment to the Associated News building, a journey of just over an hour in order to be at my desk at 7am, in time to deliver early copy for the first edition deadline of 7.15am. At that time the *Evening News* produced seven editions a day.

My first Sports Editor was Peter Watson, who didn't live far from me. I hadn't been at the paper very long when I realised just how intense this business could be. Peter seemed to be under enormous pressure. Deep into the winter months, a heavy snow drift was forecast over night, with a real danger of road and rail links into London being cut off. At the time I would write up, on the old typewriter, two or three stories overnight to use for the first edition, but there seemed little to no chance that I would be able to reach work on that particular occasion as I was, and still am, a non-driver.

Peter made the decision that he would pick me up, and that he would allow an extra hour for the journey because of the snow. So at 5am, in the pitch black, he pulled up outside the house, and off we set for London with the 'copy' in my hand ready to go.

It was a stop-start journey in the snow, but we eventually made Blackfriars Bridge as dawn broke, but there we came to a full stop. Then Peter spotted the *News* Editor in the outside lane crawling along a touch faster than us.

"Get out," Peter demanded, "jump into that car, and get that copy into the office." I did as I was told, made the few yards to the car just ahead of us, but, sod's law, we came to a grinding halt, and Peter went past us and beyond and clearly made it to the offices before us.

When I entered the editorial floor of the *Evening News*, there was Peter yelling, "Where the hell have you been?"

Denis Signey had been my mentor at this time, a seasoned journalist who had worked on national newspapers and became Jim Gregory's advisor at QPR, was once general manager at Brentford, and who edited the local paper in Maggie Thatcher's constituency and ended up with the OBE. He had been instrumental in my arrival at the *News* where Victor Railton had been legend, a man for whom I had the utmost respect and affection. Vic was my hero when I'd worked on the local *North London Weekly Herald* newspaper. Vic would pop in every Friday and I would hand him an envelope full of stories, some of which I had used that Friday in the local paper which covered predominately Spurs and also Arsenal.

My phone would often ring late afternoon and Vic would tell me a car would arrive at my home the next morning at 7am and take me to, say, White hart Lane, where such and such player would be signing that day. No-one knew but Vic. His contacts were second to none. His instructions included where to interview the player, then for me to go into the nearest phone box on the High Road, and phone over to the office every single word the player uttered in response to my questions.

"Leave off the intro," Vic would say. That evening my entire interview would appear under Vic's name, who apparently had written that Peter Taylor today signed for Spurs and said........

It was a fabulous grounding.

I was working on the *Newcastle Journal* when Vic died. I had transferred within the Thompson group from North London to Newcastle, where I covered non-league football and subbed the race cards until 2am. Blue Star won the FA Vase the year I was in Geordieland, with Blyth Spartans being in the hat for the FA Cup quarter-final draw, being paired with Arsenal, only to lose a fifth round replay against Wrexham which was switched to St. James's Park to accommodate the thousands that wanted to cheer the non-leaguers on. Because I was covering non-league football I was deeply involved in Blyth's fantastic run that season, which had seen them dispose of Second Division Stoke City away from home in the fourth round.

Newcastle were relegated that season, 1977/78, with crowds dwindling to as low as 6,000. But the gates at St. James's Park were shut for the Blyth replay and the courageous non-leaguers went out with Wrexham strolling through the game. It was vastly different at the Racecourse Ground, where Blyth should have won, but for an over-efficient linesman (they were still called linesmen at that time) spotting a corner flag falling over in the very last minute when Wrexham had taken a corner and the diminutive Blyth keeper had caught it at the near post – game over. Oh no, the corner had to be retaken. And, Wrexham equalised.

It was around five months after Vic's death that I received a call to come down to London for an interview to join the *Evening News*. It was an opportunity I couldn't turn down, and didn't. Tom Hatton had worked with Vic for decades and he was the operations man. He would make the calls, answer the bank of three phones on my desk, and generally knew people like Ron Greenwood, England manager, almost as much as Vic.

Danny Blanchflower was manager of Chelsea at this time. And although not many people, players, media, alike, understood Danny too well, I found him absolutely enthralling. Perhaps, it was because he was one of my all time heroes, captain of Spurs' flowing, entertaining and winning 1961 Double side.

Maybe it was because I liked to listen to him, because somewhere there was enormous insight, if you were able to decipher it. He didn't last too long in management, he was far too intelligent, years ahead of his time. But he did put up with me, which was something, as I was young, enthusiastic, and probably over the top, ringing managers like Danny at 6am in order to check out national daily newspaper stories for the evening paper editions. Remember the first edition copy deadline was 7.15am.

Eventually Danny's wife must have complained, because he picked me up on it and said he couldn't take any more 6am phone calls, and he told me that he had actually had a plaque made which said, "Don't take any calls from Harry before 7am". I didn't believe him. But with Danny you just didn't know.

JIMMY BLOOMFIELD
Former Arsenald and Birmingham midfielder and Orient and Leicester City manager

As a cub reporter on a group of local independent newspapers I quickly aspired to the title of Sports Editor after just one year in employment. It was a rapid promotion born out of expediency because a couple of the guys who worked on sport left for pastures new, and I was just about the only person left in the organisation remotely interested in football and sport. So, it wasn't long before, in my capacity of junior reporter, I had swapped a ladder outside of the offices in Loughton High Road to ask passers by whether they were superstitious or not, for a trip to the Orient, as Sports Editor, to interview their manager Jimmy Bloomfield.

The first time I entered the quaint ground to find the manager, I was directed to the changing rooms, where Jimmy emerged to greet me dressed only in his towel. Jimmy was an imposing figure, even without his clothes, and after a deep intake of breath, I introduced myself. Little did I know, that it would lead to a very close working relationship, bordering on a kind of friendship with Jimmy that would last to the day he died, sadly very early from a heart attack aged 49.

DAVID BLOOMFIELD
FA Press Officer

Jimmy's son David used to answer the phone to me as a toddler when I would ring the Bloomfield household inquiring after his dad, when he was manager of Orient. How strange, then, that David would turn up at Lancaster Gate as the Football Association's Press Officer. There was a mutual trust from the word go. I am sure David knew how much his dad trusted me.

David was a reasonably useful footballer, who enjoyed midfield and could pick out a long range pass if given enough time and room, of which, invariably, in press games, there was ample. I have played with him on occasions in the same England Press Team. My footballing career was pretty short. I fancied myself as a goalkeeper, having captained the school team. Davenant Foundation was a school of hard knocks, starting off next to the Salvation Army in Whitechapel High Road before relocating to Debden in Essex.

Dennis Rofe and Terry Brisley were a year older, but I played once or twice in the same team as them before they went off to enjoy professional careers.

My mum pestered the ticket office manager at Spurs to the point where he swore he'd get me a trial, and I do still have the Tottenham trial papers signed off by Bill Nicholson himself. Although I saved a penalty the day the scouts watched, Rofe and Brisley were in outstanding form, and they were the players who caught the eye. I tried training at Enfield when former Liverpool goalkeeper Tommy Lawrence was manager and was sick on the first evening and never went back. I played a couple of five-a-side games for Harlow Town during their training sessions when I covered the club for the local paper. But the England Press team was about my level, and even then, most of the time I spent on the bench next to Scottish import Paddy Barclay.

In one of the few games I missed, as I was getting older and was deliberately kept out of the loop when the games were on in case I turned up, Trevor Brooking ended up in a brawl, retaliated and ending up with a black eye for his trouble. I am sure that never happened to him in 20 years at West Ham!

My greatest claim to footballing fame was playing for Russia in a European Championship press tournament match which ran simultaneously to the main even that day. There were only about a dozen Russian journalists covering the event, but half of them were still travelling from different venues, and failed to make kick-off. As England always had a big squad, a few of the usual substitutes were loaned out to Russia, including myself and Celtic's centre half at the time Roy Aitken, who probably shouldn't have played without his club's permission and was also no doubt not insured. In the England team were the likes of Bobby Charlton and former Ipswich Town striker, Paul Mariner, who had not long given up playing and was still lean and fit. One sliding tackle I made on Bobby Charlton will always stand out, but it was a painful experience when Mariner raked down the back of both my Achilles when he leaped to win a high ball. Lovely chap Paul, but a fierce competitor whenever he was on a football pitch, as I discovered to my cost.

After a good interchange of passing between myself at left-back and Roy, I ended up in front of goal where Colin Gibson looked like a beached whale and had no chance of bouncing up to get to a loose ball just a yard from his line. It was the only goal I ever scored in a press game, but it was for Russia – against England! At half-time the rest of the Russian journalists arrived and I made way back to my place on the England bench.

At the end of the game, the Russian 'coach' presented me with one of their shirts as a memento of having scored against England.

BEST OF BRITISH!

LIAM BRADY
Former Arsenal and Republic of Ireland midfield genius

My relationship with Liam has been up and down, presently down.

When I was in my infancy as a football writer with the *Evening News*, match reporting was a hectic affair. Tom Hatton sat beside me, and I would hand him a piece of paper with a few scribbles on it, and he would dictate it to the copy taker inside the office. It was then set in the old fashioned hot metal and fashioned into a page, and printed so fast, that an hour after the end of the game you could queue up at a station or the local news agent and buy the *Pink* edition.

I used to love the *Pink* when I was a kid, buying it on the way home from a game, queuing for half an hour if I had to if it was ever late. I never thought then I would be writing the reports I would so fervently cut out and stick in my scrapbook. But that frantic rush to get the reports out didn't last long for me as the *Evening News* shut down after about a year that I worked there.

Long enough, though, to fall out with Liam Brady.

After filing a match report you would hang around the drafty club corridors, or in the car park, or whereever you could, to catch the players when they emerged form the dressing room and grab an quick interview.

After one game involving Arsenal, I caught sight of Liam and called him over for a brief chat. He took a disdainful look at me and referred to my match report in the *Evening News* a couple of weeks earlier. I remembered how much praise I had given Liam for a wonder goal he'd scored against Spurs.

But he pointed out, "You described me as British – I am Irish", and stormed off.

He forgot to mention that I had actually described him as the "Best of British".

Anyway it was a terrible error and had clearly upset him. You have to be thick-skinned to get on in this profession, and I had learned the thicker the skin the better. When Liam had finished as a player and turned his hand to the media, he was far more amenable to the press and I bumped into him at Heathrow airport and spent a very pleasant and highly entertaining journey to Nice in his company. He told me how much he hated helicopters to the point of never travelling in them, but that was by far the most convenient means of transport from Nice to Monte Carlo. Liam had a home in Monte Carlo, while I was travelling there on a match assignment. Liam asked me if I would allow him to drive me to Monte Carlo instead of taking the chopper. I agreed.

The route was a guided tour of the mountainous region, and seemed just as hazardous, if not more so, than taking the helicopter. But after so much time in his company I got to know him better, as you would expect, and a lot of preconceived ideas about him vanished. I enjoyed travelling with, and thought this would be the start of a sound working relationship. However, it didn't last long. Liam became the head of the Arsenal Academy, where a very good friend of mine, former Arsenal midfielder Paul Davis, was beginning his career as a coach. Unfortunately Paul had been over looked for promotion in favour of an Academy newcomer Steve Bould, who Liam felt was better suited to the task, but Paul felt he had been held back because, generally speaking, there is a lack of advancement for black coaches and managers, and I had signposted the fact, in my column, that there is no black or ethnic representation on the FA Council or any executive committees, so Paul turned to me and I put his feelings into print.

The mere suggestion of a racism slur got Liam extremely hot under the collar, as you might expect, and the *Mirror* headlines at the time didn't help his mood, or lower the temperature in the numerous telephone conversations that took place between the two of us on this issue.

David Dein did his best to convince me that there was no racism involved. David, being a good Jewish boy, insisted that Arsenal would not tolerate racism of any description. He was very close to Paul and he was employing Liam. He made some valiant attempts at being a peacemaker. Whereas Paul was in a difficult position and refrained from making any formal complaint, numerous friends of Paul contacted me to tell me exactly what they thought about it. However, the net result was Liam was angry, and told me never to darken his door again. We haven't spoken since.

As for Paul, he left Arsenal and now works for the PFA.

RICHARD BRANSON
Mega-rich business mogul

Branson's Virgin were the sponsors of Crystal Palace when they reached the 1990 FA Cup Final against Manchester United and I arranged to interview Richard Branson on the Wembley pitch prior to the game. Quite a coup at the time and it was an honour to meet him. He turned up in a large Range Rover with his wife and children on board to see Wembley's Twin Towers, and I found Richard to be a very approachable guy. I have since met him a couple of times at the *Mirror's* Pride of Britain awards.

BRAZIL IN BRAZIL

ALAN BRAZIL
Former Ipswich, Spurs and Scotland striker turned radio pundit

Alan has always been wonderful fun whenever I have appeared on TalkSport, chatting over the day's agenda-setting football news. Mike Parry turned to TalkSport after a stint as the FA's Press Officer, and was also good for radio banter whenever I appeared with him.

Alan spent some considerable time at the World Club Championships in Rio, but unfortunately, as I was at the tournament in Brazil working for BBC Radio FiveLive, I didn't spend too much time in his company, which was a shame because I am very fond of Alan and Mike and would gladly socialise with them. Alan and TalkSport were classed as the 'enemy' for, not only were they a rival sports chat programme, but BBC Radio FiveLive had bought the rights in the proper manner, while TalkSport promoted themselves as if they were actually covering the event. In reality Alan sat in his room in our hotel, covering the game from the TV!

SIR TREVOR BROOKING
Former West Ham and England midfield maestro

I've known him since he was plain old Trev, a loyal star for the Hammers, then as a TV pundit, and more recently in his role as an administrator. Now Sir Trevor is a leading figure at FA Headquarters in Soho Square, and he hasn't changed from the highly articulate and intelligent, yet unassuming guy I first came across at Upton Park – despite the odd fight on the football field (see DAVID BLOOMFIELD).

AGENTS ARE LEECHES

KEITH BURKINSHAW
Former Spurs manager

One of the many Tottenham managers I have enjoyed a close working relationship with and a Yorkshireman like Bill Nicholson, Keith took his job very seriously. Even though he was in charge of the club back in the 1980s, he hated agents and their growing influence within the game even then and once called them 'leeches'. Keith's condemnation of the way they operated within the industry still occupies so much of the game's administrators' time and energy. I for one see little reason for their existence – unless it is to circulate the funds. Of course there are some outstanding and honourable agents, but I am positive they are in the minority.

TERRY BUTCHER
Stalwart Ipswich and England centre-half

Terry relates so many funny stories about his exploits as a player at Ipswich under Bobby Robson and also as an England star under the same manager, that it isn't long before he has you in stitches. Many times I have shared the evening and night's entertainment alongside Terry and many other journalistic friends such as Alan Green and Mike Ingham from Radio 5.

Terry never tires of telling one story about England's exploits on the way to the semi-finals in the World Cup of Italia 90. To alleviate all the boredom, he led the team in eating a back-to-front meal, which had the England manager completely flummoxed. They all began with the coffee, followed by dessert and worked their way back to the starter. Often Terry would come down to the meal early to sit there as what looked like the best-dressed England player, replete in his England blazer, collar and tie – but would have nothing on below the waist.

But there is a very serious side to Terry, the centre-half synonymous for spilling blood for his country. He has coached for several years with Motherwell, north of the border, but he was often flying south for TV documentaries or radio debates, or to be a TV and radio analyst. Now he has left the frozen north and flown to the ultimate southern destination – not London or Ipswich, but Sydney, where he took over as coach in August 2006 succeeding former Germany winger Pierre Littbarski as manager, with Maurice Malpas taking over from Terry at the Scottish club.

The last time I actually saw Terry, he was in a dark and dingy Chelsea nightclub – actually it was during the day – when he was filming, just ahead of me, for a TV documentary on Wayne Rooney to coincide with the 2006 World Cup finals.

C

RICHARD CABORN, ALISTAIR CAMPBELL, BOBBY CAMPBELL, SOL CAMPBELL, ERIC CANTONA, SIR BOBBY CHARLTON, JACK CHARLTON, RAY CLEMENCE, MAX CLIFFORD, LORD SEBASTIAN COE, ANDREW COLE, CHARLIE COOKE, GARTH CROOKS, ADAM CROZIER, JOHANN CRUYFF

CABORN OUT TO CATCH BETTING CHEATS

RICHARD CABORN
Labour Sports Minister

Of the many Sports Ministers during my time as a journalist, both Conservative and Labour, no-one has had a worse start than when Richard was caught out not being able to answer any of the questions about sport put to him on a radio interview just after he was appointed. But he's made a big comeback in my eyes, and I have grown to respect his abilities as he has progressed in the job, listened to advice, and come back strong with his initiative to organise the Independent Commission into European Football.

The Minister of Sport made a guest appearance on my World Cup podcast show for NTL during the 2006 finals. With his tight schedule he was unable to come into the studios for the as-live broadcast on the Friday evening, so we made special arrangements for when he was available, at 9am on a Wednesday morning. Only George Cohen of the other scheduled guests was free at that time to appear with him. We also did a pre-record link up with PR guru Max Clifford. It turned out to be one of the best shows, with the Minister promising to approach Gordon Brown for tax concessions for the entire nation if England won the World Cup! He probably felt it was a safe bet that England couldn't.

Among the topics under discussion on the show was the Minister's well-intentioned backing for the Independent Commission's European Review, an initiative designed to bring in wholesale measures to take the game forward. His thinking is that a European initiative would gain EU backing and, once endorsed by UEFA, would have to be introduced by the Premier League ad FA.

One of the measures the European Review has been looking closely at has been salary capping, or compelling clubs to spend a restricted proportion of turnover on players wages. Controls on agents, and a 'fit and proper persons test' rather more rigid than the current ludicrous self-certification system in operation in the UK, are other issues high on their agenda.

Caborn has also led the way in trying to clean up betting scams in sport. He has been seeking police assistance to access mobile phone records to track down the betting cheats. The FA had been investigating the betting scam surrounding Harry Redknapp's return as manager of Portsmouth and the FA's Compliance Unit wanted to access data on mobile phones to finalise a case. The Minister is determined to provide as much help as possible to keep the game clean.

ALISTAIR CAMPBELL
Labour spin doctor extraordinaire

I worked with Alistair on the *Mirror* where he was the top political writer and, as a Burnley supporter, he naturally took a great deal of interest in what I might be up to. In fact I always had him marked down as a wannabe football writer. Far from the maniacal control freak that many of the media love to paint him as, I found him a charming guy and highly accomplished journalist. I do have to say that it did surprise me when he ended up the Prime Minister's right-hand man.

BOBBY CAMPBELL
Former manager of Chelsea and Fulham

I knew Bobby when he was manager of Fulham. Recently I bumped into him in Surrey outside a Virginia Water estate agent's office. He has a family home in Sunningdale and his boy is making his way in the world of tennis.

It was also a pleasure to spend time in Bobby's company en route to Belfast for George Best's funeral (see George Best), and indeed travelled back with him. It's guys like Bobby who have so much to give back to football, and yet the industry doesn't seem to have a niche for this vastly experienced and knowledgeable coach.

SOLD TO ARSENAL

SOL CAMPBELL
Spurs, Arsenal, Portsmouth and England man-mountain of a centre-half

I have known Sol since he was a boy at Spurs, where I always admired his skills and I got to know him better whenever the England squads assembled for major tournaments. I once bumped into him in the Cartier shop in Knightsbridge, where he was wearing a woolly hat tucked down over as much of his face as he could, clearly not wanting to be recognised.

Sky Andrew, his agent, wanted some balanced media coverage at the time of Sol's contentious move to Arsenal, as his client was going through a torrid time with the

Tottenham fans, which was hardly surprising. I was only too willing to help. Sky is one of the few agents who I trust unequivocally. Equally he trusts me. He knows he can confide in me and that I wouldn't let him down. I believe that a good journalist has to achieve a high level of trust with contacts, who sometimes become firm friends. There is no harm in a trade off. If Sol was going through a torrid time and Sky wanted help, he knew he could always come to me. However, he also knew he would have to come up with a story that would satisfy my thirst for the big exclusive. In return I would adopt a sympathetic approach toward Sol, but it must be empathised and Sky was told this from the very start; I would only give Sol the benefit of the doubt if I believed he deserved it. If I felt he was merely being greedy, then I would say so.

Sol really wanted to move to better himself, something that he could hardly say in public, as Spurs fans would have wanted to crucify him. But he wanted to play Champions League football, to test himself at the highest level, and with all due respect to Spurs, he couldn't have done that at White Hart Lane. In retrospect, I am sure that the Spurs fans can see that, and their animosity toward him has subsided with the passing of time. Equally, no-one is irreplaceable, and Ledley King has all the attributes of turning out to be as good, if not better, than Sol.

A WORD TO THE WISE

ERIC CANTONA
Eric The King

Howard Wilkinson was manager of Leeds United at the time they were playing a vital European tie away from home. As usual I was part of the travelling media corps. The day before the tie, it is traditional for the manager to hold a media press conference, and at least one player would be on 'media duty', the arduous task of facing the press, something that few, if any, players enjoy around the globe. It is, however, a task they are forced to fulfil, although some do actually refuse.

Naturally enough, the outrageously skilled and enigmatic Eric was the player of the media's choice and Howard was among the more obliging managers. He had a reputation of being a 'blazer', one of the more traditionalist team bosses, always booted and suited, only in a tracksuit on the training ground.

As we entered the hotel room to prepare for the press conference, Howard caught sight of me and brought me over to meet Eric. "Here's a reporter you want to be very careful about," were Howard's first words. Naturally enough that was a starting point guaranteed to put you off your stride, which is probably why Howard did it. I just smiled and told Eric I didn't have a clue what he was talking about. But I got the impression from Eric's face that he had been well briefed by Howard prior to the conference and the Leeds United manager had clearly tipped him off about me.

To a large degree Howard probably wasn't wrong.

SIR BOBBY CHARLTON
One of the greatest footballers this country has ever produced

Most definitely someone I would class as a friend. Not many journalists can boast the honour of actually sharing a dressing room with Sir Bobby, but I have played alongside him, and once against him, for press teams in my time.

When we ran onto the pitch, it was incredible to think that Bobby looked so fit and trim despite his age. I asked him how he did it. Simple, he replied, just warm up properly. "I see so many of these games, and everyone just rushes out and starts running around, and is pulling up with a muscle strain within a few minutes, the secret is stretching and warming up properly." Sound advice from an old pro. It was also a great pleasure to talk to him in a relaxed atmosphere at the after match meal laid on by our hosts.

I have also dined with Bobby at many sponsors' functions, once alongside Pelé, and have the ball with both their autographs on it to prove it. That's one of the perks of being in my line of work and, as a bit of a collector, I have been able to pick up some fantastic memorabilia.

Pelé and Bobby have shared the same sponsor for Word Cups, MasterCard, and at a central London hotel, a small hand-selected cohort of international football writers gathered to interview the two great men over a relaxed lunch. Pelé was late, as usual, but once he got there, he didn't want to leave, and had to be dragged away by his entourage to ensure he caught his flight.

JACK CHARLTON
England World Cup winner turned coach of a successful Republic of Ireland team

Jack turned up with a number of the other '66 World cup winning England team for the launch of my World Cup book 'This Time', and he certainly made an impact. During a Q & A at the Sports Café, where the event took place, Big Jack never held back in his analysis of Sven's England and their deficiencies prior to the finals in Germany. In fact such were his comments about Rio Ferdinand and Sol Campbell that they made back page news the next day.

When Jack first spotted me at the pre-event lunch at W'Sens restaurant, he said, "Boy you look thin, much thinner than the last time I saw you."

I am sure he thought I was Bob Harris. He has never been good with names.

So, as there are a few Harris's in journalism it must be tricky for the old bugger.

Bob Harris has written numerous sports books, mostly football and cricket, so as Big Jack was at a book function, he could probably be excused for the mistaken identity. Little wonder, then, he thought I had lost considerable weight because Bob, who was once Sports Editor at the *Sunday Mirror* and a football writer on *Today*, is a fat old so-and-so.

RAY CLEMENCE
Former Liverpool, Spurs and England keeper, now England's goalkeeping coach

Keith Burkinshaw and Peter Shreeves were pacing up and down at the airport. I was part of a small contingent of football writers who had accompanied the Spurs party on one of their European excursions on the way to winning the UEFA Cup. Keith and Peter were serious types, especially the manager, Burkinshaw. Shreeves, a former taxi driver, had a much more sociable streak to his nature, but Burkinshaw was a deadly serious Yorkshireman. So, on the morning of our return to England, it was hardly surprising to find the pair together in an agitated mood. But it went on for quite some time, and it dawned on us that the flight was being held up for some reason. It soon became apparent what was going on. Enter Ray Clemence being supported by Spurs staff dragging him along toward the departure lounge. The England goalkeeper had a stupid grin on his face, as he was bellowing out a song.

Ray did not stop singing at the top of his voice, all the way up the stairs of the plane, as he was helped to his seat. Once seated he fell off into a deep sleep and all fell peaceful again. Except for Burkinshaw's mood. He was fuming.

Clemence had been out all the night before and had got back to his hotel bedroom just as the Spurs party had left for the airport. Oblivious to the time, he went to sleep and was still in his bed when a couple of the Spurs staff were assigned to return to the hotel to find him.

Peter asked us if we would oblige him and not report this incident. We agreed. It was a vastly different era back in the early 1980s. For a start these days the media party no longer travel with a team or stay in the same hotel. The barriers have been growing higher over the years, keeping apace with the way the media has mush-roomed. Now there can be five or six representatives from one newspaper, whereas back then there was just one. It was more controllable. We would often go out drinking with the players ourselves, and we would keep their minor indiscretions to ourselves. Hence no-one has ever heard about Ray's boozy flight home until now.

MAX CLIFFORD
The sharpest, most expensive and most successful PR in the business

Max represented Faria Alam during the media explosion which surrounded the revelations of her affairs with Sven and then FA Chief Executive Mark Palios (see Colin Gibson). Max also handles the PR for Crystal Palace chairman Simon Jordan. Boy, does he need it. Max assures me Simon is a genuine guy. Until I discover otherwise I am happy to accept Max's recommendation.

Max played a pivotal role in Steve McClaren being appointed as England coach in the spring of 2006 by controlling the media furore over revelations of McClaren's extra-marital affair. Within days of the news being made public in a most calm and controlled manner, McClaren had been offered the job after 'Big Phil' Scolari had declared himself unavailable (see 'Big Phil' Scolari).

One of McClaren's fellow candidates for the England job, Bolton manager Sam Allardyce, has since admitted that he wished he had been represented by Clifford at the time, as he feels it tipped the balance between McClaren and himself for the job. Sam has since employed Max to look after his affairs, following the infamous 'bung' revelations on the BBC's *Panorama* programme (see Craig & Sam Allardyce).

One of the things I find fascinating about the way Max works is the fact that he does all his business on trust and a handshake. He never has a contract with any of his clients. He has done business that way for 40 successful years. He also tells me he has never pitched for a job. All his clients have, in fact, come to him. And when you consider his list includes the likes of the Beatles, Frank Sinatra, Marlon Brando and Muhammad Ali, that's no mean recommendation!

I once appeared on *Richard & Judy* with Max talking about a football-related topic, something to do with Paul Gascoigne and his various problems. Of all the TV programmes I have appeared on, and they account for probably all of them that might have some football content, Richard & Judy were by far the most sociable hosts. I have never before, nor since, had a dressing room with my name on the door, a personal dress advisor – who incidentally insisted on changing my tie because it was label identifiable – and there was a lovely gift-wrapped present of Molton Brown smellies to take back for the missus.

After the show at their South London studios, there was a very welcoming party with drinks and excellent nibbles shipped in from an up-market restaurant. Max had plenty of gossip, but I swore I would not repeat it. Can't wait for my next invite!

OFF YOU COE!

LORD SEBASTIAN COE
Olympic double gold winner, who won a seat in Parliament and then London the 2012 Olympics

While covering a game at Oxford United, when they were entertaining Chelsea, I picked up this tale from the gateman, who told me that renowned Chelsea fan Seb Coe had turned up at his main entrance gate without his ticket just a few minutes before kick-off. Seb had to collect his ticket at the other side of the ground, but was running so late, thought that he would be instantly recognisable and therefore would gain entrance.

"Where's your ticket?" inquired the gateman.

"It's round the other side for collection, but there's only a few minutes before kick-off, don't you know who I am? I'm Seb Coe".

The gateman, quick as a flash, responded, "Well, if you are bloody well Seb Coe, it won't take you a second to run round there to get your ticket in plenty of time, now will it!"

ANDREW COLE
Goalscoring striker with a host of Premiership clubs

There are always some people in the game with whom I am never going to have much of a rapport, and Andy, sorry Andrew, Cole is one of them.

The animosity dates back to when Glenn Hoddle was manager of England and he made the observation that Cole needed five chances to score a goal for his country. It was Hoddle's peculiarly off-beat way of explaining why he didn't rate the player as highly as the pundits who had been pushing his case for inclusion into the international side.

One of my *Mirror* columns explained precisely what Hoddle was trying to say – and agreed with him. Since then Andy, sorry Andrew, has not had a kind word to say about me. But statistics don't lie. And Hoddle wasn't the only England coach not to pick Cole, his former manager at Newcastle, Kevin Keegan, barely gave him a look in either.

ASHLEY COLE
Subject of the most tortuous transfer saga of modern times

Ashley finally got his much vaunted move from Arsenal to Chelsea, the deal delayed until late on deadline day before the 2006 summer transfer window closed (see Jonathan Barnett). There was even more bitter wrangling behind the scenes before a swap with William Gallas plus £5m was agreed between two clubs now at open war. Two weeks earlier I had predicted in the *Express* that the deal would go through, but only if it included a swap with Gallas. That was quickly poo-pooed by our major rivals, but it eventually came to pass.

Ashley then chose to tell his side of the sordid story in his autobiography, *My Defence,* that was finally published once he moved on. Extracts were serialised in *The Times* and earned the expected universal criticism.

CHARLIE COOKE
Chelsea's 1970s Wizard of Dribble

I enjoyed Charlie's dribbling skills when I watched the game as a boy, and have met him a few times now. Charlie is a particular favourite of my wife Linda, who was weaned on the Chelsea team of the 70s and I had great pleasure in arranging a picture of the two of them together, which Charlie, ever the good sport, readily agreed to pose for.

GARTH CROOKS
Double FA Cup winner with Spurs, now interviewing for the BBC

Garth, who conducts those loquacious post-match interviews for BBC TV, is someone within the industry that I would describe as a friend, as well as someone I would admire and respect greatly. He doesn't have universal appeal within the written press, but then again, nor do I.

ERIKSSON WILL REPLACE FERGUSON

ADAM CROZIER
Former Chief Executive of the Football Association

Adam fancied himself as a footballer, and we have shared the Wembley dressing room when he was the FA's Chief Executive as we played in the same team in a match arranged by sponsors to mark the closing down of the old Wembley. Adam was aggressively pro the building of a new Wembley on the old Wembley site. Even though he was a Scot, he had a wonderful 'feel' for English football and I thought he would make an excellent Chief Executive. But his decision to quit the traditional Lancaster Gate for the chrome and steel of Soho Square was a mark of his move into the 21st Century that not every one of the FA traditionalists shared. He became too powerful, by-passing the leviathan committees, and eventually he lost the internal power struggle and was dispatched to reinvent himself at the Royal Mail.

We crossed swords on many occasions. For example, Adam believed the England manager Sven-Göran Eriksson when the Swede told him that the had not been courted by Manchester United. As a result Adam authorised the FA's media department to issue a press statement rebuking one of my exclusives that Eriksson had been in talks with United's Chief Executive of the time, Peter Kenyon, to succeed Sir Alex Ferguson who had announced his retirement. Eriksson similarly issued a statement, insisting that neither he, nor his agent in the UK, or any representative abroad, his uncle, aunt or mum or dad, had been in talks with Manchester United.

Months later I revealed how Eriksson had initialled an agreement to become the next Manchester United manager, and how he was a mere week away from making an appointment with Crozier to tell him, when Sir Alex performed his famous U-turn and decided to stay and Kenyon felt he couldn't go against the wishes of the fans and backed away from appointing Eriksson.

Adam rang me to sound me out about the validity of my stories. I explained to him that, if necessary, I could prove it. He realised his error. However, he was pragmatic about it, managers are renowned for listening to job opportunities, but it should have been a lesson for the FA when next it came to issuing a press statement in support of Eriksson. Which turned out to be a denial about his affair with David Davies' personal assistant, a certain Faria Alam!

Of course I also broke the story that the Machiavellian plotting inside the FA would eventually topple him as Chief Executive and it was not surprising that we haven't spoken since. But Adam should appreciate that you mustn't shoot the messenger.

CRUYFF TO TAKE OVER AT THE BASEBALL GROUND

JOHANN CRUYFF
Dutch master and inventor of 'Total Football'

Robert Maxwell enjoyed his football. He owned Oxford United, then Derby County, with his son Kevin becoming chairman of Oxford. He also tried to buy Watford from Elton John, made a bid for Spurs and, having failed there and before he became the proprietor of the *Mirror*, tried to buy Manchester United.

Maxwell also responded to a request from the then Spurs chairman Irving Scholar to utilise his expertise to advise the club on TV rights. Maxwell urged the chairman to realise that they owned a product that the TV companies were buying on the cheap and that ITV and BBC were operating a cartel to suppress the price. He predicted that the combined rights of all the big clubs in the then First Division would be worth a fortune. Not even Maxwell envisaged that one day the Premier League, yet to be formed at that time, would earn in excess of £1billion from TV rights.

More often than not, Maxwell would consult my opinions on topics as wide ranging as TV rights, the value of players' contracts, and his many potential footballing acquisitions. It was an exhilarating time, a fascinating insight into the inner sanctum of football's high finance.

There were also a hat-full of surprises with Maxwell at the helm of the *Mirror*.

Having a hotline to his chief football writer clearly suited Maxwell and there were plenty of times when my phone rang that he summoned me to his office, and I knew there was something quite extraordinary going on.

The call that arrived one day to attend a meeting in Maxwell's private apartment proved to be one such occasion. It was more than a shock to be introduced to Johan Cruyff after the butler admitted me. Of course, I was a fan of Cruyff the player. I just loved his skills when he starred for Ajax, Barcelona and for his country. He performed in one of the greatest ever Dutch teams, and certainly the best team to have participated in, but never to have won the World Cup. Then, I knew him well enough when he turned to management, and I spoke to Gary Lineker, then at Barcelona, about Cruyff and his conflict with the Dutch coach.

But I never expected to be engaged in such an intimate set of circumstances with Cruyff as the one that took place between just the three of us. Maxwell confided in me that he was extremely interested in a project being put forward by Cruyff to co-own a small Dutch Second Division club, to finance the arrival of some key players, and to develop the club into one of the most powerful in Europe utilising Cruyff's reputation and expertise.

"What do you think, Harry?" he inquired.

I imagine that Maxwell valued my advice because, surrounded by 'yes' men as someone of his ilk is used to, he normally got a very straight answer from me, irrespective of how political incorrect it might be.

"Not something I would recommend," I suggested, as I pointed out that it would probably cause some major concern, if not hostility, within UEFA, if Maxwell began a process of cross-border ownership. What would happen, I ventured, if your Dutch club drew Oxford or Derby County in a European Cup competition some time in the future? The possibility of attracting scrutiny from UEFA, as well as the FA and Football League, scuppered that deal for Johann.

But, all was not lost, I proceeded to suggest that English football would be enthralled by a Dutch coach plying his trade within our so insular shores.

"What a good idea", beamed Maxwell. "Would you be interested?"

Cruyff: "Well, yes I would".

Maxwell: "How about Derby County? My son owns Derby County, they are a top club."

Cruyff: "Ok, I will consider it."

The back page of the *Mirror* for the next day was taken care of. Mission accomplished as far as I was concerned. A story that might come off, but would set the agenda for a few weeks, that was for sure.

When the Derby County manager Arthur Cox saw the headlines the next day, which just happened to be a Saturday, a match day, you can imagine his response. I got a call from Maxwell that morning to inform me that Arthur was none too pleased with his chairman, and not too happy with me either.

By the tone of Maxwell's voice, I don't think he particularly cared, but Uncle Bob didn't really want to offend people like his Derby County manager and he told Cox it was just a publicity stunt and he need not have worried. However, I know that had Cruyff come back and formally accepted the position, then poor old Arthur would have been out of a job.

D

KENNY DALGLISH, DAVID DAVIES, DAVID DEIN, KERRY DIXON, GREG DYKE

KENNY DALGLISH
Liverpool and Scotland legendary striker and winner of the Premiership as manager of Liverpool and Blackburn

Kenny was driving to work as usual, on his way to the training ground, listening to the radio. He was just TWO games into the new season as manager of Newcastle United and, although it had been a disappointing start, he could hardly have anticipated the shock as he listened to the main item of the sports news – soon to become the No.1 news, let alone, sports lead. The broadcaster read out the front page of that morning's *Daily Mirror,* Thursday 27 August 1998... "Gullit Set To Take Over From Kenny".

In fact the back page was more definitive... "Newcastle Axe Kenny for Gullit."

Kenny applied the brakes, pulled over into a lay-by, and contacted his chairman. The Newcastle United manager was advised that it would be best to skip that morning's training session and come into the St. James's Park offices. Kenny knew the game was up when he heard that instruction.

I was on my way to Heathrow Airport that morning to cover Chelsea's match against Real Madrid in Monte Carlo in the Super Cup Final. ITV contacted me and asked whether I would appear on their morning main news programme, as the Dalglish-Gullit story was going to be their main item because, while the *Mirror* had Gullit signing up for Newcastle, the paper's main rivals *The Sun* had Gullit going to Spurs in its back page lead story. ITV's 'angle' was the Battle of the Tabloids, and they had Brian Woolnough, the chief football reporter of *The Sun*, discussing his back page lead, and then I would talk about mine.

Now, this was a toughie. You can never be 100% sure of any story coming off as there are so many imponderables. And this one had plenty.

The night before the story broke, there had been many people who doubted it. Inside my own office there were plenty of doubters. Editor Piers Morgan was off and his stand-in editor was having kittens about a story that just had to be right. Sports Editor Keith Fisher, though, was backing me to the hilt. He was the only person I was prepared to confide in exactly how I got my information and from whom. He convinced the deputy editor that I was right.

I wanted to keep my information so close to my chest that I didn't even contact Ruud's UK representatives Jon and Phil Smith, who were personal friends of mine, and whom I trust implicitly. I didn't want to compromise them.

However, once the first edition had gone to press, I contacted, first Jon, and then spoke to Phil. They must have been shocked that I knew what was going on, but they told me that I should be very careful as it was not true.

I sat at home for hours wondering why I was taking such a huge risk. The words of the Smith brothers echoed in my mind. Could I be making the biggest blunder ever?

So, next morning, I was hesitant to be cocksure that I had got it right, particularly as Brian is such an experienced journalist. Perhaps he might have had the right story.

So, on the ITV news item I was circumspect and held back from being gung-ho that my story was on the nail. I simply explained that I was confident of my sources, and used the old get out "we shall see what happens in the next 24 hours."

By the time I had arrived in Monte Carlo, the news was breaking that Dalglish had been sacked. Fifty per cent right.

Then came the news that Gullit had flow in to Heathrow from Amsterdam. All I needed was the other 50% to be right. I was tense

I found out later that the reasons that Jon and Phil were more negative than positive about my story was that Ruud's wife-to-be Estelle was dead against him signing for Newcastle. Estelle had loved living in central London, close to Harrods and all the up market restaurants. She was far less attracted to the north-east outpost of England.

Ruud, though, wanted a way back into the Premiership to prove Chelsea wrong to sack him. He was motivated, but it was for all the wrong reasons.

He took the job, and the news-breaking article earned me the accolade of Sports Story of the Year in the awards jointly run by Sport England and the Sports Writers Association, which is now called the Sports Journalist Association.

SVEN, THE FA AND FARIA ALAM

DAVID DAVIES
FA Executive Director

It is often cruelly remarked behind his back that "if the bomb dropped, I'd like to be standing next to David Davies."

Well, he has been one of the games Great Survivors, but justifiably so. I have always felt that he is one of life's most charming individuals, and also has the good of the game at heart. For me he is greatly missed now he has quit the FA at the end of the World Cup.

Teflon David has been embroiled in his fair share of controversies; backing Manchester United to take part in the World Club Championships, backing the 2006 World Cup bid, and perhaps his greatest claim to fame, asking Sven-Göran Eriksson, his great friend, whether he had been having an affair with his very own Personal Assistant, Faria Alam, or, as she became known within Soho Square, 'Fire Alarm'.

Whatever was said between Sven and David was the central issue on which the FA Board felt that their England coach had mislead them into issuing a false statement and it almost decided them to kick out the England coach in the wake of the Alam scandal.

Caught in the middle, it was then left to David, following the dismissal of Chief Executive Mark Palios, who had also been having an affair with Faria Alam, to stand on the steps of Soho Square and declare how good a coach he considered Sven, which was not the best of timing, as the plotting was going on to get rid of the England coach. The knives turned on David as a result, but he survived and then opted to leave of his own volition once the World Cup had run its course.

PRESS PARANOIA

DAVID DEIN
Vice-Chairman of Arsenal

When David first joined the Arsenal board, I was the first journalist to interview him. From that very first day David hasn't changed much, he is paranoid about the press.

David and I are always having debates about press coverage, although he might describe some of our discussions as 'rows'. As I have always said to David, he is quick to ring me to complain if there is anything critical I have said about either him or Arsenal, but of the 99 times out of 100 when I have either praised his football club or him personally, he has never called to thank me. Nevertheless, I like David. He is a charming man.

I have followed his career in football and watched him rise to become an influential figure within the Football Association, and for some, such as Sir Alex Ferguson, perhaps too powerful. There are those who mistrust his motives and question his involvement in certain decisions, such as that to approach Luis Felipe Scolari rather than his own manager Arsène Wenger to replace Eriksson as England's Head Coach, but I believe he has the good of the game at heart.

In the game's corridors of power, the in-fighting is just as fierce as in the political arena. David's biggest 'political' and indeed personally-motivated opponent has been Ken Bates. They have rarely seen eye-to-eye.

KERRY DIXON
Chelsea's goalscoring hero of the 1980s

Kerry is one of a multitude of former players to try his hand in the media, mostly covering his former club working for Chelsea TV. During his playing career, I had a fine rapport with Kerry and that has continued as he has reinvented himself in the media.

IS THE BBC RACIST?

GREG DYKE
TV guru

Greg interviewed me some time ago at Stamford Bridge for a football documentary he was fronting, and so I have got to know him. He is a real enthusiast and I bumped into him often on the Shuttles between Heathrow and Manchester when he sat on the Old Trafford board. Now, the former Director General of the Beeb is involved with Brentford.

In 2001 Greg famously labelled the BBC 'hideously white' and incapable of retaining staff from ethnic minority backgrounds. Greg is now non-executive chairman of the Bees, but still retains his affection and affinity to the Red Devils. He insists he is a lifelong fan of Brentford, as indeed he is of Manchester United. Interesting if the two should meet up in the FA Cup.

TREVOR EAST, MARTIN EDWARDS, PAUL ELLIOTT, DOUG ELLIS, SVEN-GÖRAN ERIKSSON

SETANTA TAKE ON SKY IN TV WAR

TREVOR EAST
TV Executive

Trevor is a top TV executive, who has also shared a boardroom with Robert Maxwell at Derby County. He was poached by Irish cable company Setanta from Sky to spearhead their negotiations for Premiership live TV rights and it worked.

Premiership chairmen celebrated selling the live rights to 138 matches to BSkyB and Setanta for a staggering £1.7 billion, with the Irish PayTV station securing two of the precious packages to end Sky's monopoly and soon to elevate the name of Trevor East to one of the most powerful men in sports television.

The bumper three-year-deal, which kicks off in August 2007, represents a 66 per cent increase on the previous exclusive contract with Sky worth £1 billion over three seasons. Clubs stand to earn a staggering £28 million a year each from 2007, putting to rest any suggestion that the game's gravy train could be rolling to an end. What is all the more remarkable is that the increase in income has been achieved even though the Premier League had to end Sky's 14-year grip on the elite game following an agreement with the European Commission.

Sky won only four of the six packages, consisting of 23 live games each, put up for auction in 2006 with Setanta picking up two of the last three packages up for grabs. Under the terms of the deal with the EC no single broadcaster was allowed to win all six packages, so Sky's dominance was set to end in any case. Although they paid £1.3 billion to retain the most sought after first-choice packages, including the prime 4pm Sunday slot consisting entirely of first-choice games, the fact they have lost 46 matches will be seen as a major blow. Setanta paid £392 million for their bundle of rights and the failure of NTL, through their new Virgin TV enterprise, BT or ESPN to secure any rights shows how determined they were to make their mark on the English market. Setanta will show their 46 live games on Mondays at 8pm and Saturdays at 5.15pm and have set up a seven-day-a-week sports channel to showcase their variety of rights, which include Scottish Premier League football, rugby and American sports. In addition to the Sunday 4pm slot, Sky will show the majority of their 92 matches at 12.45pm on Saturdays and on Sundays at 1.30pm.

The agreement with the EC, following months of negotiations, allowed the Premier League to change the way they sell their rights and to exploit recent developments in technology. It also ensured a fevered interest from companies eager to end Sky's control of football on TV. Sky put a brave face on the loss of their dominant position, with sources indicating that they had lost the two packages they had least interest in retaining.

Trevor East, played down any suggestion Setanta had paid an inflated price for second-rate matches. "It's not just about first picks," he said. "Every package will have some gems in there. We're thrilled to get two packages. It's not a question of taking on Sky. There's enough room in this market for both of us."

Three weeks later the League tied up a joint deal with Sky and BT for the rights to show the remaining 242 matches. Under the terms of that deal, the games can be shown in full, but in the majority of cases, not until 10pm on the evening of the match. One match every Saturday can be broadcast from 8.30pm. They will be available for a period of 50 hours. The service is designed to appeal to fans of those clubs not featured live by Sky or Setanta who are prepared to pay a one-off fee to watch a match in its entirety, without having to pay a regular TV subscription. Securing the rights was a major coup for BT, who will now use Premiership football to drive their move away from traditional telephone services and into television and home entertainment. BT are launching a new broadband television service called BT Vision. Customers will be able to buy a set top box, which uses broadband to transmit channels provided by major broadcasters, such as BBC and Paramount. The box will also provide services such as video on demand and, now, pay per view Premier League football. BT have not said how much the set top box or each match will cost, but are expected to make an announcement later this year ahead of the service starting in August 2007.

So after all that, any fears that English football was heading for a recession were emphatically swept aside.

EDWARDS VISITS PROSTITUTES

MARTIN EDWARDS
Former Chairman of Manchester United FC

Sometimes issues outside of your control can spoil a very good relationship. As the then Manchester United chairman climbed out of his car outside one of the swankiest beach side hotels in Rio, I greeted him warmly like I had always done. Martin's reaction was cool to say the least. Together with a couple of my 'rivals' I was heading into the same reception for his Manchester United team at FIFA's inaugural World Club Championships in South America in 2000, where the accompanying media had also been invited.

Edwards complained bitterly to me about the *Mirror's* front page exposé of his nocturnal habits on the trip, which had appeared in London that morning and he had got wind of. The *Mirror's* campaign against Manchester United opting out of the FA Cup to play in the tournament was a bad enough, but reasonably legitimate, stance, which even Martin had to accept. But when my paper also exposed issues relating to his private life, that was the point at which he had lost all reasoning.

Martin blamed me directly and personally and told me in no uncertain terms not to darken his door again. I told him it had nothing to do with me, and I had no knowledge of the news department's story, let alone any input into it. That didn't seem to cut any ice, and he stormed off. I have never spoken to him again to this day.

ELLIS TO SELL VILLA

'DEADLY' DOUG ELLIS
Chairman of Aston Villa FC

For the launch of Doug's autobiography, Langan's Brasserie in Stratton Street, London played host to five tables of dignitaries including an appearance from Michael Howard, who had hot-footed it from the House where he had just taken part in a major vote. 'Deadly' is so well connected that the Aston Villa chairman can name a handful of Royals as his 'friends'.

The oldest chairman in the game had been negotiating for some time to find a buyer for his beloved Villa. The battling 81-year-old underwent six major life-saving operations in the summer of 2005. After undergoing a triple heart by-pass, Ellis was back with the surgeon for more painful and necessary surgery on the eve of Villa's home game against Chelsea at the start of the 2005/6 season, but he told me that he would be there to watch Villa take on the double champions-elect, despite all the pain and discomfort.

After 37 tumultuous, contentious years and rebuffing half a dozen previous takeover bids, Ellis told me that he would only agree to sell Villa if the new owners guaranteed to inject substantial fresh cash into the Midlands giants. Ellis effectively had total control, with a 33.5% stake in Villa, and had previously rejected all-comers by attaching stringent conditions before he would consider relinquishing control. Key to the intricacies of a Villa takeover has been the investment by Jack Petchey, formerly a director and shareholder at West Ham, and subsequently chairman of Watford. Petchey reinvested in Villa when the share price was £1.10p, the current shares are trading at £4.80p, and the takeover consortium would need to offer a premium price of £5.80p to tempt Ellis. Petchey, whose company Treffic held 21%, would collect £12m from the takeover, with Ellis taking £20m plus. That would value Villa at close to £65m and, considering Roman Abramovich paid £60m for 100 per cent of Chelsea, that will be seen to be a handsome return for the shareholders.

Of course Abramovich also took on £90m of debt at the Bridge, while Ellis has courted controversy for keeping one of the healthiest balance sheets in the Premiership. Villa are debt free, and few if any of the Premiership elite can boast a clean balance sheet, plus an untouched £20m overdraft facility and 100 acres of freehold land potentially worth £30m.

Doug has now finally sold up to American billionaire Randy Lerner. Having appointed Martin O'Neill and brought in a new wealthy owner, Doug had accomplished what he had set out to do. Like Manchester Untied, the Midlands club had been bought by an owner of a States-side sporting francise, with Lerner the owner of the Cleveland Browns.

Lerner took a majority holding in Aston Villa after buying up shares from Doug and Jack Petchey. According to a statement to the stock exchange, Lerner initially bought 59.69% of the club's shares after having his £62.6m bid for the club accepted. His advisor is Keith Harris, former chairman of the Football League, and who had been so deeply involved opposing Glazers takeover of United.

Comparisons have been drawn between Lerner and Glazer, but Harris insists the two takeovers are totally different. "From the fans' point of view, they have welcomed him," Harris said. "The Villa fans want change. Randy has inherited a club without borrowing huge sums of money which would be needed to service a debt."

SVEN FOR SPURS

SVEN-GÖRAN ERIKSSON
Former England Head Coach

Sven-Göran Eriksson was poached by the FA from Lazio as the first foreign coach for the England national side, but he might have been coaching in English football much earlier.

Ah yes, of course, you might recall that Blackburn Rovers had actually 'signed' Eriksson, but the cute Swede talked them out of pressing home their contractual obligations when the better post at Lazio cropped up. But, I can now reveal, that Blackburn were not the only club who nearly got the Swedish coach.

Eriksson might easily have joined Spurs.

Alan Sugar was doing his best to find the right coach for Tottenham. He'd had his fingers burnt by Gerry Francis and Ossie Ardiles, but before he went for his own version of the foreign option, Christian Gross, came the chance to recruit Eriksson, whose exploits around Europe hadn't quite registered too high on English football's Richter scale.

I was waiting outside the gates of England's training ground at Bisham Abbey with the rest of the media awaiting entry to the usual format of events prior to an England match – open training session/press conference – when my mobile rang. It was an old friend Bryan King, whose wife came from Scandinavia, where he lived and worked and had become somewhat of an expert on football in that part of Europe. He wondered how Spurs were getting on in their search for a new coach, and I told him, that they couldn't find the right candidate.

"How about Sven-Göran Eriksson?" ventured Bryan.

What a great idea, as he had a growing reputation built on steady progress through a number of European countries, such as Sweden, Portugal and Italy. I had heard glowing reports of his laid back managerial style, but I didn't think for one minute he would be keen on England.

"Oh yes, he would be," continued Bryan, "I know him very well, and I have spoken to him recently and he would love to come to England. Do you think Spurs would be keen?"

Immediately I contacted Alan Sugar. Naturally enough, the Spurs chairman hadn't heard of him, and really I didn't expect that he would have. Alan suggested he would make some enquiries and come back to me...

The next day Alan called back and told me that he had consulted with people and that Eriksson was not for Spurs.

So instead Spurs fans were treated to the appointment of a certain Christian Gross, who arrived via Heathrow, and took the tube, waving his travel card for the photographers. It wasn't long before it was suggested that everyone hoped he had taken the precaution of buying an instant return ticket.

Gross came with a wonderful reputation, recommended by Jürgen Klinsmann's agent, who just happened to be the same agent as for Gross. There have been a few foreign coaches since Gross who have not been given a chance by the British media because of their pigeon English, and the black humour and mimicry that attracted. In reality it was dreadful results which did for Christian at Spurs (see Christian Gross).

Eriksson has proved himself to be an astute, if not inspired, club coach, and he did transform an England team in crisis at the shock resignation of Kevin Keegan. He may well have proved to be a huge success as Spurs, a club that has had to wait an awful long time of the arrival of a foreign coach, Martin Jol, who has proved capable of pulling them together.

The majority of the media didn't take too kindly to Sven The Swede pitching up to take over the England team; there was still a residue of feeling to bring back Terry Venables kicking around. It amazed me that for years the Venables Acolytes still agitated for him to make a comeback. Personally I thought Glenn Hoddle had more chance of a second coming. However, Venables has been rehabilitated as Steve McClaren's assistant in the new England set up.

Not long after Eriksson became England coach and I switched from the *Mirror* to the *Express*, the *Express* proprietor Richard Desmond asked me to invite the England coach to one of his roundtable lunchtime get-togethers, which normally include a couple of 'faces'.

Richard had gone through the normal channels, but hadn't got very far. I made a call to the appropriate people, and Sven agreed to the meeting.

Richard has a truly wonderful penthouse office overlooking the Thames, with the kind of glorious views you would expect from such a vantage point. There was an impressive drum kit in the corner, and before Eriksson's arrival, Richard gave the few who had turned up early a quick session. He's not bad, actually.

The lunch, it has to be said, was a shade disappointing. Sven seemed less than enthused. As we learned more about the first foreign coach to the national team, it became apparent that he came alive in the company of women, and was far more dour, bordering on boring, in the presence of men. I brought along my Pelé biography, a book I am particularly proud of having written, especially as I had the great man's endorsement. Martin Townsend, the *Sunday Express* Editor, present at the lunch, observed that Sven seemed less than impressed by virtually everything that went on.

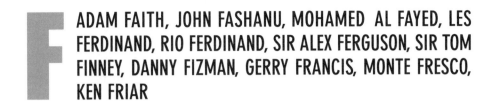

ADAM FAITH
Former pop singer of the 1960s and entrepreneur

In the mid-1990s Adam ran a TV station that specialised in business news, the only one of its kind at the time, and showed a great deal of interest in buying a stake in the website that FiveLive's Alan Green and I had set up, The Voice of Football. VOF kept going for some considerable time without any financial backing, with a number of potential investors, like Adam, showing interest in it. I met Adam at the Dorchester with his agent to discuss the project, and we met a couple of times after that. Although we didn't finalise any 'deal', we struck up a good relationship. I was devastated to hear the news that he had died in a hotel room in Stoke-on-Trent whilst on a theatre tour.

JOHN FASHANU
Former Wimbledon footballer and host of TV's 'Gladiators'

John is one of the most articulate footballers you are ever likely to meet. He would often call me at home, if he was ever in a spot of difficulty. We had a mutual trust. He gave me one of my best ever interviews when I was writing a series of articles about racism in football, at a time when the black players were loathe to come forward to discuss such a politically delicate issue. The articles earned me a Race In The Media award, and a congratulatory letter from non other than Neil Kinnock, who was then Labour Party leader.

AL FAYED PROFFERS GOLD

MOHAMED AL FAYED
Chairman Mo of Fulham and Harrods

The Daily Star's chief football writer, Danny Fullbrook, is a life-long Fulham fan, so when the Cottagers got promoted, I asked him to co-write a book about their first season in the Premiership.

I made some approaches to Mohamed Al Fayed's aides and was eventually invited along to his private suite of offices inside Harrods to interview him for our respective newspapers and also to introduce ourselves ahead of penning a tome about his club. During the interview, in which he regaled us with stories about his footballing prowess as a youngster, Mo told us he had something for us, and one of his aides left the room and returned with two gold bars. I thought I was going to be offered something as an inducement to write a good book about him and his club and was just getting ready to refuse the proffered gifts, when the secret of the gold bars was revealed. Unfortunately for us inside the gold packaging of each lay just a huge block of chocolate.

LES FERDINAND
'Sir Les' to his friends and a goalscoring legend to the fans of QPR, Newcastle and Spurs

One of the most genuine guys in the game. I enjoyed interviewing Les at length, when his agent Jon Smith made arrangements for us to meet at a hotel. Nicknamed 'Sir Les' because of his gentle demeanour for such a powerfully built centre-forward, now that his career is over Les is attempting to break into the media, notably with his appearances as a guest pundit on TV. It's proving to be a competitive sector of the media with so many ex-footballers trying their luck in the TV studio, such as Graeme Le Saux, Gavin Peacock and Paul Parker. There is a tendency for players, not long out of the dressing room, to be over protective of what they still see as their fellow players when voicing their opinions. Les and Graeme need to be more outspoken. Personally I feel that the main terrestrial broadcasters, like BBC and ITV, are missing a trick, as they need a journalist or two in the mix to be a touch more provocative.

RIO IS INNOCENT

RIO FERDINAND
Manchester United's often lackadaisical centre-half, who has more talent than he knows what to do with

I have met Rio a number of times when he has been on international duty, but I also bumped into him outside Peter Jones in Sloane Square one day while he was shopping in Chelsea. Rio had a bad press, quite deserved at times, because of his failed drugs test. But I was one of the few football writers to give his version of events. Rio was unable to discuss the issue because of the seriousness of the FA charges and all the legal issues surrounding them. But Rio is represented by Pini Zahavi, the Isreali agent, who was formerly a football journalist himself, and who knows me well enough to trust me with highly sensitive information which I wouldn't put out into the public domain without his approval and consent. On this basis I was fully conversant with Rio's defence against the charges. It enabled me to write a series of hard-hitting articles surrounding Rio's missed drugs test. On balance Rio got a raw deal. The then FA Chief Executive Mark Palios was out to make a stand on drugs and Rio was the scapegoat. While the right message must emanate from within the FA, it also has to be fair, and I am not convinced that Rio ever got a fair hearing. Several other players on the Continent who actually failed a test, rather than missed one, were far more leniently treated than Rio. It is a measure of his courage that he has made such a remarkable comeback and played an integral part in England's World Cup odyssey in Germany in the summer of 2006.

FEEL THE FERGIE HAIR-DRYER

SIR ALEX FERGUSON
The best manager in the business, equipped with the famous hair-dryer

When still just plain Alex Ferguson, after he'd delivered the first championship to Old Trafford, a celebratory lunch was arranged by one of his old pals, journalist Steve Curry. A group of chief football writers enjoyed his company, and Sir Alex even allowed Neil Harman from the *Daily Mail* to be part of the group, despite the fact they had fallen out. After the highly convivial lunch, Neil and Alex were seen to have their arms around each other, proving he can forgive and forget, contrary to popular opinion.

Ferguson has enjoyed a tempestuous relationship with the media, periodically banning a newspaper or two and the odd broadcaster from his press conferences, a kind of sin-bin punishment for something he has taken offence to. A BBC documentary that involved his son Jason, has meant that he refuses to give post-match interviews to *Match of the Day*, much to the annoyance of Gary Lineker.

Sir Alex has blown his top with just about every journalist he has come into contact with – including myself. My experience of the famous Fergie hair-dryer came on the steps of the stand at Selhurst Park, not far from where Eric Cantona had performed his infamous Kung Fu attack on a fan who had been berating him after a red card. It was there that the Manchester United manager chose to turn purple in the face and launch a tirade of four letter abuse in my direction. He had been inflamed by a *Mirror* article on the morning of that particular match discussing the Cantona incident and talking about the security issues, which Alex felt had only served to potentially provoke a delicate issue. I tried to point out that it had been written by one of my *Mirror* colleagues in the north, and the first I had known about it was when I, too, read it in the *Mirror* that morning.

Unfortunately, Fergie firmly believed, that everyone associated me with the *Mirror* at that time, as if everything the paper did or printed, was somehow connected to me, or that I must have influenced it.

The rant got progressively worse and more abusive. But I cut Fergie off in his prime by telling him that I wasn't prepared to even discuss it any longer as it had nothing to do with me. That seemed to make matters worse and he swore at me a few more times before opting to depart the briefing with the senior football writers, which he had agreed to do after his main press conference.

Ferguson often tests you with such rants. He expects an almost grovelling apology and then perhaps he will take you back into the fold. He received no such apology from me. But the nature of my job meant that I didn't need to speak to him on a regular basis, nor attend his press conferences if he chose to bar me or my paper.

However, I have never taken his outlandish rant seriously, nor have I allowed it to detract from my enormous respect for his achievements that put him at the summit of all time British bosses. In fact I wrote a book about Ferguson, interviewing around a hundred of those who knew him best, to analyse the man and his career. Just about everyone had fallen out with him at one time of another. If it's not journalists, he is berating his own players or, as in the case of David Beckham, kicking a boot in his direction.

SIR TOM FINNEY
Legendary England winger of the 1940s and 1950s

One of the prized pictures on my wall has Sir Stanley Matthews on one side of me and Sir Tom Finney on the other. Two of the most famous wingers together at the same time, and a photo opportunity I was not going to miss. The same thought occurred to the *Mail's* Brian Woolnough and he too is in the same shot. The arguments will rage about who has been the greatest British footballer of all time and most would point straight to George Best, with Bobby Moore in second place, but Matthews and Finney would most definitely be in my top five along with Kenny Dalglish.

DANNY FIZMAN
Arsenal Director

Danny must be one of the least known directors and majority shareholders in football anywhere in the world. Outside of Highbury, few fans, if any, would probably have heard of him. He is never quoted, never seen on TV and he shuns the media. But on a number of trips covering the Gunners in Europe, I have had the opportunity to speak with Danny. You will not find a more loyal Arsenal supporter anywhere. He is a diamond geezer. Well, pardon me for the pun, his business is diamonds.

GERRY FRANCIS
Former England captain and manager of Spurs and QPR

Gerry once invited me to the Playboy club in London as the venue for an interview for my first ever book, *The Treatment of Football Injuries*. Gerry was the England captain of his generation and had been treated with alternative medicines and manipulation techniques for a back complaint, so was able to give me a unique insight into how those techniques had helped a top level footballer. I got to know him much better when he became Tottenham manager.

MONTE FRESCO
Legendary photographer

Monte was recognised as the most famous sports photographer of his generation. It was a privilege to work with him for so long on the *Mirror*, until, after so many Sports Editors, he got fed up with his pictures either not being used or his 'credit' by-line being reduced in size or again not even used. He quit to go freelance and sign up for a photographic agency. Monte is a good friend as well as a colleague and I will, perhaps, remember him most for when we went on assignment to Tirana, two of the first sports journalists ever to be allowed into Albania.

England had been drawn against Albania in their 1990 World Cup qualifying group and had never played them before. I thought it would be a coup if we could get in to the country ahead of the tie. It wasn't easy. But I knew Kevin Maxwell had an office in Paris and I thought with his family's Eastern European connections, they might be able to pull a few strings. After a few weeks of nagging Kevin, he eventually, through some diplomatic means, got the go-ahead to send Monte and myself to the Albanian Embassy in Paris to apply for accreditation. We found this tiny embassy in the back streets of the French capital, and it was like something from a James Bond novel as we entered the dark, dingy, rooms with their smell of intrigue and met the counsel who went through our documents and asked a number of questions before stamping our passports with the appropriate visa.

Monte took some pics of me at the near Champs Elysee with the documentation to illustrate the series of articles we were now planning for the paper.

We made our travel arrangements and on arriving in Tirana, we were met by a driver who was clearly part of the nation's secret services. He hardly left our side during the entire three day trip. We were warned not to bring any glossy magazines into the country that might be construed as western decadence, and we were told it would be unwise to take any pictures unless they were authorised.

Monte took pictures of the stadium where England were to play, featuring the less than basic conditions in the dressing rooms, where the hot water rarely worked. We learned that the star Albanian internationals travelled to the games by bike. We sampled the England team hotel and tried the food. There was an extensive 20-page menu with just about everything on it. Unfortunately they didn't seem to be serving any of it that particular day, but chicken was on.

We ordered our starter, main course and dessert, and waited for some considerable time, wondering what the delay could possibly be as we were the only ones dining that evening. All three courses came at the same time. None of the locals probably ordered more than one course, or could afford to.

It made a very interesting feature. Bobby Robson's England escaped with a 2-0 victory en route to the semi-finals of the World Cup in Italy.

KEN FRIAR
Arsenal Boot Room stalwart

Ken Friar is one of the unsung heroes of Arsenal, and was one of the most influential and authoritative figures of their back room staff until he eventually retired. It has been an honour to have known someone so dedicated to the Gunners for so long. And I say that as a lifelong Spurs fan!

Ken was one of the old school characters, almost of an age far removed from the present, more cynical and commercially-led game. Ken was always hard to prize information from, but you were never misled by him. This is an object lesson for any budding sports journalist, or indeed, any reporter. Know your contacts, and trust those who can be trusted.

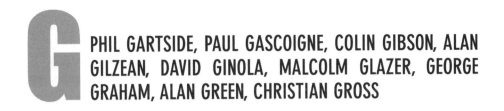

PHIL GARTSIDE, PAUL GASCOIGNE, COLIN GIBSON, ALAN GILZEAN, DAVID GINOLA, MALCOLM GLAZER, GEORGE GRAHAM, ALAN GREEN, CHRISTIAN GROSS

PHIL GARTSIDE
Chairman of Bolton Wanderers

The Bolton chairman showed during *Five's* coverage of Bolton in Europe during the 2005/06 season that he can be media friendly, but I have had a run-in with him over his manager Sam Allardyce and his links to his agent son Craig, which I questioned in an article in the *Express*. (See Sam & Craig Allardyce)

Phil is also an FA Board member, so it was natural that he should be sensitive to my exposé on Big Sam and Little Craig. His call to reproach me for having the gall to question such a relationship must have lasted two hours – even by my standards this was an epic. It didn't start off too well, with threats of legal action, but Phil eventually calmed down and at least we agreed to disagree. The issue centred on the transfer of former Everton player Idan Tal, who was back in Israel and was available on a free transfer. Three agents were linked to Tal, and it was a messy business, certainly questionably open to the potential for abuse, just as Big Sam was being sounded out by FA Chief Executive Brian Barwick as one of the contenders to succeed Sven-Göran Eriksson as the England Head Coach. Phil was most miffed by the *Express* investigation into the activities of Craig and the other agents, one of them unlicensed, and it was also at the time that Lord Stevens had been appointed to head up the enquiry into Premier League transfers.

I still feel I was right to raise the issue, but Phil assures me that Big Sam is an honourable man, despite the allegations in the BBC's *Panorama* programme.

PAUL GASCOIGNE
Everyone's favourite Geordie, with more hang-ups than a switchboard operator

Larry Harrison is a fictitious journalist at the *Express*, whose name might remind the reader of someone, that appears in the recently published novel *Burksey: the Autobiography of a Football God* by inspirational comedy writer Peter Morfoot. The book is about a Gazza-type footballer, the anti-hero, Stephen 'Burksey' Burkes, whose ridiculous antics bring him to the forefront of national popularity. Burksey's late 1980s success is down to his superagent, Dave Green; a fiction which is based in fact.

Mel Stein, who was Gazza's minder and agent for more than a decade, was responsible for Gazza shooting into the superstardom stratosphere, using Gazza's personality and antics to put him right in the public eye. Stein also wrote the authorised biography of Paul Gascoigne and in it he said, '*The Sun* started Gazzamania officially with their constant use of the phrase, but Harry Harris in the *Mirror*, had probably been responsible for coining the phrase almost a year before. All *The Sun* was doing, as it did so often, was reflecting public opinion.'

Gazza was a favourite player of mine, to such an extent that when I got my first PC at the *Mirror*, and had to use a password, I chose G-A-Z-Z-A, and I then used it throughout my stay there.

When Robert Maxwell made his pitch to buy Spurs, he wanted to have his picture taken with Gazza. He also loved the idea of owning the club where Gazza played.

As Stein wrote, 'On 9 September, the morning after the Derby game, the headlines were not so much about Paul's hat-trick as Robert Maxwell's bid for Tottenham. Paul's reaction was immediate: 'I'm not playing for that fat bastard. If he takes over then I'm off' (see Johann Cruyff). He knew the appalling way Maxwell, when owner of Derby, had treated Arthur Cox, knew that football to him was an ego trip rather than a passion, and wanted no part of it.

'Harry Harris of the *Daily Mirror* phoned me on behalf of his newspaper's proprietor to ask if there was any chance of a photo of Gazza with Maxwell if the deal went through. 'No chance', was the reply.'

As the battle for control of Spurs hotted up, it finally came down to the wire between Maxwell v Sugar. Ironic, as Maxwell was my ultimate boss, and Sugar would eventually become a close associate, albeit some considerable time after the dust had settled on the in-fighting to gain the Spurs shares.

Stein wrote, 'But Maxwell was still playing his own game, and whilst no formal proposal had been made, he was still using the *Mirror* to sway public opinion in his favour by its campaign to keep Gazza, as a national treasure, in the country of his birth. Harry Harris, chief football writer of the *Mirror*, was recalled from aboard.'

Mel was referring to how I was summoned from Malaysia, the last port of call for a summer England tour in 1991, to help Maxwell orchestrate his final pitch to buy Spurs (See Gary Lineker).

It was my idea to focus on Gazza, whom Venables had lined up for a move to Lazio. And, I am sure, Maxwell's pitch to keep Gazza had resonance with Spurs fans, who were devastated that he had to be sold off to pay off the debts. It nearly worked, but Sugar won the day, which was probably for the best for all concerned in the long run given the later revelations about Maxwell's plundering of the *Mirror's* pension schemes.

COLIN GIBSON
Former sports journalist and FA Head of Communications

Colin and I struck up a close working friendship as on-the-road football writers, when I worked for the *Mirror* and he was the Chief Football Correspondent for the *Telegraph*. Together with Steve Curry on the *Express* and Stuart Jones on the *Times*, and then Neil Harman on the *Mail*, we formed The Morris Men, thus named because we seemed to dance to the same tune and on occasions we shared the same 'inside' information.

We experienced some truly unbelievable escapades, usually involving other journalists. Once, as the Morris Men enjoyed a touch of the Sardinian sun prior to the start of the Italia 90 World Cup, the Chief Football writer for the *Star*, who shall remain nameless, strolled along the beach to find me, all booted and suited and carrying his luggage. Having sought me out, he announced that he was going home because he wasn't feeling too well, and wanted to thank me for all my help, compared to some of the journalists he could mention who had done everything they could to make life difficult for him. I was later told that he had something akin to a nervous breakdown. I have never seen that particular gentleman again ever since that moment of madness on the Forte Village beach.

It was a sad day when Colin announced he had been offered a post as a Sports Editor of the *Telegraph* and had decided to accept. It was never quite the same without the chief organiser and social arranger within our group.

Colin advanced to become Sports Editor of the *Daily Mail*, and when he heard I was leaving the *Mirror* for the *Express*, he took me out to lunch and offered me a post on the *Mail*, but he was unable to pull it off.

His next move was to become Head of Communications for the Football Association. He enjoyed the World Cup tournament in 2002, but quickly became one of the high profile victims of the Sven-Göran Eriksson-Faria Alam affair. Mark Palios, once it became public knowledge that he had also been sleeping with Miss Alam, lost his prestigious post as Chief Executive and Colin quickly followed.

Colin's mistake was to try to make a pact with the devil, a Sunday newspaper, to protect his FA employers by spinning a particular version of the story which was not precisely the truth, but it backfired horribly. It just underlines the pitfalls even for a vastly experienced journalist like Colin, to deal with Sunday newspapers when the stakes are so high.

When I first started out, editors often called the sports desk, and its personnel, the 'Toy Department', because of the softer touch toward journalism, compared to the more hard-nosed aspects of news gathering.

Nowadays, of course, the two extremes of journalisms are rapidly merging, but even now there is less edge to sports reporting than news. That's why it was a grave error of judgment on Colin's part to attempt to strike a deal with the sector of a newspaper that generally takes no prisoners. Colin would have continued for many years in his role as the FA's head of communications had he not been so naive as to attempt to pull off such a clandestine deal behind the scenes.

Once it began to go pear-shaped, he inevitably became one of the victims. Usually, a journalist will always abide by the 'off the record' understanding that exists between the reporter and his contact. Here, it was different. It was experienced journalist to former journalist, and it seemed the unwritten code went out of the window, and Colin with it. The tables were turned on a journalist – by a journalist.

For me that stinks. In some quarters, no doubt, there would have been immense satisfaction. Colin, in his former life as head of sport for the *Daily Mail*, would have made enough enemies who would have rejoiced in his downfall at Soho Square, particularly in the way that it occurred.

Colin's other passion is cricket and he was a fair performer in his youth, and he has now reinvented himself as the head of communications for the Cricket Board of England and Wales.

MISSING THE BOAT

ALAN GILZEAN
1970s Scottish Spurs striker

Sometimes you can miss a story that's right under your nose.

I was so nervous about presenting a bag full of footballs to the lucky Weekly Herald prize winners on the White Hart Lane pitch before a game, that I didn't notice how one fan had run onto the pitch and kissed the feet of legendary striker Gilly.

The first I knew of it was when I picked up the *Evening Standard* the next day and there was the picture on the back page. You can't win 'em all!

IS GINOLA WORTH IT?

DAVID GINOLA
Outrageously talented French winger for Spurs and Newcastle. Many felt him a luxury, but David believed he was worth it

David Ginola hiring Cherie Blair, the Prime Minister's barrister wife and an expert in employment law, to bring a case against Aston Villa and John Gregory, made the front page of the *Mirror* in one of the more offbeat of my footballing stories on 15 August 2001. It made all the TV and radio news bulletins and was inevitably followed up by all of our rivals.

The image-conscious Frenchman, as famous for his L'Oreal adverts and his flowing locks as for his flowing football, was contemplating an amazing legal fight with his club claiming he was subjected to defamatory remarks about his physique. Gregory had publicly accused the Frenchman of being overweight and lacking professionalism after his poor display against Liverpool in January 2001.

Professional Footballers Association Chief Executive Gordon Taylor had been in touch with the Villa boss and then chairman Doug Ellis in an attempt to resolve the matter, while Cherie Blair, also spoke with Taylor.

"Cherie Blair rang me before she went to Argentina with her family," Taylor was quoted as saying in the *Mirror*. "She wanted to check out footballing procedures." Taylor then spoke to Gregory. "He told me he was entitled to do with his players as he wished," he said. It came to nothing, but is a good example of the types of ego which create problems in the modern game that simply didn't exist thirty years ago when I first started reporting on football.

MALCOLM GLAZER
Billionaire American owner of Manchester United and Green Bay Packers

Although I have never met Malcolm Glazer, I have come to know a number of his aides and advisors extremely well. It has been refreshing to be briefed by City types who seem to be much more amenable to telling the truth than I often experience within the football industry. They steered me towards believing that the Glazer family would buy Manchester United and they didn't let me down. My series of articles on the Glazer saga proved to be rewarding as they led to highly commended awards two years running. The first year the story was recognised with a Highly Commended in the Sports Journalists Association Sports News Reporter of the Year category, the following year, as the story was concluded, it earned runner up in the Sports Story of the Year awards.

GEORGE GRAHAM
Controversial former Arsenal, Leeds and Spurs manager, sacked at Highbury for his part in a 1990s bung scandal

George was known as 'Stroller' as a player and had a reputation as a ladies man and a rebel, who was once sent home by his Chelsea manager for misbehaving along with a group of the stars of that era. Ironically Graham the manager was the archetypal disciplinarian, only fall to from grace at Arsenal when he was hung out to dry over the bung scandal.

When Graham later popped up as Spurs manager, I felt it was a strange choice for Alan Sugar, and told him so at the time. When Alan rang me to tell me he had definitely appointed Graham as his manager, I was sitting in the press box in Monte Carlo watching a Super Cup game, and told the Spurs chairman that he had appointed an outstanding manager, one of the finest of his generation, but he was also appointing a man who would never be taken to the heart of the Spurs supporters and it would all end in tears. Alan, as was his nature, became very defensive about it, and, although to a degree, he shared my reservations, he explained how he had left it to the so-called professionals on his board and the overwhelming recommendation had been the appointment of Graham.

Graham did win Alan his sole trophy as Spurs chairman, the League Cup in 1999, but eventually, inevitably Graham was on his way out.

And, of course, as usual I got the blame for Graham's sacking.

As it turned out, I did play a hand in Graham's departure, but purely an unwitting one as I was merely doing my job – in pursuit of a good story.

I noticed Graham on the ITV local news programme *London Tonight* complaining about his budget, the fact that he couldn't spend as much money as he had wanted. This was a sore point with Sugar, who was often criticised by the Spurs fans for not spending enough, when in reality during his reign his club was among the biggest spenders in the country. I knew this would hit a raw nerve and pursued the matter, tracking down David Buchler, the club's Executive Vice-Chairman, for a reaction.

It proved to be a pretty powerful one – and was clearly the prelude to a confrontation between George and the Board that led to Graham's departure.

Buchler might never have responded publicly if I hadn't been successful in tracking him down, as an article in the *Sunday Telegraph* at the time reported in graphic detail. Colin Malam's analysis of how Graham came to be sacked included a section devoted to my involvement in the affair, as he wrote....

'The strangest thing about the whole affair is the rather implausible explanation Buchler gave for the appearance in the *Mirror* on Friday – the day every other newspaper eagerly carried Graham's complaint about a 'limited budget' – of an exclusive story quoting the Executive Vice-Chairman as telling the manager to shut up. According to Buchler, it came about quite by chance.

"It so happened that when I came out of a meeting on Thursday night at about 6pm," he said, "I put my phone on to ring my wife. I pressed the green button and, instead of getting my wife, Harry Harris, the *Mirror's* chief football writer, had just phoned in. He asked me if I knew about Graham's remarks. I said "no" and added that it was not the sort of thing I wanted to have discussed in the press. I really didn't think that the press should know about the intricacies of a meeting."

That didn't just happen by coincidence. I must have rung Buckler's mobile number a hundred times that evening, maybe even more, determined that I would get hold of him, knowing the fragile position of Graham at that time, and the delicacy of his remarks. Colin Malam pointed out that to publicly express concern about having a limited budget is an old managerial trick to prise more cash out of the board, but not at Tottenham, and not at that time. Graham knew the score, it was as if he was pressing the self-destruct button.

So just three weeks before the 2001 FA Cup semi-final against Arsenal, Graham was sacked when Buchler called him in the next day for an explanation of his comments.

Did I play a part in Graham's sacking? Colin Malam seems to think so, and I am not going to argue with such an esteemed football writer.

THE VOICE OF FOOTBALL

ALAN GREEN
BBC Radio FiveLive's opinionated, but entertaining Irish commentator

Greenie and I set up an internet site called Voice of Football that enjoyed a million hits in the first week. We kept it going for some time, before it became so much of a time burden that we sold out to Sportal and continued to write columns under the VOF title. Despite all the trials and tribulations of trying to run what amounted to a business as well as proving the content and still doing our day jobs, Greenie and I never fell out and we have remained firm friends.

A GROSS MISTAKE

CHRISTIAN GROSS
Swiss former Spurs coach

Alan Sugar and I had a bit of a falling out over the appointment of Christian Gross (see Sven-Göran Eriksson). I was trying to push him in the direction of Sven-Göran Eriksson.

That was a fair argument, but I had my doubts whether a total unknown in the UK, would stand much of a chance, particularly whether he would be accepted by the fans, or indeed the media.

The whole arrangement just didn't sound right to me and I made my views known to Alan, which didn't make me very popular at the time.

As soon as he arrived at Heathrow and caught the tube to Seven Sisters station, you just knew Gross would end up being a figure of fun. He lasted a mere 9 months before my prophecy of an early sacking became a reality. Alan didn't thank me for saying, "I told you so."

TONY HADLEY, ERIC HALL, MATTHEW HARDING, KEITH HARRIS, RON HARRIS, THIERRY HENRY, JIMMY HILL, GLENN HODDLE, KATE HOEY, JOHN HOLLINS, JON HOLMES, DON HOWE, ALAN HUDSON, GEOFF HURST

TONY HADLEY
Spandau Ballet's charismatic singer

You have to hand it to then *Mirror* editor Piers Morgan, his initiative The Pride of Britain awards was inspired, and it attracted a galaxy of stars, with Tony Blair hosting the glittering occasion.

One year I found myself 'hosting' a table on behalf of the newspaper that contained Ronan Keating and Tony Hadley, both the pop stars had an enormous interest in football. It was quite embarrassing because they seemed to know who I was, but I was struggling with the finer details of their music backgrounds. Unfortunately, I am so one-dimensional, so preoccupied with football, my job really being a paid hobby, that I know so little about 'real life' outside of the sport. So being far from an expert on the music industry I decided to slip away on the pretext of going to the loo, to ring my wife Linda who I knew would fill in all the details. Armed with all the data I felt much more comfortable.

Tony told me of his strong Arsenal allegiance, and I have kept in contact with him since that first meeting, ringing him in the States to tell him that we would be voting for him when he won the TV competition, *Reborn In The USA.*

ERIC HALL
Football's 'monster' agent of the enormous cigars

It's hard to distinguish between Eric Hall the football agent, and Eric Hall the music hall sideshow. He represented Terry Venables for a time, then his only high profile client was Dennis Wise.

I got hold of a series of dubious invoices that Eric submitted to Tottenham when Terry was Chief Executive, some of which appeared in the *Mirror* during the course of my investigations in Venables' financial dealings that lead to a full FA investigation. Hard to be friends after that. (See Terry Venables)

One of my treasured pictures alongside the legendary Bill Nicholson, during the height of his career as Spurs manager. Magical. I went on to persuade a very reluctant Billy Nick to write his memoirs, which we did in conjunction with my *Daily Mail* colleague Brian Scovell. (See Bill Nicholson)

Starting out with a weekly show on Hospital radio at Whipps Cross in Leytonstone.
My co-host was the football writer from the rival local paper the *Guardian*, Steve Tongue, who is now the highly respected football correspondent of the *Independent on Sunday*.

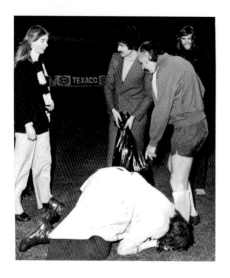

One of my most embarrassing professional moments. Before Alan Gilzean's testimonial, as I concentrated on the task of handing out the footballs, I didn't even notice a Spurs fan rush onto the White Hart Lane pitch and kiss Gilly's feet. The next day, I knew all about it as the picture appeared on the back page of the rival London evening paper. (See Alan Gilzean)

The Mirror had this picture taken in their studios for promotional purposes. 'Star' writers, including myself, John Blake, the legendary Marjorie Proops, Anne Robinson and Joe Haines, the political writer, featured in the campaign.

Spurs manager Terry Neill and I had a bet about who would be the quickest round the perimeter of the White Hart Lane pitch. I shot off into a shock lead, but I quickly ran out of steam and Terry finished the easy winner. He would never have lived down losing to the local sports reporter! (See Terry Neill)

A chance to interview one of my boyhood heroes, Spurs full-back Cyril Knowles, in the back of a cab during my days as a novice football reporter for the local *North London Weekly Herald.* This is one of the pictures I specifically told the publisher could not be used under any circumstances – just look at that Jason King look alike on the left, how embarrassing!

These were the days that, wherever the England squad went, the press corps were right with them. There were far fewer of us back then and we travelled with the players, shared the same hotel etc. Not any more, of course. On this trip to Egypt in 1986, where else would one go for a photo op? The Pyramids to ride a camel.

The former *Mirror* proprietor Robert Maxwell pops down to the editorial floor on hearing that Channel 4 boss Michael Grade was visiting, re-living his days as a *Mirror* junior reporter. 'Captain Bob' had a reputation for being an office bully and at times it was hugely justified, but he could also be charming and marvellous company.

Enjoying a drink and a laugh with Maxwell. He once offered me the editorship of the *Mirror*, but I declined as I knew it was not for me (See Robert Maxwell)

Still my favourite footballer - Pelé.

Gazza failed to turn up for this specially arranged photo shoot in the *Mirror's* own studios, so the sports editor's bright idea was for me to be Gazza, posing alongside Italia 90 heroes Gary Lineker, David Seaman and Paul Parker.

Visiting exotic locations is one the perks of the job, but when England were drawn against Albania in the World Cup for the first time, it was off to Tirana, and that, believe me, is not one for future holiday venues. (See Monte Fresco)

Interviewing Gary Lineker at Heathrow Airport before we all departed for a sneak preview of his new life in Japan with Nagoya Grampus 8. (See Gary Lineker)

Winning The Press Gazette Sports Journalist of the Year award for the first time in 1993.

The press team played their own European Championships in Sweden and it will be easy to spot our 'ringers' Sir Bobby Charlton and Big Ron Atkinson! (See Trevor Brooking)

Some of the media covering England's pre-Euro 96 trip to the Far East pose on the Great Wall of China. (Clockwise from back left) Mike Ingham, Henry Winter, Steve Curry, Gary Newbon, Alan Green, Neil Harman and myself. This trip, of course, sparked the infamous 'Dentist's Chair' story

Highly Commended in the Sports News Reporter of the Year award in 1997.

With co-author Danny Fullbrook (standing) of the *Daily Star* (a big Fulham fan) I wrote a book commemorating Fulham's first season back in the big time. Mohamed Al Fayed graciously came down from his office to take a peek at the book's launch at Harrods. Al Fayed enjoyed himself so much he stayed, posed for these pictures, and even signed a few autographs. (See Mohamed Al Fayed)

On assignment, watching Trinidad & Tobago fail against the USA in their final qualifying tie to reach the 1990 World Cup. Dwight Yorke starred for T&T at the age of 16, but finally realised his dream by coming out of retirement to play in the 2006 World Cup in Germany. This is a picture of the incredible crowd queuing to get in on the morning of the match that took place in the early evening. (See Dwight Yorke)

Showing off my skills to then England manager Glenn Hoddle (right) with the *Mail's* Brian Woolnough looking on in admiration. At least I think that's what he's thinking…

Bungs... Sports Minister Kate Hoey raised questions in the House about the culture of corruption, giving me a mention in the Commons.

Sometimes you might need a hard hat with Kenneth Bates! Only joking, Ken. He proudly showed me around his vision of Chelsea Village while it was still being built.

Chesterfield were docked nine points after my *Mirror* investigation into their bungs, but the players didn't appreciate it very much and showed their feelings after their final match of the season when striker David Reeves removed his shirt to pay his own special tribute. (See Graham Bean)

Before the 1999 FA Cup final, Ruud Gullit afforded me an exclusive interview at Newcastle's training HQ in Northumberland.

Piers Morgan at the *Press Gazette* British Press Awards night celebrating after his team of *Mirror* journalists won four prestigious awards. Piers leapt on stage with a waste paper basket to symbolise what he thought of the *Sun* and to take the Mickey out of his rival Editor Stuart Higgins.

Pictured with the League Cup trophy, the last Cup won by my boyhood team, Spurs

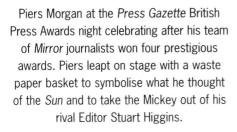

The four *Mirror* winners in 1998. It was a proud moment for me to win the Sports Reporter of the Year Award, the second time I had been honoured in these awards.

I've had my ups and downs with Dennis Wise, but this was one of the ups when,
as Chelsea captain, he afforded me an exclusive interview prior to the 2001 FA Cup Final,
which we conducted in the stand at the Bridge. (See Dennis Wise)

One of the journalists who I believe deserves enormous respect is investigative reporter Mihir Bose.

Receiving The Silver Heart from Gary Newbon, the master of ceremonies at the
Royal Variety Club of Great Britain's lunch time bash. I was awarded a lifetime achievement
award for Contribution to Sports Journalism in 2004.

Guests on one of my ntlworld World cup web cast shows were (from left) former Charlton
manager Alan Curbishley, Crystal Palace chairman Simon Jordan and Samsung Mobile
director Mark Mitchinson, whose company sponsor Chelsea to the tune of £55m. Other
guests during the five show series included Minister of Sport Richard Caborn, Everton
chairman Bill Kenwright, former referee Jeff Winter, 1966 World cup heroes Geoff Hurst and
George Cohen, plus PR guru Max Clifford, Harry Redknapp, Mick McCarthy, Peter Bonetti,
Paul Parker, and agents Pini Zahavi, Athol Still, Jon Smith, and Colin Gordon.

reproduced by kind permission of Mirror Group Newspapers

Appearing as a cartoon character, portrayed as a confidante of the central character in the Scorer strip cartoon in the *Mirror*.

I was at Wembley as a youngster to watch the Boys of 66 win the Jules Rimet trophy, so it was a personal thrill to have so many at one of my recent book launches.
(From left) Martin Peters, George Cohen, Jack Charlton and Gordon Banks.
Martin I have known since his playing days at Spurs, while it has been an honour to have got to know George on a personal level.

Winner of Sports Reporter of the Year in the British Sports Journalist Awards organised by the Sports Council and the then Sports Writers Association.

It's been a hell of a career with plenty of exclusives, exposés, memorable moments and some hairy ones as well. But I wouldn't have swapped it for anything.

MATTHEW HARDING
The man who took on Ken Bates at Chelsea, but sadly died in a helicopter crash before the entire scenario played out

Harding arrived at Chelsea with a £5million loan to finance the rebuilding of a new stand, and he backed chairman Ken Bates with the recruitment of Glenn Hoddle as manager, and the acquisition of internationals Ruud Gullit and Mark Hughes that changed the dynamics of the club, taking it forward to its next significant stage after all of Ken's hard work.

But Matthew wanted more, much more. He craved control of the club and Ken wasn't going to give up easily. Matthew was the Terry Venables of the boardroom, affable, amenable, approachable, and would happily be the media's drinking partner. In contrast Ken was seen by much of the media as hard work. While most sided with Matthew, I backed Bates. Matthew appeared to be the People's Choice, but that was to underestimate the loyal following Bates had created over many years of striving for the good of Chelsea.

And, when you dug a little deeper, Matthew's CV was a touch tainted. Of course there is no point now in speaking ill of the dead, and Matthew suffered a tragic end, dying in a helicopter crash on the way back from a Chelsea away game. But he did have a good sense of irony. After one match at the Bridge, I was standing in the corridor waiting to interview one or two of the players, when Matthew strolled past catching the eye of all the journalists he knew. He stopped and spoke to them, then he spotted me, the author of several articles championing Bates' cause. "Well, Harry, I would just like to personally thank you for all your help and support." With that he smiled and walked off to see Glenn Hoddle in his manager's office.

KEITH HARRIS
Former Chairman of the Football League

The former Football League Chairman, and huge Manchester United fan, is wonderful company, a fascinating character, and highly respected in City circles. Not one of my usually footballing contacts, Keith is more of a trusted friend, and they are few and far between.

Keith was genuinely keen to make a contribution in preventing the Glazers from buying Manchester United. He provided me with a wealth of interesting data to help me with a series of articles on the Glazers' £800m takeover, that really few people ever thought would come off. Keith had his doubts, but always warned me not to underestimate the Glazers' resolve. He was right.

A ROCKET FROM RON

RON HARRIS
Chelsea's Chopper

Chopper can still be pretty cutting with his comments – his opinions are as savage as his tackles – and I have received a Chopper rebuke in my time.

Ron rang to respond to an article that appeared in the *Express* quoting Ken Bates at great length talking about some of the players of the 70s. The then Chelsea chairman was keen put a stop to everyone harking back to the past, and also was none too pleased with some of the comments attributed to Chopper about how everything had improved with the arrival of Roman Abramovich. Bates' comments hit home with Ron, who rang me to complain and had a right old rant. He even threatened legal action because some of the Bates remarks were potent. Ron was upset because Bates' comments came the day after the death of one of his 70s team-mates, which prompted the hard man of that team to let rip in response. His attack on Bates was never going to result in anything other than instant retribution. I reported soon afterwards that Ron had been sacked by the club.

Chopper first caught up with me when I was a guest of Samsung Mobile in a challenge match played at Stamford Bridge and Ron was guest speaker. We met again when he popped into a meet and greet at the Samsung Mobile executive box at the Bridge when I was a guest of Samsung Director Mark Mitchinson. Wherever and whenever we bump into each other he still remains as indignant as though the article was written yesterday.

When we last met up at the Gatwick Hilton for a dinner function; he could not get the Bates issues off his chest quickly enough! "Look," he told me, "I have never been sacked by Chelsea, but I did lose my £5,000 a night job as an after dinner speaker down at the Bridge as a result of your article. And, let me tell you, I never apologised in writing for that article about Bates despite what he said at the time."

HENRY WINS FOOTBALLER OF THE YEAR FOR RECORD A THIRD TIME

THIERRY HENRY
The greatest modern footballer and goalscorer

The day after Thierry's wonder goal in Madrid in the Champions League in 2006, I was having lunch in the Landmark Hotel in London with agent Jon Smith when in strolled the Arsenal icon with David Dein's son, Darren, to dine about four tables away. Thierry was still deep into new contract talks with Arsenal, spearheaded by Dein snr, with the player clearly being advised by Dein jnr. Darren Dein is a lovely lad, an expert in sports law, so I left the two of them to their own devices. But when Thierry was leaving he came over to the table and we talked for a while.

I complemented Thierry on a goal I told him was the best I had seen in that season's Champions League. He modestly shrugged his shoulders, and said he felt it would be a tough second leg. I agreed, but a lot would depend on whether Ronaldo lost a bit of weight. As it turned out Arsenal were in control and then went on to produce another outstanding performance in the first leg of the quarter-final at Highbury against Juventus. After that I voted for Thierry as Footballer of the Year for 2005/06, an accolade he subsequently won, making him the first player to do so on three occasions.

JIMMY HILL
Football's greatest survivor, having worked for BBC, ITV and now Sky after a career playing for Fulham and as manager and Chairman of various clubs

Sky TV's Sunday morning chat show is where I usually meet up with Jimmy to spend some quality time discussing the big issues in football, provoked by the back pages of the Sunday papers.

Jimmy Hill's Sunday Supplement takes place in Jimmy's mocked-up kitchen, where only the croissants and orange juice are real. It's one of the shows I enjoy doing, the only problem is that sometimes it feels as though an hour isn't long enough, especially with the Ad breaks in between. Make no mistake, the debate continues during the adverts. In fact it starts around an hour before transmission and would carry on for hours afterwards if we didn't all have to dash away from Sky's Isleworth studios.

Vic Wakeling, head of Sky Sport, made the decision to scrap Sky's original Saturday night media show, *Hold The Back Page*, in favour of the gentler *Jimmy Hill's Sunday Supplement* hosted by the genial, but opinionated Jimmy with a great deal of concern from the journalists that it wouldn't work. The new show features regular guest Brian Woolnough of the *Mail* plus two guest football writers.

But Vic has been proved right. With *Hold The Back Page* there were always four major football writers around the table, all trying to score points off each other. Sometimes it lead to slanging matches, and often it would get quite nasty depending on the mix and there were shows where some pundits insisted on talking over what you were trying to say, and I pitied the audience, who probably couldn't make out a single word of it.

How long before Vic comes up with yet another format, only he knows.

GLENN HODDLE
Genius midfielder with Spurs, whose coaching career has seen him in charge at Swindon, Chelsea, Southampton, Spurs, Wolves and, of course, England

The day Glenn Hoddle was sacked as England coach I shared the entire day of gloom with him and his agent Dennis Roach, pacing up and down his London terraced Town House in Queen's Gate, Kensington, awaiting the decision from the Football Association. It was a stressful time, just pondering the outcome, and when the verdict finally arrived Glenn was visibly shaken, devastated, having become the first England coach to be dismissed for non-footballing issues.

The catalyst for Hoddle's exit had been a media campaign against him.

He returned a hero from the 1998 World Cup in France, where David Beckham had been sent off against Argentina and 10-man England had put up a courageous fight in their second round match, but gone out on penalties.

But a poor start in the following European Championship campaign saw the anti-Hoddle faction get to work. Hoddle was savaged for his World Cup Diary, even though it had been co-written by the FA's own Head of Communications David Davies. In it Hoddle hadn't said very much more than was already known about his well publicised confrontation with Paul Gascoigne when Hoddle had left Gazza out of the World Cup squad, at La Manga's five star hotel, where the England coach told all the players from his initial squad selection whether they would be included in the final 23 or not.

Gazza's wife Sheryl first sold the story within an hour of being told of what happened in Hoddle's hotel room in La Manga, then Gazza did his newspaper 'buy-up', but somehow many sections of the media deemed it was wrong for Hoddle to give his full version in the book.

Ten days before Hoddle's enforced exit, I had organised an informal off-the-record lunch with the England manager and half a dozen senior football writers, who, as yet, were not committed to forcing the FA's hand into pushing Hoddle through the exit door. We gathered at Scalini's restaurant in Walton Street, and among those present were Danny Fullbrook, and his close friend on the *Daily Mail*, Ian McGarry. I advised Glenn to be circumspect with his interviews, and he was welcome to ask my advice at any time. We were, after all, old friends, going back to his Tottenham playing days when I 'ghosted' his autobiography just as he left for Monaco.

I had been in Toulon with a group of colleagues covering the under-20 tournament when we heard that Hoddle was being transferred from his beloved Spurs. Bob Harris from rival newspaper *Today* told us all that he was going to Paris St. Germain, but I knew differently. I had spoken with Glenn and knew he was on his way to Monte Carlo. I left the media hotel with a couple of other journalists to head for Monte Carlo, while Bob and one or two others, headed off to Paris. Well, you choose who you share your inside information with in this business.

There was a trust between Glenn and myself and I felt he had taken the wrong advice when he agreed to be interviewed by the respected Chief Football Correspondent of the *Times*. But the go ahead was given by Davies. To be fair to the correspondent on the *Times*, he had not made an awful lot of an off-the-cuff comment from Hoddle about the disabled; accordingly to the tittle-tattle at the time, it was toward the end of his long interview, however, one of the sub-editors on the sports desk had a handicapped child and took great offence to some of the remarks. The article was turned on its head, and made enormous impact. Yet, just a year earlier Hoddle had made similar assertoins in a radio interview, but they had made few adverse headlines because England were heading off to the World Cup Finals on a high.

Glenn swears that his comments to the *Times* on the disabled were off the record, and taken out of context. The journalist took the precaution of taping the interview, and continues to call Hoddle a "liar" for denying "I said them things" in Clinton-esque fashion. Personally I think he would be best to leave the past in the past, considering all the circumstances of the 'interview'.

Perhaps I am too much of the old school, who believes that if someone affords you an exclusive interview, you owe them back in return a degree of protection against themselves. Clearly, the modern way is to hit them hard, and not worry about ever returning for another interview. Put it this way, Hoddle would never again give this particular journalist another crack – and no doubt he wouldn't want one.

Hoddle's grievance about the circumstances of his England sacking will live with him forever, and I am sure if he makes a Premiership comeback as a manager, he would still like to return to the England post sometime in the future, and that will depend on how successful he can become. The *Times* football correspondent will then have to campaign, with all his FA contacts, hard to ensure that never happens.

I still bump into Glenn, who returns to Sunningdale from time to time and enjoys a quick lunch at Cafe Figo, where Sky presenter Richard Keys can also often be found.

KATE HOEY
Former Labour Minister of Sport

Kate was an exceptional Minister of Sport. She was proud to have become the first women to hold the post and bitterly upset when she was relieved of her duties. As an Arsenal fan, Kate certainly had a 'feel' for the national sport, and all credit to her for taking up the campaign to rid football of sleaze and corruption.

I spent a long night in the House waiting for Kate to make a speech to the few MPs still around, but it made back page news in the *Mirror*.

Parliamentary Debates, Monday 30 January 1995, in the House of Commons Official Report (Hansard) records Kate's long speech on football corruption, in which she sad: "It must be remembered that all the allegations and investigations now being discussed come from outside the game, or from newcomers to the game. Particular credit must be paid to the consistent investigative reporting of Harry Harris, of the *Daily Mirror*, to Patrick Barclay of the *Observer*, and to the *Mail on Sunday*, among others."

The Parliamentary Under-Secretary of State for National Heritage, Mr Ian Sproat, started by saying: "I must begin by congratulating the Honorary Member for Vauxhall on securing this debate and on her persistence in pursing allegations of improper payments and behaviour in the sport."

Of course The Government weren't interested then in cleaning up the game, and despite the well-meaning public utterances from the present Minister of Sport Richard Caborn, the Tony Blair government really aren't interested now.

JOHN HOLLINS
Former Chelsea and Arsenal midfield dynamo

'See You At The Far Post', has been John's catch phrase ever since I've known him as an all-action player in his days at Chelsea and Arsenal, then got to know him far better when he moved into management and coaching.

It was because of John's problems at Chelsea, where chairman Ken Bates sent him a letter notifying him that his contract would not be renewed at the end of the season, that I first came into contact with Mel Goldberg, an Arsenal fan who specialises in sports law, and who was representing John. It was refreshing to deal with Mel, and it produced a few back page headlines when I was able to report, with total assurance, the details of Hollins' advance sacking from the Bridge. As a result a friendship blossomed with Mel that remains just as strong today.

It's great to see John's son Chris being promoted from a sports presenter on BBC News 24 to the main BBC sports bulletins. You can tell his sporting background by those amusing participation features Chris performs most weeks. Chris did ask me if I would like to be one of his regular pundits, but his interview slot is invariably 7.30am which means a car at 6am, and as I can often be working until quite late at night, it isn't something I can really fit in apart from on the odd special occasion when I am delighted to appear.

THEY THINK IT'S ALL OVER

JON HOLMES
Football Agent extraordinaire

One of the game's super agents, who has represented, through his company SFX, former England captains, Gary Lineker and Alan Shearer, plus Michael Owen and a host of high profile sports stars such as Will Carling and David Gower. Jon helped devise the game show *They Think It's All Over* and is on the programme's credits, but his company lost its top client David Beckham, who was lured away to 19, the management company that looks after Mrs Beckham.

Tony Stephens also worked for SFX, an offshoot of an American parent company, specialising in top clients such as Beckham. Although Stephens remains as a consultant, the England captain opted for a change of direction in his management company as well as his career when he moved to Real Madrid from Manchester United. But the split was acrimonious. Beckham was still under contract, claimed SFX, when he switched to 19 and compensation was paid.

SFX now sub-let to agents who work under their umbrella and share the commissions. I have known both Jon and Tony for many years, and, while Jon has branched out, moving into part-ownership of Leicester City, Tony has been more on the road discussing deals for his clients and I know I am onto a good story if I ever bump into Tony on his travels. I did just that in Cardiff once in a hotel prior to the Cup Final, and knew that a big story wouldn't be far away. And, my instincts were right. It was an opportunity for a brief chat with Tony and an arrangement to make contact later, then to pen a speculative article when the timing was right for his client. Timing can often be the key.

HOWE RESIGNS AT HIGHBURY

DON HOWE
Much respected coach and manager

Don's press conferences were always illuminating when he was Arsenal manager. One always stands out as he delivered an honest appraisal of his team's failings. Then, as he left the room, he came up to me and said. "oh, and by the way, I've resigned", knowing that I knew him well enough to be sure he would take such an honourable path and was about to ask him the question. He pre-empted my question, gave me the answer, and walked straight on.

Terry Neill relied heavily on Don when he was in charge at Highbury, and there are few better strategists in the coaching fraternity, especially when it comes to organising a defence.

ALAN HUDSON
Rock and roll midfielder with Chelsea and Stoke in the 1970s

I spent many a happy hour, literally, propping up the bar in The Big Easy on the Kings Road in Alan's company. Although he likes a drink, Alan he has made every effort to put his life back on track after an horrific accident that almost claimed his life when he was hit by a car while crossing the road.

Alan has been one of those former players who has hit hard times and irrespective of how hard they try to find a new career just cannot seem to make ends meet.

Alan tried his hand in the media, writing a weekly column for the *Stoke Sentinel*. He also wrote a compelling autobiography, *The Working Man's Ballet* published by Robson Books, but an attempt at a follow up book based on the modern day Chelsea with throwbacks to the past, badly backfired with problems over financing the publication. The book was rejected by all the mainstream publishers, but Alan was determined to go it alone and put his own money into the project. I attended a launch of the book in a Chelsea restaurant organised by some of Alan's friends and there was a good turn out, an auction, and every effort to publish the book, but Alan finished up being evicted form his mother's flat in the World's End estate, Chelsea and moved out to Cyprus.

A BRIGHT SPARK

MARK HUGHES
Welsh centre-forward for Manchester United and Chelsea

A Barcelona lunch with Mark Hughes is one of the more pleasant memories of an off the record briefing with a footballer. In 1987, Mark invited The Morris Men, the journalists who always stuck together during this era, Colin Gibson of the *Daily Telegraph*, Steve Curry chief football writer at the *Express*, Stuart Jones, the football correspondent of *The Times*, and myself at the *Mirror* to talk with him candidly.

Mark knew Steve and Colin best, as they are both avid Manchester United fans. Mark was going through a tough period out in Spain, and clearly wanted a move back to England, but didn't want to go public with his views. Instead, the tapas lunch was arranged in a very fashionable part of town, and, well-briefed by Mark, we were able to put his point of view across perfectly accurately without every quoting the source, which, of course, was Mark himself.

He spent the following season on loan to Bayern Munich, before returning to Old Trafford in 1988 to become an integral part of Alex Ferguson's revival of Manchester United, going on to win plentiful silverware, including United's first European trophy for 24 years, the 1992 Cup Winners Cup, scoring both goals in the final in a 2-1 win over – Barcelona.

GETTING THE LOW DOWN

GEOFF HURST
Hat-trick hero of the 1966 World Cup Final

Geoff wasn't Chelsea manager for long, but I had a very good relationship with him, and if I asked the right questions he would always give me an honest answer, which is all that you can expect from a manager as a reporter. He got used to my method of holding back a pertinent question and tackling him with it in private, instead of at a press conference. Geoff would take me into a separate room, with the hot water pipes overhead, to have a private word and invariably I would emerge with a good enough story for the back page. Now Sir Geoff is an ambassador for the game and I still see him quite often.

MIKE INGHAM

MEDIA WARS

MIKE INGHAM
BBC Radio FiveLive's Chief Football Correspondent

Mike, together with FiveLive's other senior commentator, Alan Green, would be welcome any time at Chez Harris. Mike's wife Laura, and Alan's other half, Brenda, have all become personal friends through our association going back far too many years to remember.

If there is anything I miss coming off the road and becoming the columnist for the *Daily Express*, it is their company on a routine and regular basis. They are both not only wonderful broadcasters and journalists, but also fine guys. It does annoy me, though, that there is so much animosity between the varying branches of the media. Invariably, it breaks out into open hostilities, particularly when the media are on England duty, and especially during the major tournaments when the media are billeted together for such long periods.

The big divide between the varying media groups go back a long way. Basically the written press require their own briefings and interviews, quite separately from radio and TV. The broadcast media are instantaneous, and if the written press do not have any additional interviews, press conferences and the like, then they know that the material is 'old' news because it has already been broadcast on radio and, these days, live on Sky and then later that day on BBC and ITV news bulletins.

Sometimes the problem has spilled over and can become very personal.

However, I have never been as concerned as some of my colleagues, as this is an issue that should be sensibly sorted out in advance.

Michael Hart, the highly rated football correspondent for the *London Evening News* for so many years, is another good friend and a trustworthy journalist. But he has also been caught in the cross fire, as an evening paper is obviously on the streets ahead of the following morning's daily papers – and there has often been conflict over this issue. It eventually reached the ludicrous stage where Michael was allowed to ask, on his own, the first few questions, and then not allowed to use any material from the rest of the media conference. It got as petty as that.

J

SIR ELTON JOHN, CRAIG JOHNSTON, CLIFF JONES, VINNY JONES

ELTON TO SELL WATFORD TO MAXWELL

SIR ELTON JOHN
Genius songwriter and musician, self-confessed diva and former Chairman of Watford FC

It's not the kind of call you receive everyday.

"Come up and see someone special I want to introduce to you," boomed that familiar Maxwell voice.

As I made my way through the usual security screens, requiring a special key in duplicate to enter a door off the editorial sector to make my way to the Maxwell-only lift, I was wondering who it could be this time. It wasn't an every day occurrence that Maxwell would make the mysterious "come up and see me, I've got a surprise for you" call, but it did happen now and again.

Then, as I was greeted by Maxwell's butler and shown through to the extra-large drawing room section of the apartment, there was Elton John.

Of course I knew of Elton because of his ownership of Watford, but he was somewhat of a recluse and rarely, if ever, gave interviews. I immediately thought there might be a unique opportunity to have a chat with the chairman of Watford.

Then, Maxwell made the grand announcement.

"I have agreed with Elton this morning to buy Watford Football Club".

Wow. That was definitely something that didn't happen every day.

But the alarm bells sounded instantly. Maxwell already owned Derby, his son Kevin was Oxford United chairman; this isn't going to get past the Football League.

Now I knew why I had been summoned.

Of course I was going to interview Elton. It was imperative, as Maxwell saw it, that Elton explained, naturally in the columns of the *Mirror*, why he wanted to sell out to Maxwell and why it would be such a good thing for football if he did.

Elton's interview made quite a splash the next day, but so too did the inevitable reaction from the Football League, and ultimately Maxwell's purchase of Watford was blocked until such time as he could sell Derby or Oxford or both, and eventually the Watford purchase fell though, but not without many more column inches for many months to come and a huge fallout with then Chelsea Chairman Ken Bates. (see Ken Bates)

CRAIG JOHNSTON
Former Liverpool striker and inventor of the Predator football boot

Craig had a flamboyance and vision as a Liverpool winger, but more imagination than I ever imagined until I met him. Craig came to me at the *Mirror* touting this weird idea of putting strips of rubber on the end of a football boot. Naturally I was unconvinced, but Craig told me how he had tested his invention exhaustively, getting John Barnes to use it to shoot at goal and how much he thought it would improve swerve when the ball was struck.

I was still unsure. However, Craig can be very persuasive, and I always have an open mind. I took the concept to Robert Maxwell, who, like me, didn't really have a clue whether Craig's invention worked or not, as it just seemed so far fetched – simple strips of rubber on the toe of a boot to revolutionise sporting footwear? Maxwell seemed positive enough, but nothing came of his interest. The next thing we knew, Craig had sold his idea to boot manufacturer Adidas and the revolutionary Predator boot was born. The next time I saw Craig, he was developing a superior proto-type, and was involved in other incredible concepts. Craig was truly one of the game's greatest innovators of recent years.

CLIFF JONES
Spurs' goalscoring winger of the 60s

Cliff was one of my boyhood idols as part of that wonderful Spurs Double Team in 1961, and his courage and enthusiasm shone through as a player and was still there many years later when he was working as a fitness instructor and coach at the local Harringey Sports Centre. I was just starting out as a football writer, and still fancied myself as a goalkeeper, although having failed miserably to make it to any professional level, I found myself playing in a five-a-side tournament, with Cliff taking part for one of the opposition sides. His feet were so quick it was impossible for me to judge which direction the ball was going and he scored five times past me.

Even now, Cliff's mind is as sharp as ever and he can still recall my goalkeeping prowess. In fact, he's such a well-mannered guy, he manages to mention it without even bursting into fits of laughter and derision.

VINNIE JONES
The bad boy of British football

A BBC crew came to the house recently to film my views on the day Vinnie Jones bit the nose of my *Mirror* colleague, Ted Graham, and drew blood.

The news reporter had made the mistake of approaching a rather drunk and garish Vinnie in the breakfast room of the Dublin hotel close to the Lansdowne Road ground where England were about to play the Republic of Ireland in February 1995. It had been such a late night out for Vinnie and his friends that they returned to the hotel being used by the media in time for breakfast. Vinnie had already insulted Gary Lineker that evening and, as I had been sitting at the opposite end of the restaurant, I had heard all the shouting and kerfuffle.

Vinnie could get up to all sorts of tricks, but everyone was shocked by the violent attack on the *Mirror's* news reporter, who was there covering the game for his newspaper.

Much later that day England's game had to be abandoned because of violence caused by a section of hooligan fans inside the stadium. So, Vinnie's attack became even more pertinent on a day of hostility.

Vinnie was sacked by the *News of the World* as their columnist as a consequence of that attack. The Editor at the time was Piers Morgan who later become the *Mirror's* Editor and while fronting a TV series called *Tabloid Tales,* covered an item, 'Vinnie Jones Bit My Nose'.

JORDAN SUES DOWIE

SIMON JORDAN
Perma-tanned Crystal Palace Chairman

When the Crystal Palace chairman strode into the studio sporting huge sunglasses, a glowing tan and expensively designed hair, you just wanted to loathe him. But who said, "don't judge a book by its cover?" Simon might look more than a touch flash from the outside, but once you get to know him, you realise that he can be warm, charming, and great company. That's my first impression of the Simon Jordan who appeared as a guest on my Hold The Back Page web and pod casts during the World Cup on www.ntlworld.com.

He was good value, controversial, witty, pithy, articulate – and out of the ordinary.

Simon was in the TV studio alongside former Charlton manager Alan Curbishley and my final question was, "where did they see themselves in five years time?" Alan said, naturally, that he would expect to be back in management sooner rather than later. But the show concluded with Simon's comments. We were beginning to run out of time, even though it was not actually live, the screening for the web casts were as-live, so I had to come up with a suitable ending.

As Simon said he wanted to take Palace into the Premiership, I butted in and closed the show with "I sincerely hope so..." Unfortunately Simon hadn't quite taken my hint about coming to an end, and he uttered just one final sentence..." then I can disappear into the ether, up my own backside."

Of course, my concluding phrase was, "I hope so."

He looked shocked, if not a touch hurt. But, all credit to him, he could see how it had occurred, and he enjoyed the joke along with everyone else.

I am sure, come the editing, the final amusing pay off, would have been drowned out, in any case. At least that's what I told him and he seemed suitably reassured.

During the break between the web and pod-cast recordings, Simon discussed his feud with his former manager Iain Dowie. Dowie had left Palace after failing to win them promotion back to the Premiership the season after relegation citing a desire to move to a club nearer his family in the north. Imagine Simon's surprise that Dowie popped up but a few days later as manager of Charlton. Now Charlton is further north than Norwood, but both are south of the river Thames!

It was not an issue that I included in the recordings because Simon had only recently aired his views in great detail through the press and there wasn't an awful lot more he could have said. And anyway, by this time, it was all in the hands of lawyers and he had been advised not to say any more.

However, Simon was happy to discuss the whole affair off the record, and it was illuminating to hear all the finer points of the case. Clearly, his stunt in issuing a writ to Dowie for leaving Selhurst Park under false pretences during his media unveiling as the new Charlton manager was something I hadn't seen before.

Subsequently Simon had made numerous public utterances about his views of how he had been misled by Dowie and Simon then told me how Dowie had counter-sued claiming defamation. He then looked deadly serious and extremely angry when he wrapped up by saying he would not back down and would fight all the way to the courts. Given how expensive such legal action can be, multi-millionaire Simon, who made his cash in the early boom years of the mobile phone revolution, was prepared to make Dowie suffer financially as he believed in his cause wholeheartedly.

ROY KEANE, KEVIN KEEGAN, GRAHAM KELLY, NIGEL KENNEDY, BILL KENWRIGHT, BRYAN KING, JOE KINNEAR, JÜRGEN KLINSMANN, MICHAEL KNIGHTON

KEANE WALKS OUT OF WORLD CUP

ROY KEANE
Former Manchester United captain. The definitive angry young man of the 1990s, the most driven footballer of his generation

Arguably one of the biggest World Cup revelations to emerge from the tournament in Korea & Japan in 2002 was the story I broke of Roy Keane's bust up with Republic of Ireland manager Mick McCarthy and his extraordinary return from the finals before the competition had even started.

The tale of Keane's acrimonious confrontation with McCarthy, followed by Keane's early World Cup exit, and fallout from the Irish international team has since been the subject of several TV programmes, numerous articles, radio debates, a book and was even portrayed in a West End production.

Express Sports Editor Bill Bradshaw and I decided that, with the time difference between the UK and the Far East, it would be a good idea to have a man positioned over here making calls to find out what was going on behind the scenes. That was me.

On one occasion, I was checking out a tip about something completely different and spoke to an agent whom I trust to give me the honest answer. During the conversation, I inquired about some of his clients who were on World Cup duty.

He told me: "You will never believe this, but just around midnight one of my guys was just leaving the bar of the Irish hotel when he bumped into Roy Keane, who told him that he might as well say goodbye there and then because he would be off in the morning."

He was right – I didn't believe it. Who would? It was just a couple of weeks away from World Cup kick-off and the teams were still preparing for the big day. No-one would walk out so close to the World Cup.

I remembered being in the Dutch camp to hear Ruud Gullit's farewell press conference when he walked out amongst undertones of racial divisions within the camp. But I had never heard of anything like this involving a British team.

As the huge media entourage actually at the event slept, or partied, I was busy checking out this incredible lead, having alerted Bill to the breaking story I was working on.

Keane's agent was the highly respected lawyer Michael Kennedy, who also represented David O'Leary among others. I didn't have a particularly close relationship with Michael at that time, but knew him well enough to place a call to his London offices.

"Not true", he told me with great authority. Of course, he pointed out, if all I had said about a row with McCarthy over training facilities and a threatened walk out the next morning was true, surely he would know about it. And he didn't.

Back I went to the source of the story. Because of the time difference, it would be pretty late here in England before they woke up in Japan, so I really need to be 100% sure of my facts to run with this story in our first edition, which went to the presses at around 8.00-9.00pm.

My source told me that the player concerned was a sober type and had not been excessively drinking that evening, was highly intelligent and would have related the conversation with Roy with incredible accuracy.

Good enough, I felt, to go with the story, and Bill backed me up – as usual.

Bill's vast experience as an on-the-road journalist gave him an astute insight into how these kind of stories can never be guaranteed and how on occasion you have to go with your hunch.

As a back up, I began making calls to the Irish team hotel at the crack of dawn. I rang and asked to speak to Mick McCarthy. He declined to come to the phone, but dispatched his assistant to speak to me. I put the facts to him, and, although he didn't deny them, he wouldn't confirm them either, but pointed out that meetings were on-going, and they hoped to persuade Roy to stay. Fine, so trying to convince him to stay, meant that he had threatened to walk out. That was confirmation in my book. I had my exclusive – and what a story! We ran it as the back page 'splash' and added the comment for the latter editions.

Our rivals first got wind of the story when they saw our first edition, and then the Irish team hotel was bombarded with calls. Roy was persuaded to stay, albeit for just a couple more days, before he was eventually packing his bags – just as we said he would do. From the day of our story for weeks, months and even a year later, that story set the sports pages agenda across the national press and earned the *Express* and myself the Sports Writers Association Sports Story of the Year 2002.

KEEGAN HAS A SENSE OF HUMOUR!

KEVIN KEEGAN
Mighty Mouse. Twice European Footballer of the Year and England captain before managing Newcastle and England

Kevin was my type of player, self-made into a wonderful goalscorer, and as a manager his philosophy was to attack and entertain. Then, when out of his depth as England manager, he quit in the Wembley dressing rooms after losing to the Germans in an opening World Cup qualifying tie.

Don't you just miss KK? He's also got a sense of humour. I contacted him once at Newcastle to ask him if he would comment on an article I was doing about changing hairstyles, and he did. Few people in the game have had more changes of haircut and, of course, he had set the standard with one of the first full footballers perms.

FA TO INVESTIGATE FOOTBALL BUNGS

GRAHAM KELLY
Former Chief Executive of the Football Association

Appearances can be deceptive and, although Graham was extremely over weight when he was FA Chief Executive, he used to turn out for media games and looked reasonably sprightly for his size. He did try to pound the streets around Lancaster Gate to get his weight down.

After a serious illness, Graham lost several stones, and looked a shadow of his former self. I talked to him about writing his autobiography, but at that time I had an awful lot of commitments and someone else wrote his book for him.

There was one occasion in the early 90s when Graham allowed me to deliver files in a big black case, marked with a huge *Mirror* logo, on our investigation into irregular payments and dodgy invoices in football. Graham seemed keen to clean up the game and we were pictured together outside the FA and inside his office and he promised to act upon our findings and we reported his interview in great length in the paper.

But the FA, under Graham, did not, eventually, push the boat out in this area and it took the accusations by Luton manager Mike Newell in early 2006 to finally spark a proper investigation into bungs.

NIGEL KENNEDY
Maverick violinist and Aston Villa fan

One of the world's greatest violinists is a mad Villa fan, who stayed at the Forte Village during Italia 90, where I got to know him very well and we ended up playing doubles together against Gary Lineker and Ron Atkinson on Centre Court in front of a handful of on-lookers. Big Ron was devastating at the net, where he didn't have to run too far, but not too hot on his ground shots. Gary, being a naturally athlete, was by far the best of a very average bunch and just about carried Big Ron over the victory line!

BILL KENWRIGHT
One of Britain's greatest Theatre Producers and Chairman of Everton FC

As a theatre impresario Bill has a vastly different attitude toward the media than most chairmen. When I pestered him endlessly to tell me what was the likely outcome of his battle to try to keep Wayne Rooney at Everton, he told me that, however much it would grieve him to have to sell him, Rooney would always end up at Manchester United. I can only thank Bill for his help as it allowed me to correctly predict the transfer well before the deal was signed and sealed.

BRYAN KING
Former Millwall goalkeeper

Ken Bates has a poor reputation among journalists, and is often depicted as miserly, but Ken can be greatly misunderstood and I have known him to be partly to acts of momentous kindness.

Bryan, the old Millwall keeper, was playing in a media match I helped to organise at Stamford Bridge, for unless I had a hand in arranging these media games, invariably I would never be picked to play – I was that bad.

It turned out to be a good game, with a reasonable crowd, but when Bryan came rushing out to make a save, he snapped his Achilles and was carried off.

Incapacitated for weeks, Bryan missed out on some lucrative coaching in the Caribbean, and other work he had lined up during the summer. When I told Ken of Bryan's plight, my information is that the then Chelsea chairman made sure Bryan wasn't out of pocket by too much. A grand gesture and the sort of thing that Ken does not get enough publicity for.

JOE KINNEAR
Former Wimbledon and Nottingham Forest manager

Joe was the pin-up boy of the Spurs team that won the FA Cup in 1967. He then then became an outstanding manager and he was a jolly nice bloke to socialise with, and I like him a lot.

Unfortunately, Joe is responsible for one of my biggest howlers during my time at the *Mirror*. Joe was coaching abroad and wanted me to write an item in my column informing everyone back home how well he was doing and wouldn't it be great idea to hire him in England. I was more than willing to oblige, but in the article I suggested he had a wonderful lifestyle, to go with his managerial success, from his luxury apartment "overlooking the Himalayas".

Yes, I hold my hands up... not easy overlooking the Himalayas, is it?

Joe was coaching in one of the world's most unlikely spots at the time, Mongolia, and was just about forgotten back here. But I like to think I helped him a touch, and when he eventually returned to English football, it wasn't long before he was managing Wimbledon and making an impact there.

But, much like the elephants in those Himalayan parts, journalists never forget. Now and again there is some old scrote who can remember that far back and brings that one up.

JÜRGEN KLINSMANN
Germany's 'diving' striker, who lit up the Premiership in his one year with Spurs

When he was the golden boy of German football I interviewed Jürgen during the 1990 World Cup Finals in the team hotel, along with a handful of other English reporters. Yet, when he emerged from the lift, he wanted to know which of the writers was from the *Mirror*. He looked me straight in the eye and said, "Ah, you're the one I am supposed to worry about."

Not at all, I told him. But he didn't seem to look reassured.

When he turned up on Alan Sugar's yacht and ended up signing for Spurs, I thought it was a tremendous coup, not just for the North London club, but for English football, even though he had been experiencing a goal-drought during his spell at Monaco.

He was such a captivating new addition to the Premiership scene that I decide to write a diary of his first season at White Hart Lane. It was certainly an uplifting experience, even if somewhat unexpected for a German to sign for a predominately Jewish club, with a Jewish chairman, and a high percentage of Jewish support. They do, after all, call themselves "Yids".

But Jürgen showed he had a sense of humour when he 'dived' in a unique goal celebration that ended up being copied by virtually everyone for a while. It was Jürgen's way of mocking the critics who for years had taunted him as a player who dived. Compared to some in the English game at the moment, that accusation now looks laughable.

However, I saw a darker side to Jürgen's character. All my efforts to seek his approval for the book, maybe for him to endorse it in some way, perhaps write a foreword, came to nothing. In frustration I opted for the direct approach and the next time I was at White Hart Lane, I hung around the entrance area where the players pass by from the dressing rooms to the stairway taking them to the Players Lounge. It's the perfect vantage point for reporters hoping for a quote or two. I asked Jürgen if he would stop for a chat, but he was most reluctant to continue the conversation as soon as I mentioned the book, even though I explained that the publishers were happy to make a contribution to one of his favourite charities and for him to see it before it went to print to show him that it was an upbeat celebration of his first season with Spurs.

Only later did it dawn on me that one of the reasons for his reticence is that he didn't plan to hang around too long and had known that he might be heading off to a bigger club for more money, I don't know. Perhaps he was protective of his own image and was not interested in any unauthorised book.

I didn't hold it against him as I voted for Jürgen as Footballer of the Year, an honour which he won. But just before he received the award, it was announced that he was quitting Spurs and heading to another country.

No wonder Alan Sugar threw his Spurs shirt in the bin in disgust.

Alan told me how Jürgen and his agent has been in his Chigwell home discussing how best to persuade Jürgen to stay on, but it became clear that even though the player told the chairman he was happy at the club, he would be invoking a clause which gave him a way out if he wasn't... well, happy!

Sugar could have contested it, but there's no point keeping a player who wants to go, and Sugar was not in the mood to make him too much of an extravagant offer to stay considering he had rescued him from his gloom in French football and Spurs had resurrected his career.

Yet, remarkably a year later when Spurs were in trouble and in danger of relegation, Jürgen came back to the rescue.

MICHAEL KNIGHTON
Ball-juggling, alien-seeing, wannabe owner of Manchester United

Michael invited around to his London offices to reassure me of his credibility to buy Manchester United, but my exposé into his finances just about killed off any hope he had of buying the club.

He tried to win over the fans by juggling the ball in front of the Stretford End, but he found it much tougher to juggle the books. He naturally suspected that Robert Maxwell was behind my revelations about his finances because the *Mirror* owner had once wanted to buy Manchester United himself. Well, Michael was right to a point. Maxwell was very interested in my articles, but he hadn't instigated them.

FRANK LAMPARD, MARK LAWRENSON, FRANK LEBOEUF, MATT LE TISSIER, GRAEME LE SAUX, DANIEL LEVY, GARY LINEKER, RICHARD LITTLEJOHN, RUPERT LOWE, DES LYNAM

NEW LAMPS FOR OLD

FRANK LAMPARD
England and Chelsea's goalscoring midfielder

Young Frank turned up for a lunch to promote a book penned by Alan Hudson that was attended by a handful of the Chelsea legend's friends, including Frank Lampard snr. It was held, appropriately, in a Chelsea restaurant, and although the book was destined to cause Hudson more grief than good, there was a good turn out, with Derek Dougan volunteering to front an auction to help raise some much needed cash for the former Chelsea midfield ace who was about to be thrown out of his mother's flat in the World's End estate on the Kings Road.

I had known Frank snr for many years going back to his West Ham days when I worked on the *Evening News*, and I have always enjoyed the story about the two Franks when Claudio Ranieri signed the West Ham player for Chelsea for a then record £11m.

Claudio telephoned Frank snr to enquire whether Frank jnr was doing his best to shed a few extra pounds, and Frank snr had assured him he was working out in the less-than-glamorous location of their garage to keep in trim.

With the two Franks at lunch, I should have taken the opportunity to find out whether it was true. But it was a social gathering. George Best, his son Calum, and agent Phil Hughes also popped in, and George sat next to me for a chat. He had a pint glass in front of him, and someone had filled it with white wine. The event was being filmed and I suggested to George that he should ditch the wine, but he didn't seem too concerned.

It was at that lunch that he asked me whether he would consider writing the third of a trilogy of books he was signed up to pen for Ebury press. The publishers had put forward Hunter Davies as the ghost writer, someone I would have the utmost journalistic respect for, but George had met him and they had not clicked, George suggested that Hunter wanted too much control over what was to be written and kept putting words into his mouth. I am sure Hunter will have much better luck with Wayne Rooney and his £5m five book deal with Harper Collins, which he has agreed to ghost the first tome of.

As it turned out I did ghost George's latest, and as it turned out, last book, *Hard Tackles & Dirty Baths*, and it was an honour for me to do so.

A LORRA LAWRO LAUGHS

MARK LAWRENSON
Former Liverpool defender who is now as classy on the Match of the Day sofa as he was in his playing days at Anfield

Mark Lawrenson and I have shared the same BBC World Cup seat for a TV chat, and it is not until you actually appear with him, that you realise how professional and accomplished he can be. He always does his homework, he knows his stats, and that always makes him a formidable panelist if ever there is a disagreement during the programme. He is also cool and full of well-informed opinion.

I often bump into Mark at weekends when I am at BBC Centre for either Radio FiveLive studio discussion programmes, for BBC News 24 programmes, or even the late night main stream news bulletins. He is always polite and approachable, a real gentleman.

I knew him also in his other life as a player for Liverpool, but not particularly well, because I was just starting out at the top level of newspaper reporting. But I knew him much better when he was manager of Oxford United, and Robert Maxwell's son Kevin was his chairman.

One Oxford United board meeting was held at Holborn inside the *Mirror* building, no doubt because Kevin was so busy with his daytime job, working for his father. Kevin had little experience of running a football club and clearly relied on either his father's advice or the professionals within the organisation. But there was one occasion when he wanted advice on an issue other than the opinions being voiced within his own board. He contacted the sports desk and asked Keith Fisher and myself to come up. We had no idea a board meeting had been convened and it was quite a shock too for the Oxford directors and their manager, Mr Lawrenson, to see two *Mirror* journalists entering the room and then being asked their views about how the club should be run.

FRANCK LEBOEUF
France and Chelsea centre-half

Franck 'I Won The World Cup' Leboeuf was far more humble and down to earth when he first arrived at the Bridge.

He loved playing at Chelsea from the word go and was an instant hit with the fans. He couldn't believe how, when he first arrived in the capital, men, woman and children would come up to him and hug him and welcome him to the club. He told me that one day he hailed a cab and the driver, who was a big Chelsea fan, became incredibly overexcited when he got in the back. Franck was going home and the driver asked if it would be OK to make a quick stop off as it was on the way. Franck was quite laid-back and agreed, but couldn't believe it when the cabbie stopped at his own house in Fulham, brought Franck in to meet the family and made him stay for tea!

He was seeking positive publicity as he told me how little respect he had received in his home country. He liked the fact that I admired him as a footballer and had given him some terrific write-ups in my match reports. Together with our wives, we dined along the Fulham Road and Franck was highly approachable and very down-to-earth. But after a while at Chelsea Franck thought he had taken a step up in the world and he became far less approachable as a consequence.

When he first arrived Franck was relatively sober dresser, but quickly became extremely flamboyant. But fame quickly went to his head. He was no longer open to dinner invitations from my wife and I, and was soon mixing in far more glamorous circles.

When I first met him he came across as a fun character, albeit with a chip on his shoulder about how he had been criticised and perceived in France. But Franck became arrogant and aloof to those who had helped him adjust from the outset to English football.

He also joined the new fashion of shaving his head...slap heads, as they became known in the mickey-taking world inhabited by the cockney wit of Dennis Wise's Chelsea. Franck told me at the time that he was fed up with worrying about little gaps appearing on his head and just decided, one day, to shave it all off. It suited Luca Vialli and also suited Franck.

Even so, I have fond memories of Chelea's era of 'Sexy Football' under Ruud Gullit and Franck was one of those players who will always be remembered for putting some much needed glamour into West London football.

GRAEME LE SAUX
Guardian reading England, Chelsea and Blackburn defender

Graeme has always been a touch different. I remember once, when he played at Arsenal whilst at Blackburn, catching sight of him rushing through Highbury tube station.

At Stamford Bridge he enjoyed the Chelsea lifestyle, lived locally and I often spotted him in the local restaurants. A highly intelligent guy as well as talented performer, it was always a pleasure to bump into him 'off duty' for a private chat.

MATT LE TISSIER
Southampton's all-time hero

The then Tottenham chairman Irving Scholar once confided to me how Terry Venables had persuaded Matt Le Tissier to become a Spurs player and actually produced a 'signed' contract, which the manager tucked away in the safe ready to produce at the end of the season when Le Tissier's contract with the Saints had expired, so he could register it with the football authorities.

According to Scholar, his manager had to apologise for finally having to accept that the gifted midfielder, whose boyhood hero was Glenn Hoddle, would never actually wear the white shirt of Spurs.

Le Tissier had a change of heart, or rather his wife and family persuaded him not to quit the south coast, and Le Tiss begged Venables to rip up the contract, which he agreed to do.

I reminded Le Tissier of that story when he came round to my home in Virginia Water, when we met up along with one of my journalistic colleagues, Danny Fullbrook from the *Daily Star*, who has worked with me on some book projects in the past. The Publishers had commissioned us to ghost Le Tissier's life story and we spent around two hours discussing a few of the chapters. In fact Danny took a considerable amount of notes as we asked Le Tissier a number of reasonably innocuous questions.

Everyone departed quite upbeat about the project and we were all determined to make the book as much fun as possible with as many amusing anecdotes that Le Tissier could recall. Danny set about transcribing the notes and had prepared two of the chapters, when I received a call from Le Tissier's agent, who explained that he had once again changed his mind. Now I knew how El Tel had felt.

Le Tissier gave no explanation, at least none that his agent was prepared to pass on. I explained that we had gone to an awful lot of trouble, so the agent should tell Le Tiss we have written two chapters, and that he should look at them before ditching the autobiography.

The message came back, "tell them to f*** off if they don't like it, and I don't care if they have already written two chapters."

Charming.

DANIEL LEVY
Former Spurs Chairman

I had some dealings with Daniel long before he became Spurs chairman, and maybe I hoped to push him toward making an investment in the North London club.

Together with Alan Green, I had dinner with Daniel and his then secretary Tracy, soon to be comes Mrs Levy, to discuss an internet project than Alan and I had started up called Voice of Football.

Tracy is a big Spurs fan and I tried to persuade Daniel to increase ENIC's portfolio of European football clubs with the purchase of Spurs. He wasn't too keen at that time, but I must have sowed the seed, as he eventually made Alan Sugar an offer he couldn't refuse.

GARY LINEKER
England striker turned top BBC sports presenter

As the pictures show, I interviewed Gary at Heathrow Airport just before he boarded the plane for Nagoya for his first visit to the home of his 'J' League club, Grampus 8, after agreeing to a highly lucrative deal. Three chief football writers, through Gary's agent Jon Holmes, had arranged to accompany the striker to Japan and when British Airways discovered that we were being welcomed by Lineker and his agent, we were upgraded to first class on JAL; it was quite an experience.

The media had a lot of time for Lineker. He always made himself available, he was articulate, and had a charming smile. He was clearly destined to become a media star once he finished playing and indeed he has fulfilled that ambition more than he could have ever imagined.

I had probably personally seen all of Lineker's England internationals – bar one. That was the second time he scored four times in one game for his country – against Malaysia in June 1991.

It was coming to the end of a very long tour of Australia, New Zealand and the Far East. We all arrived in the sweltering heat of Malaysia in the evening and headed straight to the hotel.

The next day it was hard to get motivated for the build up for a friendly against a team you knew England would hit for however many goals they felt in the mood. The humidity was high, and I felt as though I had had enough.

The Morris Men were together as usual, Neil Harman of *The Mail*, a new recruit to the happy band of travellers, Steve Curry, then the chief football writer at the *Express*, Colin Gibson of *The Telegraph* and Stuart Jones of the *Times*. We would take turns to organise the night's social activities and, on arrival in Singapore, it was my duty to sort out the venue for the evening meal and then the light entertainment that would follow. Usually I would avoid such an assignment, in the hope that Colin would carry on as usual and take over. Colin was the chief organiser as well as the Chief Football Correspondent of his newspaper.

But even the charming Colin was bored in arranging the meal, so I booked the four of us into the hotel's Japanese restaurant, which had a reputation for excellence. Everyone seemed to approve of my choice.

I went back to my room to a shower and change.

No matter how irrelevant England's matches may have appeared, as this one did against Malaysia, because of the travelling and concentrating on the games, the build up, the previews, the match reporting, the follow up on team selection and the communication with an office several time zones away, it was a very time consuming business. With so many games, it was becoming increasingly harder to spent time rooting out the big exclusives. It wasn't impossible, it was just becoming more impractical, so the big exclusive stories were becoming fewer and further between.

Due to the intensity of covering England, I had completely forgotten that I was trying to convince *Mirror* owner Robert Maxwell to make a bid for Tottenham Hotspur as chairman and 26% leading shareholder. Then Chairman Irving Scholar was on the verge of selling out with his partner Paul Bobroff and Terry Venables wanted to take control and was looking to every conceivable consortium to raise the funds without much success.

"Why don't I find out what's going on there," I thought.

I rang Scholar. He informed me that Alan Sugar was hovering in the background to back Venables with a bid and told me it was Maxwell's last chance if he was still serious in his aspirations to win Spurs. Aha! My excuse to ring Maxwell had instantly and miraculously presented itself.

It didn't take long to hook Maxwell back on the takeover trail of Tottenham, and when I told him that Alan Sugar was going to beat him to it, he quickly ordered me back from Malaysia to orchestrate the start of the media coverage of his formal bid to buy Spurs. Maxwell would obviously lean heavily on my inside track of events inside White Hart Lane, my close friendship with Scholar and how best to keep the FA and Football League at bay because of Maxwell's son's ownership of Oxford and his own control of Derby County.

The travel company who had organised the media to follow the England team had a representative in the hotel, I called his room, and luckily he was there, changing for dinner. I told him that I needed to make arrangements right there and then to return to London. He came back and said there was just one available seat left, first class, to Heathrow. When I reported that news back to the sports desk, they were hesitant whether Maxwell really wanted to go to such enormous expense to get me home less than a week before I was due back anyway. The word came down from Maxwell's office, that he had personally authorised the expense.

I rang Colin, and told him not to expect me for dinner – I was going back to London. "Surely you can come to dinner before you go in the morning", suggested Colin.

"Sorry, I am actually going this minute – bye."

It wasn't until I landed 20 or so hours later that I heard the news that Lineker had bagged four in England's predictably easy victory. It was a big regret of mine, as it was the first England game I had missed in many, many years. (See Irving Scholar)

As for Gary, I followed the latter part of his plying career in Japan with interest, and when he finally quit as a footballer, it came as no surprise to me that he made the grade in television and has become the accomplished anchorman of Match of the Day.

Not too long ago I was dining in Cafe Figo, one of my wife's favourite lunch-time spots in Sunningdale, very close to where we live. We hadn't been seated for more than ten minutes when Gary and a friend strolled in and sat right beside us at an adjoining table, Gary continuing his chat, completely oblivious to who was sitting next to him.

You can imagine his shock when he realised it was me! I think initially he thought I was trying to uncover something about his recent split from wife Michelle. But as usual he was the perfect gentleman, as charming as he is on TV.

I have know Gary for a long time, all through his family's struggles with baby George's leukaemia and it was sad. I felt for the family when Gary and Michelle broke up. That kind of story has never interested me.

RICHARD LITTLEJOHN
Daily Mail **columnist**

Rarely do you come across journalists you admire as true professionals and gifted writers, who are also just jolly nice blokes. Richard is one of the few. He's always been a life-long Spurs fan and I know how much he would have loved to have put a consortium together to have had a big stake in Spurs. Maybe one day.

RUPERT LOWE
Southampton's hockey-loving former Chairman

The much-maligned former Southampton chairman had more than his fair share of detractors, but I liked his tenacity to try something outside the norm, such as the appointment of Sir Clive Woodward as Saints' Director of Football. However, Woodward's arrival upset then manager Harry Redknapp and it wasn't long before the unexpected occurred and Redknapp made the most unlikely return to Portsmouth from whence he came.

Redknapp's return to Fratton Park, a year after he made the incredible first move along the South Coast to Saints, sparked allegations of a huge betting scam involving many well-known people, including a former England international turned TV pundit and even a current England player, who all made a killing as they allegedly placed their bets in the full knowledge that Redknapp was headed back to Pompey. As Lowe himself put it in a letter to the FA, "The betting situation is, in my opinion, also unacceptable and brings with it a very unpleasant and unprofessional smell. It may not technically be insider trading, but it is equally unethical and will, in the long term, drive supporters away from football if allowed to continue. It would not be difficult for the FA to instigate an investigation into this matter and get the truth." That investigation never happened in any serious sense, of course, despite my attempts to get to the bottom of why.

I also never quite got to the bottom of the time I spotted Rupert Lowe at Madrid airport.

I had been invited over to Madrid to attend the glittering launch of David Beckham's autobiography, *My Story*. I travelled back to the airport with Garth Crooks, who had been interviewing Becks for the Beeb. We shared a glass of wine or two while waiting for our flight, only to catch sight of Rupert wandering around the airport. He eventually came over for a brief chat and we were dying for him to do that as we were curious as to why the Saints chairman should be in Madrid on his own. His explanation was that he was out there talking to a player about a possible transfer to his club.

I sensed a sensational story – could it be Zidane or Roberto Carlos moving to homely Southampton?

Strange, though, that there was actually no agent in tow or, indeed, any of the usual entourage that normally accompanies club chairman on those sorts of missions.

And, as you might expect, it came to nothing. Mysterious.

DES LYNAM
TV's most charismatic sports presenter

Charm in abundance belongs to Des, at least that's how the public see him on screen, but in the many times I have met him, he is just as charming off screen as he is on it. A real gentleman.

M

GARY MABBUTT, MALCOLM MACDONALD, LAURIE MADDEN, TERRY MANCINI, DIEGO MARADONA, LAWRENCE MARKS, RODNEY MARSH, ROBERTO DI MATTEO, SIR STANLEY MATTHEWS, ROBERT MAXWELL, FRANK MCLINTOCK, STEVE MCMAHON, DAVID MELLOR, BRIAN MEARS, PAUL MERSON, PAUL MILLER, SIR BERT MILLICHIP, BOBBY MOORE, PIERS MORGAN JOHN MOTSON, JOSE MOURINHO, ALAN MULLERY

THE MIRACLE CURE

GARY MABBUTT
Spurs defender who inspired a generation of diabetic kids to take up sport

Gary's harrowing experiences as a diabetic – like losing consciousness at the wheel of his car and missing a game because he passed out at home without any help at hand – are among many episodes detailed in the book I wrote for him many years ago called *Against All Odds*.

Once, when I invited Gary to the *Mirror* and he was sitting with me in the Sports Editor's office, his blood-sugar levels fell drastically. At first he rambled, then became incoherent and then virtually passed out before we called 'medical'. A bar of chocolate was the miracle cure to raise the sugar content of his blood, and within seconds he was fine. I had witnessed a 'miracle' – just as his thousands of fans did every time Gary took to the field of play.

SUPERMAC: YOU'RE RUBBISH

MALCOLM MACDONALD
SuperMac, Newcastle and Arsenal's rampaging centre-forward

SuperMac and Peter Shreeves were 'guests' in a media team I played in at Queen's Park Rangers back in the 80s when the First Division club had a synthetic surface. I enjoyed playing on the astroturf, starting off at centre-forward alongside one of the country's greatest ever goalscorers, who after a while turned round and was heard to say, "I have seen players who cannot kick with their right foot, I've seen players who can't kick with their left foot, but until know I have never played alongside someone who can't kick with either foot." After that I stopped kidding myself about my footballing prowess.

LAWRIE MADDEN
Former Sheffield Wednesday midfielder

Lawrie might have been a journeyman footballer but he was one of the first ex-pros to turn his attention to a career in the media. I appeared on a few radio debates with him some time ago. Unfortunately for Lawrie he had the idea of switching to the media far too early, as the real explosion of alternative work for former footballers and managers has mushroomed the bigger Sky TV's football coverage has become. Sky has a large rostra of 'faces'. Their *Gillette Soccer Saturday* show has three or four on duty in the studio all afternoon, commenting on their individual games via a monitor on their desks. Sadly Lawrie has not maintained his media presence, although he paved the way for today's plethora of former footballers-turned-pundits.

PRESS WARS

TERRY MANCINI
Former QPR and Arsenal midfielder

Terry has close connections with a travel firm who specialise in football-related trips to La Manga, the hotel complex which England use regularly as their training camp. Terry has helped organise one or two media trips, and if he didn't know it before, he sure knows it know, the press can be extremely demanding at times. But the quality of the golf on the resort definitely makes up for all the hassle he has had to endure.

Trying to organise a media trip for a major tournament must be a logistical nightmare for his travel company. Just try to get two or three journalist to agree on just about anything would take a minor miracle, so, how about getting about a hundred or so to agree! No chance.

Dissention inside the travelling media corps is something that can often be quite intimidating for those organising the travel arrangements. On any trip, it could take just one chief football writer ending up with an inferior room to one of his counterparts on a rival newspaper to declare World War three! Woe betide the organisers if the flights are delayed, or even cancelled. The reaction is often quite volatile.

Then there was a famous occasion when a travel agent (who shall remain nameless), who came highly recommended by one or two journalists, did a runner with all of one newspaper's cash and failed to finalise the itinerary for the trip leaving them to rearrange the whole shebang again. Perhaps that was a modicum of revenge for all the hassle people like Terry have suffered during years of organising media trips.

THE HAND OF GOD

DIEGO MARADONA
Genius footballer, or drug-crazed lunatic?

Ossie was panicking. Diego was fast asleep and Ossie was pacing up and down the hotel lobby. "Typical Diego," moaned Ossie, "always asleep, always late." But this was an impotent assignment, it was Glenn Hoddle's testimonial and Ossie Ardiles had arranged for none other than Diego Maradona to play for Spurs at White Hart Lane that night.

Ossie had brought me with him for a pre-arranged exclusive interview with Diego himself. The original idea was to meet to up reasonably early at the hotel, speak with Diego for a few minutes with Ossie interpreting, and then I would make my way to the game and leave the two Argentineans to chat over old times over afternoon tea.

When Diego eventually emerged from the lift with his entourage crammed in behind him, there was barely enough time to make it to the ground from central London.

Ossie suggested that I accompanied them, and there was just enough time for a quick photograph with Diego, his wife, Ossie and me outside the hotel.

Ossie drove, Diego was in the passenger seat, and I was on my own in the back, armed with just a notebook and biro. Diego's entourage followed in a couple of limos. I asked the questions and Ossie translated as we drove.

Diego was just a kid when he first got into the national side and Ossie looked after him, like a father figure. I knew that Diego would be as honest as he could be under these circumstances, when I got round to the pertinent question about his Hand of God goal against England. He confessed, for the first time, that he accepted it was handball, but he refused to back down from his belief that it was divine intervention because he hadn't intended to handle and had jumped to try to head the ball. At least he had gone part of the way to confessing it was handball, and that was sufficient for my story.

I also asked him if he would one day like to play in English football and he was very positive that he would, and if he did he would like to follow Ossie to Spurs. I know the club made some attempt to see if it was possible, but it never really come close to coming off. Again, though, what might or might not have happened in the future, it was headline news for me that Diego wanted to play in England.

Recently the BBC invited me to a hotel in Covent Garden where they were filming for a documentary on Diego fronted by Gary Lineker, which in itself made headline news as Gary also asked him about the handball. There was much media criticism that Diego had been paid £50,000 for this particular interview. The BBC executives I spoke to said it was much, much less, but no doubt it came close with all the travelling and expenditure involved.

LAWRENCE MARKS
TV Scriptwriter extraordinaire

Lawrence was a news reporter on the *North London Weekly Herald* group of newspapers when I was covering football. We both worked in the paper's offices, a stone's throw from White Hart Lane and would, most days, chat about football over lunch in one of the greasy-spoon cafes along Tottenham High Road.

On occasions we would treat ourselves to a proper restaurant, but not too often. We were poor young journalists back then. Lawrence gave up on journalism to take the gamble on comedy scriptwriting in unison with his friend Maurice Gran, and together they become one of the nation's best ever sit-com writers, owning their own production company. Shows such as *Birds of a Feather* and *Goodnight Sweetheart* have, needless to say, made them millionaires.

I have been a guest at Lawrence's home, and meet up with Lo & Mo on occasions. They invited me to the TV studios to watch an episode of *Birds of a Feather* being made, with the usually after show party. We have all been threatening to work on a football-related book project together and I am sure one day that we will.

RODNEY MARSH
Outspoken pundit, whose views cause as much trouble as his tricky wing play with a host of clubs

Rodney sat behind me at Stormont Castle during George Best's funeral. It was hardly the occasion for a proper chat. Rodney is someone I would like to get to know better.

He has a habit of getting himself into trouble. He annoyed Bradford fans when he claimed the club would be relegated in their first Premiership season of 1999/2000. And when Paul Jewell's men stayed up thanks to a last day win over Liverpool, Rodney was forced to eat humble pie and have his hair shaved off in front of the baying Bradford hordes.

Then he was given the push by Sky after making an distasteful joke about the Tsunami on their programme *You're On Sky Sports*.

He also clearly angered a good friend of mine, Sir Alan Sugar. Rodney's criticisms of Alan when he was Spurs chairman, would often throw the Amstrad boss into a rage. He felt Rodney was not fully conversant with all the facts and misunderstood his motives. To be fair, Rodney showed the kind of attitude that the majority of Tottenham fans shared during Alan's reign. It is only since he sold up part of his shares that the Spurs contingent have come to appreciate and recognise the contribution he made to stabilising the finances. In fact, under Sugar, Spurs' levels of expenditure on player purchases were far higher than most people were prepared to give him credit for – including Rodney.

ROBERTO DI MATTEO
Chelsea's Italian Stallion in Ruud Gullit's sexy midfield

Roberto will always be a Chelsea legend, recalled with deep affection down the Kings Road for his wonder goal in record time at Wembley when he won the FA Cup for Chelsea and broke a 26 year wait for a trophy.

But he will also be remembered in the Fulham Road for his attempts at being a restaurateur. While still in his prime he became part owner of one of the Fulham Road's landmark Italian restaurants, San Frediano's, which was a grand old-fashioned establishment that my wife Linda and I enjoyed very much when we used to live in Elm Park Gardens in Chelsea.

Roberto invited us both to the opening of a hip version of the restaurant, and it looked as though it would be a hit, particularly as it would inevitably be frequented by the Chelsea stars. But the competition in Chelsea is so fierce with so many trendy bars, restaurants and cafes. After around 18 months Roberto and his partners sold up and opened a less expensive, pizzeria-style restaurant aptly named 'Friends', in Hollywood Road, just off the Fulham Road, and that proved more popular. Again, another opening, and most of the Chelsea players turned out this time.

Sadly Roberto never recovered his fitness after breaking his leg badly and was forced into early retirement and is now back in Rome. We miss him.

On the subject of restaurants and the team that brought the first piece of silverware to the Bridge of the modern era, the then chairman Ken Bates invited Linda and I to the Town Hall for the private celebrations after the traditional open top bus ride through the streets of Chelsea and Fulham.

Ken and Susannah invited us to slip away slightly early to join them for a more private and quiet celebratory lunch. We escaped the Town Hall hysteria through a side exit, and walked down the Kings Road for about a quarter of a mile to Leonardo's, another of those long established quaint old-fashioned Italian restaurants, although it has recently been modernised.

Ken faced a number of complaints about the route that the bus took because fans had lined the Fulham Road, but the bus did not go past. Most of the fans, though, were in great mood and when Ken entered Leonardo's he was afforded a standing ovation. We hadn't been there long before a few of the diners came over to congratulate him and a bottle of champagne was soon on our table.

After a long lunch, Ken and Susannah left, but hadn't gone very far when one disillusioned fan, still moaning about the route, poured a pint of beer over Ken's head. About 20 loyal Blues fans gave chase to the culprit, and I wouldn't like to think what they did with him. Ken might not have been very popular with large sectors of the media, but most Chelsea fans loved him for what he did for the club.

SIR STANLEY MATTHEWS
The original 'Wizard of Dribble' and arguably the greatest ever British footballing genius

Merely being in the same room as Sir Stan was an honour, but to have my picture taken with him and Tom Finney was indeed a privilege. Of course Stan incredibly played in the top flight until he was 50, but even so I can't recall much of him in his heyday, and have only seen some black and white clips. But enough to know he was a genius.

MAXWELL IS ALIVE AND LIVING IN PARAGUAY

ROBERT MAXWELL
'Captain Bob', Press baron, business magnate, football club owner, egotist and my former boss

Most people I meet in the profession always want to know "Is it true how Robert Maxwell hired you?"

Generally speaking it is true, but the tale has either been embellished down the years or some of the facts are not quite right, so few, if any, know the whole story.

I had started working on the *Daily Mail* as one of the youngest football writers. Tom Clarke, the then Sports Editor, had taken a risk with me and hired me when the *Evening News* closed down. I had worked for about a month at the *Daily Star*, after being handed a redundancy pay off from Associated Newspapers, who had owned the *Evening News* as well as the *Daily Mail*.

I got the call from Tom and, after a successful interview, he decided to take me on. But then the Associated News management asked if they could have their redundancy cheque back, if I didn't mind. Well, I did mind. I was entitled to it and, more importantly, I had banked it. I then learnt that the management had done the same with a couple of other ex-News guys who had now been taken on by the *Mail*. No doubt they thought the prospect of a new job would be so overwhelmingly enticing that I would give up my redundancy. I refused. For the next 12 months I worked on a freelance basis. Eventually I was given a staff appointment with all the benefits that went with it, pension rights etc.

Tom must have wondered at first whether I was worth it. I pestered him non-stop, with this story, or that story, with this tip I was working on, or that. I probably told him the contents of my lunch-time sandwich. Equally Tom has since told me that he did admire my relentless enthusiasm, and the quantity of the work, although the *Mail* required a certain standard of writing and it was a good education working for a paper that demanded the highest quality.

It was the perfect platform and was inspiring to work with some of the best writers of all time. What I might have lacked in terms of their quality of writing at that time,

I definitely made up with the volume of work. And, pulling out of the hat exclusive football stories seemed to come relatively easily to me to make up for any slight slip-ups in syntax.

Volume of work was supplemented by long hours and often, long after the last of the writers had headed off for a social engagement or a winding down session in the nearest wine bar, I was still at my desk, deep into the night.

One night, around 8.30pm, within minutes of the first edition deadline, the Press Association dropped a couple of lines that Robert Maxwell had bought Oxford United Football Club. Good story. But even better, suggested the night Sports News editor, if anyone could get hold of Maxwell. Quite sensibly, he doubted whether that would be possible at the best of times, but impossible so late at night and particularly when he would be avoiding the media because of this late announcement, the timing of which was clearly to ensure as little interference as possible.

That was a challenge I couldn't resist. I rang a local contact in the region and virtually begged for a private number for Maxwell. I was given a car telephone number. When I rang it, Maxwell personally responded. It was the first time I had come across that husky, deep, intimidating tone of his.

When I introduced myself, explaining why I had contacted him, I didn't get the instant brush off I had anticipated. Instead he said, "How did you get my number? Oh, never mind. What I am more interested to know is what are you doing in the office at this time of night? Aren't all of your fellow writers off down the pub somewhere?"

I told him that I had a tendency to work very late, as I was determined to get on. "I like that," he replied. "Right then, get on with it, I haven't got all night, what do you want to know?"

The interview lasted no more than two minutes, but in half a dozen questions I had got more then enough for a big story that night and a follow up the next day."

But he before he hung up, Maxwell said, "I like a young lad like you who is willing to work so hard, why not come to work with me?"

At that time Maxwell owned Maxwell Communications and in those days there had only been loose talk about him one day owning a newspaper.

"Sorry," I said, "You don't really have what I would like.'

Now, that was a challenge to Maxwell. "What do you mean, what would you want?" I told him I love working on newspapers and nothing else would do, so he didn't really have a position that would interest me.

"What if I was to double, no treble your salary, what about that?"

Sorry, not interested.

"Well, let me tell you, within a year I will own the *Daily Mirror* and I will offer you the job as my Sports Editor...." With that the line went dead.

Of course, everyone still there on the sports desk was told the exact words of this conversation, because how could you keep something like that to yourself for a minute?

The reaction from everyone, and there were only a handful of back-bench sub editors left, was that they didn't believe a word I was saying.

Round about six months later Maxwell did indeed buy the *Daily Mirror*.

"Just wait," I told everyone on the *Mail's* sports desk, "that phone will ring with that offer he promised me." Cue laughter.

And no phone call.

I was well and truly stumped. I had told the truth, something I pride myself on, because I always think it's hard to remember the lie.

About three months went by. One or two of my colleagues started to take the piss..." tell us that story again about how Maxwell was going to offer you a job." It was quite embarrassing.

Then one night, around about the same time I had rung Maxwell for that exclusive interview, the phone did ring. One of the sub-editors picked it up. "Oi, Aitch, its someone calling himself Robert Maxwell on the blower."

Right, that was it. "Haven't you guys had enough mileage out of me?" I exploded. "I told you he offered me that job, but none of you believe me anymore."

"Hello. Who's this?"

"It's Robert Maxwell."

I held the phone away and mouthed..." It's Robert Maxwell, it is Robert Maxwell."

"I told you I would buy the *Mirror*, and now I am offering you a job. Come to the *Mirror* right now. I have the Editor of the paper waiting to greet his new signing."

I told Maxwell that I was working on a couple of stories and would be finished in about an hour and half.

"Fine – will be waiting."

So, I finished up as quickly as I could and around 9.45pm made my way over to Holborn to the *Mirror* building. I was invited up to the ninth floor to Maxwell's offices there. He sat me down in this enormous office and told me he would double my salary, and that if chief football writer was the position I wanted, then that is the position I shall have. "The Editor Mike Maloney is behind the screen waiting to meet you," said Maxwell.

It all seemed rather rushed. After waiting all this time for the call, when it came it seemed so sudden that a decision had to be made there and then.

I suggested I would go away and think about it and give him my decision in the morning.

"Do you want to sign for my team," he said.

"Well, yes I do."

"Then what is there to think about?"

I told Maxwell the problem was that I should tell my sports editor Tom Clarke first. After all he had taken the gamble in giving me my big chance and the least I could was to consult with him first.

"He will persuade you to stay," said Maxwell. "We shall speak to him right now, what's his number?"

By now, it was rapidly approaching midnight. I didn't think Tom would appreciate a call at home at this time of night, although, of course, if any big stories were breaking or one of our rivals had a major story on it's back page then the sports editor would expect a routine call at this time. I didn't think it would too much harm, so I gave Maxwell Tom's number.

Tom's son answered the call and told his dad that it was Robert Maxwell on the line. Tom swore, thinking it was a typical back-bench wind up from within his own offices. He swore again when he came to the phone – only to discover it was the real Robert Maxwell.

"I am Robert Maxwell and I have your top football writer here with me in my office and I want to sign him. Will you let me have him?"

Tom was taken aback and declined to give Maxwell any answer.

After putting the phone down Maxwell turned to me and said, "I've told him, as you asked, so now will you join me?"

I asked Maxwell what Tom had said, and he assured me it would be perfectly alright. On that basis I accepted. Maxwell pulled back the screen, and he was right. The editor had been waiting there all this time just to shake my hand, or at least Maxwell had told him to do it.

I sensed there would never be a dull moment working for Maxwell.

I completely under-estimated the half of it.

As it turned out the *Mirror* already had a chief football writer in Harry Miller, but I joined on the understanding that I would be working at that kind of level, covering England games and given the space and exposure my stores demanded.

Many myths have grown as a result of my time at the *Mirror*, notably the Maxwell years.

Maxwell could switch from being charming and pleasant to being an ogre in the space of a sentence. His mood swings were hard to predict, but usually were triggered by anything that displeased him. However, for someone who was surrounded, in the main, by 'Yes men', it must have been the fact that I told him how it is, that made him warm to my opinions and increasingly trust my judgment.

One day he summoned me to his offices to break the good news – he wanted me to be his next editor of the *Daily Mirror*, not quite straight away, but he would take me off my sports desk duties, send me to a further education establishment to study business, economics etc, to prepare me for the task of running his flag ship newspaper.

He could tell I was unimpressed. In fact he was shocked by my reaction. I explained that I would better suit the newspaper by continuing to do what I did best and break big football stores for his back page, and occasionally for the front. But he seemed to have his heart set on this massive promotion for someone with absolutely no experience of working inside the office.

Then he changed tack and, instead of trying to impress me, he tried to tempt me. "Of course," he went on, "it will entail a big hike in salary, and I will personally oversee a move to a very expensive central London apartment which would be at your disposal during the week."

But I was adamant. I was not suited to it, so I wouldn't do it. I would have been out of my depth and I didn't want the job.

I know some people who later joined the *Mirror* who were out of their depth, but who had untold ambition to become the Editor of the *Mirror*. Fortunately not too many egotists made it to the very top.

Whatever Maxwell's reputation – and I have no doubt most of it is deserved – he could be a very generous boss.

There were a handful of select journalists to whom he warmed. He respected their ability and wanted to reward them accordingly. The doyen of agony aunts Marjie Proops was one; the former Harold Wilson aide, and *Mirror* political editor, Joe Haines, was another. One female editor of a Sunday title received a gift of a very expensive sports car on her promotion to the top job, while the inner sanctum of journalists were given highly ethically questionable personal salaries from Maxwell's private account. I was most definitely not one of those.

When he died, committed suicide, was assassinated – delete where applicable – there were those who questioned the legitimacy of dual salaries. But whoever suggested I was paid twice was mistaken. I had a very close working relationship with the sports editor at this time, Keith Fisher, but when he told me that he had frozen my annual increment because he was told, so he said, by someone in accounts, that I had two salaries, that was bitterly disappointing for me. Of course it wasn't true.

Anyone who had any dodgy Maxwell connections was quickly rooted out in the fallout from his death and never survived at the paper. I survived longer than perhaps any of those senior journalists who were there during the Maxwell era, and I believe that tells its own story.

It upset me about Keith, because he had come to me one day with a real problem. He had commissioned a builder to do some extension work at his home, paid him up front, only for the builder to go belly up after laying only two rows of bricks around the house.

Keith was left without any funds to pay another builder, and no matter how hard he tried, with threats, legal action etc, he got nowhere with the builder who had gone bankrupt.

Keith asked me if I could go to Maxwell for an interest free loan. I had never asked Maxwell for a penny for myself, but I asked on behalf of a colleague in desperate need. And Maxwell gave him that interest free loan, which Keith paid off through his monthly salary.

The week before Maxwell died, he called me into his office and said he planned to give me some share options in the *Mirror*. I find it astonishing that he should promise this to me and then, just a few days later, top himself. I can't help but rule out his death as suicide.

In addition, I knew a man who would prove black is white if it suited his purpose, so if he had what would appear to be an insurmountable personal problem, financial or otherwise, he was the sort who always believed he could find a method of dealing with it.

Maxwell would use the full force of the law to halt people in his tracks if he felt he was being exposed for anything, a tactic that many wealthy men turn to if it suits their purpose, as *Private Eye* found to its cost in 1986 after accusing him of trying to buy a peerage from Labour and looking like renowned East End gangster Ronnie Kray.

I had been in his company when he had taken a call and told me to leave the room because he was talking to a head of state, a Prime Minister, or someone that it was so confidential even someone he trusted could not be privy to it. So, if you ask me whether he was working for peace in the Middle East, I would say that yes he probably was. If anyone assassinated him, it would most likely be an enemy of Israel, not their secret service as it has been suggested.

Recently, on a trip abroad with Premier League sponsors Barclays, I was asked whether I thought Maxwell was assassinated, or simply fell over board.

I spent the next 30 minutes convincing the 30 hard-nosed journalists around the dinner table that Maxwell was alive and well, and living in Paraguay.

I even nearly believed it myself!

FRANK MCLINTOCK
Arsenal's double winning captain and Sky TV pundit

Frank and I got on famously until the day I named him as the 'bag man' in the infamous £50,000 bung case involving Terry Venables and Brian Clough.

'El Till', as we labelled Venables in one hard-hitting back page lead in a series of exposés into the then Spurs Chief Executive, had authorised the payment to be collected from an East End bank, brought back to White Hart Lane, and put into a bag, which Frank put onto the front seat of his car. He then transported it to a motorway service station where it was to be collected by one of Cloughie's aides, for distribution. Clough always claimed that he never actually got it all, as some went to his chief Scout, who was charged by the FA and found guilty.

The five year Premier League bung enquiry, which included as its three man team Rick Parry and Steve Coppell, handed over their extensive files to the FA. But then Chief Executive Graham Kelly decided that, as Clough was out of football and also an ill man, that he wouldn't be 'prosecuted'.

Frank took great exception to being drawn into this controversy and we didn't speak for some time. But credit to Frank, he has appreciated that I was doing my job, that I had got all my facts right, and we have spoken more recently, although hardly what I would call a deep and meaningful conversation.

96 LIVERPOOL FANS DEAD AT FA CUP SEMI-FINAL

STEVE MCMAHON
Former Liverpool and England midfielder now a TV pundit in the Far East

I wasn't at Heysel, but I was at Hillsborough. At times it is an episode in your life you prefer to hide away in the dark want-to-be-forgotten areas of your memory. To relive them are too harrowing. Just thinking about it now, it makes me shiver with grief for those who died.

I remember going to the game with three of my colleagues, the usual suspects who always travelled together. The scenes approaching the stadium were identical to those we would witness virtually every weekend; dozens of fans drinking at nearby pubs, spilling out onto the pavement, in the majority of cases doing relatively little harm.

Not long into the game, it was clear something awful was going on, but no-one really knew the scale of human suffering. But soon enough there was plenty of evidence before our eyes of a serious situation, with the game stopped and ambulance crews tending the fans behind the goal and spilling onto the pitch.

The worst part was to come; performing journalistic duties, when really it was just too sickening and morbid to want to stay anywhere near Hillsborough.

A glance into the indoor training area, which had been turned into a makeshift morgue presented me with an image that will haunt me for the rest of my life. Then I went outside to witness people rushing in different directions, searching for missing loved ones.

The homeward journey in the car seemed to last forever.

The next day, trying to write an assessment of what happened was hard, really hard – an emotional handicap.

Relatives suffered the most, ordinary fans who survived suffered as well, but no-one gave much thought to the media, who might also have needed counselling.

In the *Mirror* offices on Monday afternoon, the tension became unbearable, and I ended up in a row with the Sports Editor over the coverage of the story, and cannot even recall what the argument was about.

During the course of the *Mirror's* blanket reporting of Hillsborough, which went on for days, if not weeks in its intensity, I interviewed Steve McMahon, articulate and intelligent member of the Liverpool team that day, and his account of what occurred was extraordinarily vivid.

I ended up writing Steve's life story in a book called *Macca Can'* published by Pelham Books. I get a call from time to time from Steve wondering if I can lay my hands on any spare copies – which I can't, I'm sorry to say.

BRIAN MEARS
Former Chairman of Chelsea

Brian was the antithesis of Ken Bates. When Brian was in charge Chelsea was a media haunt, and journalists were welcomed with hospitality and warmth. The Mears family founded Chelsea and it was always the place to be for a free drink after the game. Only Ipswich Town when controlled by the Cobbolds had a reputation of being more friendly to the media. Ken, though, loathes certain sections of the media who continually target him, and he detests the 'freeloaders' in the game, which again, in his opinion, constitutes some of the press as well as the hangers on of which Chelsea seemed to have a large quantity according to Ken. When he arrived at Leeds United, Ken had the same outlook and rid himself of more 'freeloaders'.

DAVID MELLOR
Former Conservative MP, famous for his Radio FiveLive phone-in show and Chelsea shirt-wearing sex romps

David was good enough to give me an exclusive interview for my book on *Chelski – The Russian Revolution,* which focused on the business ins and outs of the takeover of Roman Abramovich. David gave me the inside track on how he had tried to bring in his own man to buy a controlling stake in Chelsea and thought he had pulled it off until the Russian arrived out of left field.

David and Ken are old mates, and David's allegiances are all true Blue, even though he began his affinity to the game by supporting Fulham. David now has a highly readable page on sport, mostly football, and generally speaking Chelsea, which appears once a week in the *Evening Standard*.

I have it on good authority that David does NOT consult Ken on a regular basis to provide him for material for his column – and if you believe that you will believe anything. However, it has been a touch transparent David, that you have regularly attacked some of Ken's fiercest enemies, such as the Isreali agent Pini Zahavi.

MERSON BLEW £108,000 BETS AND CHEATED ON PREGNANT WIFE

PAUL MERSON
Former Arsenal wildman

I got a tip from a regular source that Paul Merson had been found the morning after the night before in a Highbury executive box. There had clearly been some excessive drinking, and perhaps even a hint of drugs, as Arsenal's star player was found asleep under the table.

Irrespective of how solid any tip might seem, I always check them out thoroughly. On this occasion the degree of difficulty in establishing the possibility of drug taking by one of the country's most prominent players, with Arsenal and England, would be hard to stand up.

Paul's agents were Jerome Anderson and Geoff Weston, two guys I got on well with and trusted. But that wasn't the point, as it would not be in their interests for such a story to reach the public domain and I didn't want to put them in a tricky position if they knew and didn't want to tell me.

The best policy was to contact them and ask them outright. My source had excellent Arsenal connections and I had no reason to disbelieve him. My thought was it could be true, and until I discovered otherwise, I would approach my process of checking it out as if it were so.

I spoke first with Jerome. He knew nothing about it and he suggested I spoke to Geoff. He again was flabbergasted and suggested it couldn't possibly be true.

However, there had been rumours of Paul's obsessive drinking habits and there was always a danger it could spill over into drugs, if he was keeping the wrong company.

I knew Paul reasonably well and liked him and suggested to Geoff that I would hold back my enquiries in case it did turn out to be true to give him the chance to approach Paul and tell him I would approach the problem in a sympathetic way, if Paul came clean and talked about it.

Geoff said he would speak to Jerome and Paul and get back to me.

About a week later Geoff called me, and asked if I had made any headway in my enquires. I told him I had not made one more call as I was waiting for him to come-back to me after speaking with Paul.

Geoff said that Paul trusted me and would like to speak to me and would I be inter-ested in a story about his drinking and how he planned to fight it, maybe even going to AA? I told Geoff that Paul had confessed in a similar way to his drinking problem a year earlier in a Sunday paper, and that the *Mirror* would be most reluctant to pay a 'fee' in any case, as we had already had a tip about his wild excesses at Highbury after a game.

Geoff assured me that Paul denied being caught in one of the club's executive boxes, but was fearful of being caught out and wanted to speak to me.

The next day, I travelled to Barcelona with Manchester United for a big night of European football. I spoke with Geoff a few times from Barcelona, and about half an hour before I was due down in the lobby to depart with the rest of the media for the stadium, I received a call from him to tell me he had Paul Merson with him, who wanted to talk to me.

Paul spent the next 30 minutes starting the process of unburdening himself. He told me about the drink, he told me about the drugs, but he swore me to secrecy until he could seem face to face, as he had a lot more he wanted to tell me about.

Paul put Geoff back on the phone and we made arrangements to meet the next day, early afternoon in Jerome and Geoff's offices. I would be travelling back the next morning and would go straight there and Paul would catch up with us all after training.

I got to the agents' offices around 1.30pm, but there was no sign of Paul. He finally turned up around 2.30pm looking completely dishevelled, unshaven, and not anything like an athlete who played for his country.

Paul asked my opinion about the ramifications of any confession he would now be making to me. I told him straight that "it would be in my interest to say anything, at this point, to convince you to give me a fantastic front page story, but if you are asking me as a mate to advise you on how all this will be perceived, then it is better to confess than to be caught out. And it can only be a matter of time before you are exposed, and then the FA will ban you for some time."

Paul agreed to an interview and pictures, provided the *Mirror* paid for him and his family to leave the country immediately, to fly off to a destination where he could think, and not be hounded. I told him the *Mirror* was most reluctant to pay any fee for this interview as I had sourced the story myself, but the paper had agreed to pay all the cost of a five star hotel, flights and expenses for him to be hidden away.

Initially the paper wanted me to go with him, but Paul really needed to be with his closest family. He was actually on the verge of a breakdown.

Naturally I was proud of the story that made several pages of the front and several at the back for days on end, a story every paper was compelled to follow up.

But I was even more proud of myself for giving Paul the right advice. His con-fession touched the FA, and his tears when he was full of remorse when the FA held a press conference to highlight his problems, convinced the authorities that Paul and cases like him needed help not draconian punishment that could drive them to suicide.

I like to think I helped Paul onto the road of rehabilitation and a footballing comeback. We got together to write a book about his life and experiences and it was even more harrowing listening to his days of drying out from not just the booze, but the drugs as well.

PAUL MILLER
Spurs defender, turned business man

Paul was a no-nonsense, hard man centre-half, but surprisingly has reinvented himself as a sort of City gent. I bump into him quite often at Wentworth where he plays golf, or at Langan's, where he is involved in business lunches and it's always good to catch up and chat about the game. Paul is well connected in City circles, where there are constant rumours about him being involved in takeover bids for football clubs.

SIR BERT MILLICHIP
Long-serving former Chairman of the Football Association

Bert headed up the FA's disciplinary committee before he became chairman and nothing much seemed to flummox him, but there was just one occasion when he really did not know the answer.

In 1985, England had only just arrived in Mexico for an end of season tour to play games in the country to prepare for the 1986 World Cup finals when news reached us about the Heysel disaster at the European Cup final.

Bert realised straight away that UEFA would not permit English clubs to participate in European competition after that and he pre-empted the inevitable by announcing that the FA would take measures to withdraw English teams from European competition. It was the least Bert and the FA could do. But Bert couldn't have imagined that English clubs' exile from Europe would last so long.

HOW I SAVED SOUTHEND AND CAME TO BOBBY MOORE'S RESCUE

BOBBY MOORE
England's gentleman, World Cup winning captain

Bobby should have been an England coach, or an ambassador for the country's national sport, more hands on than, say, Sir Bobby Charlton, who has kind of assumed that role without it being officially bestowed upon him.

Bobby stayed in the game by moving into club management, but he was never suited to it. His mind was light years ahead of those players he was trying to coax into adopting a football philosophy that, down in the lower leagues, was probably beyond them. The mix wasn't right.

Bobby was managing at Roots Hall, with a Southend United club in dire financial straights, so coming up to Christmas I thought of a seasonal feature interviewing Bobby about the number of players under his charge on the breadline – and, of course, hardly able to afford the Christmas turkey.

Bobby seemed pretty busy as I tried to contact him at Southend, and when I eventually got through he sounded pretty preoccupied. When I explained to him my idea, he told me that he would speak to me at length later that day, but if I thought the players were suffering hard times because of the club's perilous financial position, I should consider the fans, who had been contributing all year to the club's Christmas Saving fund. Thousands of them been queuing overnight to recoup their savings, only to discover that the guy in charge had done a bunk with their money.

Well, it did make a good story at Christmas, but the time Bobby could spare to discuss the issue with me coincided with a long standing lunch date with none other than Ken Bates, a chairman who did not like any of his appointments turning up late, so I was my usual punctual self.

Over cocktails Ken asked his usual opener "what's happening in the bazaars?" I told him that Southend were facing crippling debts and that the guy in charge had done a runner with the supporters' club's Christmas fund, and that I had to speak to Bobby Moore about it. Did he mind if I made a very quick call. Ken agreed, but you always knew with the Chelsea chairman that anything that interfered with his precious preassigned time was putting him out, and I suppose he had a point.

Unfortunately I couldn't get hold of Bobby first time and it took a couple more tries before I eventually got through and got my interview.

Ken was distinctly unimpressed that I had been away from the table for about ten minutes. Perhaps he wasn't taking too much interest when I first explained Southend's plight because around this time most Football League clubs were experiencing cashflow crisis. "What is so special about Southend?' Bates wanted to know.

I reiterated the plight of the fans, and now having spoken at length to Bobby realised just how bad it was. There were fans in wheelchairs, families with their small children, all camped out around Roots Hall waiting for their only source of savings for presents and turkeys for Christmas. The debts were so heavy that the club probably would go out of existence within days rather than weeks. Time was running out and Bobby was pleading for some urgent assistance as part of the article I was going to write.

Ken might seem hard as nails on the outside, but inside he has a genuine soft spot if you can find it. He was willing to help. But not without a challenge. At this time he was finding it hard to contact Robert Maxwel,l who had become quite active in Football League affairs, particularly on issues of TV rights.

Here was the challenge; Bates would put up £500,000 in cash, if Robert Maxwell put up the other £500,000. "Go and ring Uncle Bob," as he and I used to call him.

So I did.

I am not sure whether Ken believed I had such direct access to Maxwell as some people had told him. Now was his chance to find out.

I rang Uncle Bob's line and spoke to his secretary, who put me straight through. I told him of Southend's plight, of Ken's challenge and my recommendation that if the pair of them bailed out Southend it would be national news – and not a bad tale for me, either, as the *Mirror* would break the story.

"Yes, it's agreed, go and tell Ken Bates".

So back I trooped. It felt as though I had spent the entire lunch on the phone – no mobiles in those days, so it was up and down the stairs to the cloakroom outside the toilets to make the calls.

Ken was wearing one of those, "You ain't got through" smiles. But when I told him it was all agreed, he was probably thinking about how to raise half a million overnight!

The next morning I reported for work to be summoned to Maxwell's offices. There Uncle Bob told me he was still waiting to hear from Ken about his half of the bargain. I told him that Ken would not let us down.

However, Bobby Moore had impressed upon me that the club had until 5pm that evening to raise the £1m loan, otherwise Southend would fold.

At midday we were already running short of time. Maxwell had still not heard from Ken and repeated attempts to contact him failed. "Sod Bates", stormed Maxwell and he gave instructions to his security staff to escort me to accounts where £1m in £20 notes had been made available for collection on my signature.

A car waited outside the Holborn building and, accompanied by suitcases full of crisp £20s, we made our way to Southend.

Bobby Moore had been pacing up and down outside Roots Hall, where the fans were queuing up, and it was getting dark by the time we arrived, beating the 5pm deadline by about five minutes.

Maxwell's final instructions as I left his offices... "take a note book and pencil, and I want you to write down every name of each and every person you hand over the money to – and interview them all as well."

"Fine," I thought, "but there must have been thousands waiting for their money."

I was there for most of that night, either writing down the names, interviewing as many as I could, or rushing to the phone to continually 'file' copy to the newspaper for the next morning's editions. That night the £1m that saved Southend made the main item on all the late night news bulletins.

Next morning Bates' money arrived as promised.

Much later I discovered that the reason for the delay was that Maxwell had insisted on a covenant giving him ownership of Roots Hall if Southend failed to repay his money within a certain time, and in all probability Ken had the same 'comfort' that a schedule of repayments had been agreed in a binding contract.

PIERS MORGAN
Former Editor of the Daily Mirror and all-round media personality

Piers supported Arsenal and I supported Spurs, so perhaps we were never destined to get on.

In fact, the first day Piers was appointed Editor of the *Daily Mirror*, he ventured over to my desk and his opening gambit was, "Ah, your the feller I've been told to be wary of."

I told him that he had been given some duff information, because all he could expect from me was stories, and all I hoped from him was to provide enough space at the back of the 'book' to give the stories a good show.

As it turned out Piers and I enjoyed a wonderful working relationship. I loved his style – brash, campaigning, eye catching, inspirational. He was young, but not inexperienced, having edited the News of the World. I always thought he would be good for The *Mirror*, and for much of the time he was. Of course we had our falling outs. And when we did, it was never over something trivial. And usually it centred around an issue when Piers turned his hand to football. During the European Champions in 1996 when England faced Germany in the semi-finals, Piers came up with a series of stunts which, you could argue, were hilarious, but equally they could be offensive. And they turned out to be rather more offensive than our Editor anticipated.

For the build up, Piers had Stuart Pearce in a tin hat and, as he began to warm to the War theme, he thought of the preposterous idea of sending in tanks to the German training camp. When someone pointed out the folly of such a move, he thought of planes dropping leaflets proclaiming an England victory.

Naturally enough when I turned up at the England training camp for the daily round of media conferences, with the press wonderfully catered for in their own tent with food and drink on tap, the radio and TV outlets wanted my opinion. The safest bet would have been to have refused, but all the papers like their journalists to appear on TV because it is free advertising. And, never one to shirk a challenge, I made a number of appearances, but always playing a Geoff Boycott straight bat.

I am sure the TV networks were fed up with me saying that editorial decisions of this nature were the domain of the Editor, so I would not offer an opinion other than perhaps to say it would not have been the way I would have gone about it had I been the Editor, which I am not. Perhaps that was sailing close to the wind, but no-one picked me up on it. Maybe also, it was because I fobbed it off with a joke, by saying "I've been told not to mention the war. I didn't mention the war, did I?"

The reaction was hostile, though, and Piers must have sensed the feedback was negative because he tried to redress the balance. He decided he would send his senior football reporters, including myself, to the Tower. Of course he didn't tell me about it, as he knew I wouldn't approve, and he was probably concerned about how strong my reaction would be.

So, he left it to the Sports Editor, David Barnforth, whom I found to be very straightforward, although some of my colleagues thought his dedication and work ethic too much to handle.

'Barmy', as he was called out of his earshot, delegated the sports news editor to summon me to the office. I must have had ten requests about my movements after the media conferences in the England camp. Was I coming back to the office? No, I wasn't. Oh, could I come back to the office? Why? Well, we would like a chat about how the coverage is going.

I could sense something was up. There was never usually this kind of half insistence that my presence was required at Canary Wharf. But the sports news editor seemed to be under intense pressure to ensure I came back to the office, and he confessed as much. When he told me that, I came in.

As I turned the corner toward my desk, there he was, a giant of a man, wielding a gigantic axe – a Tower of London Beefeater, or at least a replica of one. The Beefeater-A-Like had been waiting patiently for some time in all that gear and was almost wilting by the time I arrived.

The sports news editor asked me ever so politely, apologetically, if I minded very much having a mock up picture taken with the Beefeater, as if he was taking me to The Tower, for the *Mirror's* impertinence in the way we had covered the Germany game. "The others have done it, so surely you can?"

Actually, no way. Sorry, not interested.

By this time Piers was heading off back to the sanctuary of his office. He could tell I didn't see the funny side of this. I made it perfectly plain what I thought. "Why don't you send Piers to the Tower?"

'Barmy' interceded with some calming words, trying to be conciliatory. Then, seeing that his efforts to persuade me it was just a giggle had failed, he tried another tack, suggesting that one of his sub editors was hauled off to the mock tower, to have his picture taken, and did I mind if my head was superimposed on his body?

"Do what you want, but I'm off unless anyone objects."

The next day, there I was on the front page of the *Mirror* being carted off to the Tower, and no reader would have known it wasn't me. My wife was embarrassed, but only because my stand-in was wearing really naff shoes!

Once the tournament was over, next came the documentary crews to film retrospective programmes.

The *Mirror's* coverage of the Germany game was naturally a must investigate target. I must have been filmed for more than an hour, with the interviewer asking for my opinion on the reasons behind the coverage, the impact it had, and they were determined that I was critical of Piers. They must have asked the same question about Piers about a dozen times. Clearly, I must have let my guard slip and made it clear that I did not approve, but I had not been consulted about it, and would have argued against it had I been.

That was the sound bite they wanted. Virtually all of the rest of the interview was left on the cutting room floor. It seemed all I had said was that Piers had got it wrong.

Talk about being quoted out of context. But you cannot argue with TV, that's why Ken Bates always tells me he will never pre-record anything for TV and always insists that it goes out live, so he cannot be edited.

Piers had either seen or been told about my remark. He was none too pleased. He called me into his office and gave me a right old bollocking. On this occasion I could offer up no defence other than that I had made many other comments but they were not used. Piers put his foot down and instructed me to make no further comment about any editorial decisions which were solely the domain of the Editor. Fair enough. I did not quibble.

That was probably the only occasion Piers had to reprimand me. However our next row was our last and by far the biggest. At the end of it, after a court room appearance for me, and the threat of a full scale trial for Piers, a very angry truce was thrashed out in front of company lawyer and Piers' best mate Martin Cruddace in the lobby of a Canary Wharf hotel.

The catalyst to my final bust up with Piers was my decision to leave the *Mirror* after 18 years and join the Daily *Express*. He wasn't too pleased to hear I was going and said that it was like "Patrick Vieira quitting Arsenal to join Doncaster Rovers." The story appeared on the Guardian web site and in their media columns. Even the giveaway local paper at Canary Wharf led their page Business Week/ Wharf Media section on the 'transfer' with the headline 'Harris Scores With *Express*'. Piers was quoted again, "Harry's been a terrific football journalist for the *Mirror* for nearly 20 years, but he says he fancies a new challenge. I understand this 'new challenge' involved a salary not dissimilar to that of Zinedine Zidane's at Real Madrid."

But it looked like I would have a long wait before taking up my new position because an executive decision was made to keep me to my 15 month notice period. At the same time the September 11 tragedy occurred and Piers was wrapped up 'in the war', and was too busy to see me to thrash out my departure date. Emails didn't work and no matter how I tried to contact Piers for an appointment, it didn't work. After about four weeks of utter frustration I thought it was time to take the initiative. In retrospect, I was utterly wrong, of course, and should have waited.

Looking back, eventually Piers would have fitted me in and sorted it out amicably. But I used an internet site that I co-owned called Voice of Football to post up a blinding story about David Beckham. Somehow the *Express* got wind of this story – how they did so I couldn't possibly comment – and they used it on their front page and their back page splash.

Piers woke the next morning and saw the front pages. I was reliably told by his flat mate Martin Cruddace that he'd never been so angry. I'm not surprised.

Piers took his retribution by issuing an injunction against me leaving to work for the *Express*. I was in France at the time as a guest of Barclaycard as part of an early season media trip to a vineyard – and boy did I need a drink when I found out about their legal moves.

When I returned there was a big decision to make about whether to contest the injunction. Clearly the *Mirror* thought it was a fait accompli, but I got in touch with Alan Sugar's personal lawyer, Alan Watts at Herbert Smith, and we went to court and put up such a good fight that the *Mirror* were on the back foot from the outset.

The Judge eventually decreed that he could not settle this dispute in the form of an injunction and was to recommend it went to a full trial. Clearly, if it proceeded then the *Mirror* were not going to get an injunction to prevent me posting any more stories on the web site, or indeed, eventually being free of the 15 month notice period if I went on to successfully win the trial.

A meeting was called between Piers and myself to avert the witness box and we got together at a hotel in Canary Wharf, with Alan Watts in my corner and Martin Cruddace representing Piers and the *Mirror*. Ironically the Arsenal team were staying at the hotel to prepare for a match that evening, which put Piers in a good mood to start with. But then followed a great deal of shouting and arguing. Finally, however, agreement was reached.

Piers insisted that I couldn't leave the *Mirror* to cover the World Cup for the *Express* until, and if, England reached the semi-finals, but we agreed on the quarter-finals, and he would cut the gardening leave from 15 months to a more manageable eight months.

However, after a few weeks Piers rang me to inform me that I could actually go from January 1. He wished me well and suggested that I was still making a mistake and if I changed my mind he would welcome me back to the *Mirror*!

WILL MOTTY QUIT?

JOHN MOTSON
'Motty', to just about the entire nation, the man with the sheepskin coat and a whole bundle of trivia at his fingertips

I've plenty of time for someone like John Motson; top of his profession for so long and a likable chap. But I did give him something of a fright recently when I got wind of the fact that he was considering taking a new direction after the World Cup finals in Germany. I got the tip from a very well placed source – in fact someone who had been dining with John just a couple of weeks before and John had told him about his plans.

Not so, insisted John, when I told him about my tip. He sounded quite perturbed. I explained that it had come from outside of the Corporation, so he had no worries about anyone plotting his demise. He was grateful for that, although I am not so sure he was reassured totally as a little later John's agent also gave me a call to reassure me it wasn't true.

I discussed all the nuances of my tip, the call to John and his reaction with my Sports Editor Bill Bradshaw, and, although we both suspected there was more than meets the eye in all of this, out of deference to John, we decided not to run any speculative story, and in any case, we knew that John was denying it.

Let's see what happens.

LIKE BRIAN CLOUGH ON SPEED

JOSE MOURINHO
The 'Special One', style guru and manager of Chelsea

Jose is a particular favourite of mine. He has taken a great deal of stick from certain sectors of the media, and some of it justified, brought upon himself. But I happen to believe someone as colourful and gifted as Mourinho can only be good for English football. It will be a sad day for me when he leaves, and a much quieter one for the game in this country.

"Like Brian Clough on speed," is how I have described him. It gave me great satisfaction to chart in graphic detail his first season in charge at Stamford Bridge, which turned out to be the greatest season in the club's history, which was the subtitle to my book published by John Blake, just two weeks after the season finished. With the aid of Mark Mitchinson at Samsung Mobiles we devised a can't-buy giveaway for the *Express* of seven Samsung 600 mobiles personally signed by Jose, and it created the best response to any prize on sport in the Express' history.

Jose agreed to present the phones, and when a small boy turned up for the presentation to collect his winnings, Jose signed his boots and gave them to him.

A NIGHT ON THE TILES

ALAN MULLERY
Fulham, Spurs and England midfielder, now at home in the TV studio

Attitudes when Alan was manager of QPR were completely unrecognisable from the kind of relationship that now exists between the media and the football industry, particularly managers and players.

In Alan's time in West London, there was a far more trusting relationship. The media travelled with the team on the same plane, were billeted in the same hotel and often would socialise together. That was certainly the case with Mullery's management, but then again there were far fewer reporters who would travel with a club in Europe – usually just the one. So it was far more manageable, and controllable.

QPR were playing a European tie in Rejkjavik in Iceland and, although at first it didn't seem appealing, it turned out to be a very enjoyable three days. The Rangers itinerary meant that the party would stay over night after the match, returning the following day. Nowadays this idea is frowned upon, as managers want their players back as quickly as possible. Overnights for any English team are rare.

After the match, Alan invited the handful of media who travelled with the team to an after match meal in a English-style pub. Alcohol consumption was very much limited in this region and spirits were prohibited after a certain time. 'Mullers' had opted for this pub because he heard that, to circumvent the rule, the beer was spiked with vodka.

Most of the players and a few of the journalists left the pub for a night club, called Hollywood, where we all enjoyed a very fruitful night on the tiles.

The next thing I remember is waking up in Steve Wicks' room with a pounding in my head that I realised wasn't just the alcohol. Steve was a tall, slim, blond, very good looking guy. A very attractive girl, who had taken a shine to him, was banging on the door demanding to be let in!

We all beat a hasty retreat to the busses to be shipped back to the airport.

TERRY NEILL, GARY NEVILLE, MIKE NEWELL, BILL NICHOLSON, RON NOADES

NEVILLE LOSES IT

GARY NEVILLE
Manchester United captain, England right-back and self-styled players' shop steward

During the European Championships or World Cup, the volume of one's TV and radio appearances normally multiplies, to the extent that it is sometimes hard to remember precisely what you have said to whom. But I got a stark reminder when my mobile rang while I was with some contacts having a convivial lunch and picking up plenty of material for future columns.

"Gary Neville here. Is that Harry Harris?"

Now, you always suspect a wind up when someone who wouldn't necessarily have your mobile number, and/or wouldn't usually call you, and/or you don't actually call regularly, and/or don't in fact at all, suddenly rings out of the blue.

The tendency is to tell the caller to 'bugger off' and find out very quickly it was someone from the office.

However, my instincts told me this was, indeed, Gary Neville ringing me out of the blue. His voice was quite distinguishable. Although I had never met him, I had heard him and seen him many times being interviewed on TV.

"Yes, you've got him. Glad to hear from you, how can I help?"

"Well, you won't be glad to hear from me, you f****** c*** , I have just been told about your TV interview when you slagged off my brother, and our dad, and you are bang out of order, Phil has been left out of the England squad and you're taking the mickey out of him, I want an apology."

I was stunned. the language was quite industrial. If I was a referee I would have shown Gary a red card.

I told him I couldn't recall precisely what I had said, but I did make reference to Phil's omission not being much of a surprise, and that at least his agent Neville Neville, had one Neville going to the tournament even if the other Neville wasn't. Perhaps it was a flippant remark, I conceded, and I apologised if it caused offence, but I really didn't intend to, and sometimes things can slip out when you are doing several live broadcasts in a short space of time. If I was insensitive to Phil's grief at this time, I was sorry.

Gary called me a few more names and suggested that it was typical of us reporters and how would I feel if I wasn't picked to cover the tournament?

I appreciated his concern about his brother, and, in fact, applauded him for having the nerve to call me to tell me what he thought about it. Rather than take offence, I told him I would be extra careful about what I said about Phil being dropped from the squad. Gary told me it was too late, and that he still thought I was an "arsehole", and hung up.

Sorry, Garry. There are far too many who already think I am an arsehole, so one more isn't going to make much difference. Journalism isn't a popularity contest. Accuracy, honesty and the truth are a journalist's most potent weapons, and not everyone likes the truth. Unfortunately there are a lot of fans who do mock the Nevilles and, while that is sometimes unfair, it is nonetheless true.

TERRY NEILL
Chirpy Irish former Sours and Arsenal manager

Sidney Wale was an 'old school' style of football chairman. He never gave interviews and was rarely even pictured, let alone made public appearances or statements. However, as the local reporter on the Herald, I had known Sidney for long enough for him to trust me, and when I approached him in an empty Tottenham car park when he just happened to be on site during the week, I didn't miss my opportunity to ask him why he had chosen an ex-Arsenal man in Terry Neill to be the next Spurs manager in succession to Bill Nicholson.

"Did he play for Arsenal?" came Sidney's shocked response.

Did he play for Arsenal, indeed. Good grief, you would think the men appointing such an important employee would know his CV. Perhaps not.

I spoke with Bill about the appointment of his successor and he thought that, after a lifetime at the club, that the board would have consulted him.

They didn't. He had wasted his time sounding out Johnny Giles, as the directors opted for Terry Neill.

Still, there was never a dull day with Terry around, although he wasn't around for too long.

One sunny afternoon, for some reason, a challenge was thrown down and Terry and I found ourselves on the dirt track surrounding the White Hart Lane pitch, racing around it. I took the first bend ahead and that spurred Terry to kick in and he ended up the winner by some distance.

Terry was never going to be a managerial norm, but my relationship with him continued when he became Arsenal boss, and long after his managerial career came to an end, when he opened a wine bar-restaurant close to the *Mirror* building in Holborn. That meant I actually saw much more of Terry in 'Terry Neill's' than I had when he was in the game. After a good few years Terry sold the wine bar and headed off back to Ireland.

MIKE NEWELL
Luton Town manager

Transfer back-handers have become something of a speciality subject of mine over the years, so it was heartening to contact Mike Newell to discover that the Luton Town manager was only too willing to speak to me at length after he had 'come out' with his comments that he had been offered a bung by an agent.

I rang him at the club and he came to the phone immediately after training that morning to tell me that he also knew of directors and Chief Executives offering bungs. I congratulated him on his courage in speaking out.

Newell, one of the game's youngest managers, had returned my calls to his Kenilworth Road club because, as he noted, the *Express* has been banging on relentlessly about bungs for the past four years. "Congratulations, Mike, it's about time someone had the guts to speak out", I told him. He replied, "I didn't think it would make such an impact, I knew there would be a few headlines, but it was not my intention to open a can of worms, but I have opened a can of worms and I don't regret it one bit. In fact, this has been coming. I have been having my say about agents in the club's programme notes, but no-one has really taken much notice, because those notes have been doctored. The club were very worried about some of the outspoken comments such as calling them 'parasites'. But I am entitled to my opinion. This is not about Government's national security, it's about The People's Game, it's about supporters' money and ultimately it's supporters' money that is going into the pockets of these agents and out of the game and I do have a massive problem with that. I have a problem with the enormous amounts of money agents ask for renegotiating a players contract or negotiating the contract when we sign a player. We know what the player would want to play for us, then the agent asks for more and he wants his cut as well. I can't get my head round that at all. I know how much they ask us at Luton for, so imagine how much they ask a Premier League club – you can multiply it ten times if you want."

Newell's confession that he was offered a "sweetener" by a rival club director to sell one of his players proved to be the catalyst, along with Sven-Göran Eriksson being trapped by the *News of the World's* Fake Sheik into suggesting he knew of managers and clubs who routinely indulged in such illicit practises, for the Premier League's enquiry into transfer dealings.

Newell told me that he planned to name the club director and the agents who have tried to offer him bribes when he talked to the FA at Soho Square, which he duly did. Newell predicted he expected many people would inevitably deny any involvement: "You will get a lot of people denying it – but you don't have to be Einstein to understand why they are denying it."

FA Chief Executive Brian Barwick issued a statement, "These are very serious claims that Mike Newell has made. We welcome the fact that he has said that he is willing to provide names and details of people who have breached the rules. We have contacted Mike this morning and will meet with him early next week. If he provides us with evidence we will investigate fully. The FA takes this issue very seriously. If people have evidence we would expect them to come forward and provide it to our Compliance Department, who thoroughly investigate evidence of wrong-doing.'"

Newell has always deliberately ignored the various bung overtures made to him. "I was never interested in it. It was never intimated [how it would be paid], in a brown bag or whatever," the 40-year-old recalled. "I'm not naive. They say `We can look after you. We can make the deal go through.' If it has happened to me in League One what do you think? Don't you think it's strange certain agents do deals with certain clubs regularly?"

Newell is in no doubt the willingness to do dodgy deals is still very much active. "It's not just agents, but officials of football clubs. That is absolutely without doubt, offers to `make deals go through' with players I was trying to attract.'" He added, "Was I shocked? No I wasn't. Perhaps I should have been, but you know this kind of thing goes on. He told me there would be a sweetener if I let the deal go through, but I was determined not to sell the player. He didn't say how much the 'sweetener' would be because I wouldn't let it get to that stage – I wanted t be able to sleep at night.

Agents have offered me cuts of transfer deals. I haven't got a long list to present to the FA, but there are a number of instances that I do know about. Yes, I know I have opened up a can of worms, but it should have been opened up a long time ago."

Newell also issued a challenge, "I find it unbelievable that the journalists in this country cannot investigate what is going on – it's not Watergate or the White House they are going into,' he said. "I find it unbelievable that they just skirt round the issue. I can't believe that the FA and everybody concerned are too naive to think this has gone on."

If only he knew how hard some of us try, and how many obstacles are put in our patch.

There are a handful of investigative journalists digging around bung allegations for years, such as Mihir Bose, Tom Bower, and myself.

Since I joined The Daily *Express*, the paper has been at the forefront of exposing the transfer backhanders and dodgy agents and how they siphon off millions form the game. Let's just look back at series of exposés in the *Express* alone.

On 11 March 2004 we printed a blacked out figure of a prominent Premier League manager, who had been banned by his own board from taking part in transfer nego-tiations – and we even reported how the Premier League knew about it and had kept it hush-hush! The Premier League had been alerted to a cosy piece of self-regulation with the club taking their own internal action. We said then that the manager ought to have been exposed and prosecuted by the FA.

Nothing happened. Not even an enquiry. Yet, the *Express* knew the manager's identity, but the FA never asked us! We wrote at the time: "The manager has been told he can no longer deal with other managers and agents, or negotiate any transfer transactions without the prior knowledge and approval of his board."

The *Express* also discovered that HALF of the Premier League bosses, and even some directors and Chief Executives, had been taking transfer backhanders.

Previously we had told how Mohamed Al Fayed had sacked Jean Tigana because he suspected transfer backhanders in several big money transfers. "Show Me The Money – Al Fayed calls a halt to Marlet payments" we revealed on December 10, 2002.

"Time to call in the enforcer", we then detailed how the then FA Chief Executive Adam Crozer planned to beef up the FA's Compliance Unit – but he never quite got to grips with the problem before he was forced out.

Inside we reported "why Al Fayed fumes over the Marlet deal", and on the same page that same day "Hutchinson: I was offered bung".

Colin Hutchinson was for so long Ken Bates' transfer recruiting officer at the Bridge – but again the FA didn't want to know.

On January 13, 2005 our back page headlines screamed: "Bungs row mars Exeter's Cup Joy", as we exposed the backhanders paid to the players who were facing Manchester Untied in their epic FA Cup tie. The Ahead Of The Game column's main headline said, "Exeter's day in the sun belies murky past." We followed that up with the headline the next day "Why Exeter cover-up is so serious." But did the FA act? No.

Let's retrace one of the *Express*'s most potent investigations.

December 5, 2002. Over three pages the headlines roared "Swiss role In Angel Deal"..... "£3million Swiss miss"..... "Angel, Alpay and Balaban deals under close scrutiny"..... "Harry: I have nothing to hide"..... "All Eyes are on agents", "Clubs hire gumshoes". To be fair to the FA they even employed private detectives, while the Serious Fraud Squad refused to take on the case, but after nearly two years the enquiry petered out to nothing.

And there lies the problem with even Newell's 'evidence'. He might know what has been going on – proving it will be completely different. But at least the FA have been forced to instantly react. Let's face it, that's the least they could do. The only question the *Express* asked at the time was...why has it taken so long?

The FA came up with their answer: "People make reference to this kind of transfer abuse, but they are never prepared to name names or provide us with the evidence. They are ready to call on the football authorities to do something, but here the difference is that Mike Newell has publicly stated that he will provide us with details. It is very easy to accuse the FA of not doing something about it, but we need people who are willing to help us. And, it is not true to say that we haven't taken action, because we have."

The FA provided a list of the cases they have brought against Arsenal, Preston and a handful of agents, but it is pitifully inadequate. The Lord Burns structural Review of the FA, and don't forget this report was commissioned by Soho Square, recommended a substantially improved compliance Unit, semi-autonomous from the FA itself.

As for Newell's challenge to journalists to investigate more, if you have ever wondered why so few cases of transfer irregularities and breaches of the rules take place, and why so many culprits get away with it, then here is some evidence of the dithering, fence-sitting, prevarication, and passing the buck that goes on in football.

In my *Express* column I reproduced a transcript of a judge's summing up in a High Court case, where he went into graphic detail of how Arsenal had broken the rules in the way they 'sounded out' Gilberto Silva.

I forwarded the article to FIFA with this email:

Hi,

I am inquiring about the case of Arsenal, and their vice-chairman David Dein and a British court case in which the Judge said in summing up that there had been an approach for Gilberto Silva via third parties prior to any contact with his club in Brazil. The FA here in England has passed on press cuttings to this effect. Will FIFA now be making any enquiries, or opening a case on the Gilberto Silva transfer? Arsenal manager Arséne Wenger is now complaining about Barcelona president Joan Laporte, publicly stating he wants to sign Thierry Henry. Is this also an issue for FIFA?

I am writing an article about these issues for tomorrow's paper, so would appreciate a response some time today, if possible.

Many thanks and a Merry Christmas.

Harry Harris

And FIFA's response?

Thank you for your enquiry.

Generally speaking, we aren't in a position to speculate as to whether or not FIFA will in the future investigate a particular issue (i.e. open a case), but rather we can only address matters of fact, i.e. cases formally opened, decisions already taken, etc. Thus, in respect to the two situations you have described below, I can confirm that as of today no formal cases have been opened with the FIFA Players' Status Department.

I trust this information will be of use to you.

Regards,

John Schumacher

FIFA Media Department

Clearly this was far from answering the questions, so I emailed back.

Hi John,

Many thanks for your reply. Can you confirm that the FA have forwarded to FIFA a Daily *Express* article of two weeks ago drawing attention to a potential breach of the rules by Arsenal in relation to the Gilberto Silva transfer. (and, if and when you do take action, could you please let me know)

many thanks

Eventually, back came this reply.

Dear Harry,

Unfortunately I am not able confirm at this time if the FA has submitted any such documentation to FIFA. Kindly follow up with us in the first week of the New Year and perhaps I will be able to get further information then.

So, after the first week of the New Year, I repeated my email process, determined not to be shaken off by FIFA.

FIFA emailed yet another response.

Dear Harry,

Thanks for your follow-up enquiry.

To the best of our knowledge, FIFA has not received any such documentation from The FA concerning the player Gilberto Silva or Arsenal.

Well, now that's strange. The FA assured me that they had sent our article through. What was going on? The plot thickens.

I went back to the FA and informed them of FIFA's complete lack of knowledge or receipt of the two communiques between the FA and FIFA.

The FA emailed me this response.

We have had confirmation that we first brought the Gilberto Silva issue to the attention of FIFA's Players Status Dept back in the summer last year, and followed it up in December with further communication.

So, back to the email to FIFA incorporating the FA view.

Finally after three reminders came this reply.

Dear Harry,

Thanks for your follow up and your patience in waiting to receive further information.

FYI, as a general rule the FIFA Players' Status Department only investigates a particular matter based on either a formal complaint/claim from one of the parties concerned or at the formal request for assistance or intervention by a member association. Thus, a formal request, accompanied by compete relevant documentation, would have to be submitted to our services by the FA before FIFA could make any comment on the matter, in accordance with FIFA's role as the provider of international players' transfer principles, regulatory structures and dispute resolution.

After discussing the matter with both FIFA's Players' Status Department as well as the Media Department of The FA, I can confirm that the FIFA Players' Status Department did not formally receive the article about Gilberto Silva and Arsenal from The FA, nor any further or other documentation in this respect. Needless to say, the prerequisite for a possible intervention or assistance were not met. Any possible exchange of information regarding the relevant article may have occurred on a personal basis only as it regularly happens between members of the various organisations.

I trust you will understand our position on the matter.

Kind regards,

John Schumacher

FIFA Media Department

No, I was not satisfied and emailed FIFA to tell them so.

I told FIFA that surely they should act on prima facae cases without having to wait for someone to make a formal complaint.

But for organisations like FIFA the rules are the rules. And it's about time they were changed.

BILL NICHOLSON
Legendary manager of the Spurs double winning side of 1961

David Leggett was the outgoing Spurs specialist reporter for the *North London Weekly Herald* group of newspapers. He was off to a superior position and I was the only one left within the small newspaper group with any kind of football knowledge, and willing to take over the task, which entailed covering Spurs home and away, writing articles about the reserves and youth teams as well. As a Spurs supporter, this wasn't a job, it was a prize. Enthusiastic? I couldn't wait.

It was the summer break and manager Bill Nicholson was preparing his team for the new campaign. David had made arrangements to say his farewells to Bill and to introduce me as his successor.

Just the thought of meeting the great 'Billy Nick', manager of the first double winning side of the twentieth century, filled me with apprehension and excitement all at the same time. I took my usual route to the main Herald offices in Tottenham High Road, from Gants Hill, via the Green Line bus, but this was no ordinary journey to work. It was the day I was going to meet Bill Nicholson.

David did the customary 'handing over' and left me alone with Bill, in his offices at White Hart Lane, for a quick chat.

'Now then', enquired Bill, trying, no doubt, to be kind to the local boy who was just starting out in life as a football writer, 'when would you like to see me?'

I replied, 'as I have to write about the team each week with a Wednesday deadline and early Thursday morning for any midweek game, could I see him every Monday morning?'

There was a few seconds silence, and then Bill smiled, and leaned over, in a way that you can imagine if you were one of his players and he was about to give out an important instruction, which you had better make sure you get every word.

"Your predecessor, Dave, saw me once a season'.

There was a few more seconds silence. It seemed like half an hour.

"Come and see me Monday morning before training, here in my office, and we shall see how we go, but remember, once a season your predecessor saw me.'

Every Monday morning before training for the next SEVEN YEARS Bill Nicholson saw me and we spoke for around 15 minutes as he gave me a fully comprehensive run down on everything that went on inside the club, except, of course, those issues he wanted to keep to himself, but as the years went by he confided in me much more.

It wasn't long before a string of daily newspapers had my number and would ring me constantly for inside information. Naturally they paid me for it, but I never parted with any information I knew Bill would not want me to. I looked upon Bill almost as a father figure. My dad died of lung cancer when I was five, and there were times when I think he almost treated me like a son.

One day I turned up around five minutes late for one of Bill's Monday morning briefings. Usually I was always sitting outside his office waiting to be called in.

Bill was a stickler for punctuality and I am sure he liked the fact that I was always on time.

However, not this time.

I started to make some excuse about transport, and also pointed out that I had a problem with the one watch I owned, that it had stopped, and that had also thrown me.

The next Monday I came for my weekly chat in his office. Before I could say a thing, Bill told me, that he was upset that I was late the previous week, and even more perturbed that my only watch had stopped. He reached into his top draw, and pulled out a handsome looking case. He handed it over to me.

"Now, never tell me your watch has stopped again".

Inside was a gold watch inscribed with AC Milan, which had been presented to him by the Italian club after a European tie with Spurs. I didn't know what to say, apart from a bumbling 'thank you'.

Often I would work late at the *Herald* and walk along the High Road to catch a bus to see the bare light bulb in Bill's office which fronted onto the main road, still alight. He lived and breathed Spurs and spent more time in that office then he did at home.

When I moved on and eventually turned up at the *Daily Mail*, I became very close friends with a highly professional and honest journalist, Brian Scovell. We would normally go out to lunch together and became firm friends. Someone suggested I should write Bill's book, now that he had 'retired' from his beloved Tottenham. But Bill had never wanted to be bothered with an autobiography.

I nagged him for so long he agreed to let me come around to his house, which was in the real White Hart Lane, a long winding road off the High Road, and after an hour chatting away, he agreed to write the book. I asked Brian if he would help me write it, and he agreed. I now have only two copies of *Glory, Glory Bill Nicholson* left in my book case, one of them signed by Bill and all the Double Team who turned up for the launch of the book, which was published by Macmillan's in 1984 and commissioned by Alan Samson, a life-long Arsenal supporter, who could see the value of ensuring that Bill's memories were not shelved.

NOADES MAKES RACIST REMARKS

RON NOADES
Hard-nosed Football Club Owner, Chairman and Manager

The former Crystal Palace chairman had been a very close family friend along with his lovely wife Novello, but that all changed when I wrote a scathing, hard hitting article about Ron's TV interview in which he had made derogatory comments about black footballers, that hadn't gone down well with the likes of Ian Wright and Mark Bright, the club's rampaging strikeforce at the time.

It caused poor old Ron no end of grief, but I stuck to my guns despite the threat of being alienated from Palace and their chairman. It was a risk worth taking because the cause was a right one.

My relationship with Ron was frosty for some considerable time, but I am sure, in retrospect, Ron must regret his comments and must know I was only doing my job in reporting them.

O

DAVID O'LEARY, PETER OSGOOD, LORD HERMAN OUSLEY, MICHAEL OWEN

O'LEARY VERSUS DEADLY DOUG

DAVID O'LEARY
Former Leeds and Aston Villa manager

Working for a chairman who is nicknamed 'Deadly' is hardly conducive to a stress free existence, but David O'Leary's professional problems with Doug Ellis didn't show when the pair were together for the launch of Deadly Doug's book at Langan's and they looked at ease in each other's company. Deadly told me how he bumped into David at an airport and made a mental note that one day, when the time was right, he would hire him as his manager, and that's exactly what he did. So, Deadly would be most reluctant to sack him, but he'd said that about one or two others he showed to the door at Villa Park and the chop finally came after the well-publicised 'Player's Statement' of the summer of 2006. Villa never proved that O'Leary's hand was behind the insubordination contained within the statement, but it was enough to ensure he departed, leaving the club in disarray, up for sale and managerless a couple of weeks before the start of the 2006/07 Premiership season, although, as can only happen in football, all that changed with the arrival of Villa's very own Messiah Martin O'Neill a few weeks later.

Once the club had finally been sold to American multi-millionaire Randy Lerner, it seemed an incredible turn around from utter despair to elation had been completed.

THE KING IS DEAD

PETER OSGOOD
Chelsea and England striker known as 'The King'

Peter Osgood visited Virginia Water twice for lunches at Café Blue to talk about book projects, and he brought along a signed limited edition photograph of himself for my father-in-law Ken Udall.

Ossie put his name to a foreword to my book *Chelsea Century* published by Blake Books. He made no pretence about how he and the Chelsea faithful were enjoying the money-no-object patronage of the Russian owner. Ossie told me, "It is a fantastic time to be a Chelsea fan, to be a Chelsea player, and generally to have any connection with the club... while someone like Roman Abramovich owns the club and Jose Mourinho manages the team, it won't only be True Blue Chelsea fans fascinating by events at the Bridge. As long as Abramovich is there, the future is just fantastic, mind boggling. Chelsea have a fabulous team already and with Abramovich they can go out and buy even more great players and be a forced to be reckoned with for years to come. What Mourinho has achieved in such a short space of time as the coach is equally unbelievable. Mourinho is cocky, arrogant and confident – but all in a nice way, a positive way. The players think the world of him and there is a remarkable camerarderie among them and with that kind of atmosphere and the quality of their players, Chelsea can be a force to be reckoned with.

"I've met Jose a couple of times and introduced my son Darren to him, and he came across as one of the game's absolute gentlemen. He told me I was welcome at Stamford Bridge any time, which is more than I used to get when Ken Bates was in control of the club!

But the supporters are only really interested in the players, the results and the performances, and under Mourinho the club have an awesome team that can only get better and better and is guaranteed to fill the stadium all the time."

We talked a great deal of a booked entitled *The Bridge, Inside Out*, and spoke to Samsung Mobile's Mark Mitchinson, who was keen to help out in any way. But Ossie couldn't quite get the authorisation he needed to convince the publishers to go ahead with the project as Chelsea like to have only their own, official, authorised books sold in their Megastore.

It was a terrible shock when I heard the news of Ossie's premature death just a few months later.

LORD HERMAN OUSLEY
Chairman of the Commission for Racial Equality

Herman has been extremely active as the leader of the Kick It Out campaign to eradicate racism from the national sport, but one of his hobby horses is the fact that there is no ethnic or black representation on the FA Council, or indeed on any of the major FA committees. It is an issue upon which that I have told him he will have my total support and commitment.

MICHAEL OWEN
England's Boy Wonder from the 1998 World Cup

A number of national newspapers were chasing the story that Michael Owen was the biggest loser in England's 2002 World Cup card school.

The Sun was close when they had a blacked out picture of an England player suggesting that one of the World Cup team had lost a great deal of money. But two days later, I broke the full story in the *Express* naming Owen and the actual amount he had lost – £20,000.

Around 11.30pm, the first editions of the papers 'drop', that is they are available to all the other papers, and arrive at their offices. At midnight I was tucked up in bed when the phone rang, it was someone I knew reasonably well on *The Sun*. They wanted to know how I had stood up the fact that it was Owen. "How was I able to name him?" *The Sun* man explained that they had been chasing the story for a few days, and their lawyer's verdict was that they did not have sufficient to go on to name Owen. I told him that I was so 100% sure of the facts, that our lawyer was more than satisfied, and that I had spent a few days checking it out and had made sure there would be no legal comeback. He wanted to know how I knew there would not be a writ in the morning – but that was confidential. Rest assured, I went on. There would be no comeback.

About ten minutes later, he rang back. Not good enough for *The Sun's* night lawyer, he was afraid.

What I couldn't tell him at the time, was that I had spoken directly to Owen's agent and told him that I knew for sure it was Owen, and that I had spoken to two England players who had confirmed it to me, and that I was satisfied it was him. The agent came back to me and, after taking advice, felt it was important for me to have the story right throughout, and I was given one or two important facts, which I guaranteed would be included in the article.

The Sun would have paid absolute fortunes for that story, and the *Express* got it first – for nothing. Fortune favours the brave.

P

MICHAEL PARKINSON, RICK PARRY, PELÉ, STEVE PERRYMAN, MARTIN PETERS, DAVID PLATT, DAVID PLEAT

MICHAEL PARKINSON
Chat show host, raconteur and eminent sports writer

Michael is a first rate sports writer in his own right and is presently the President of the Sports Journalists Association. In the past we have shared the rostrum at the SJA awards, and I have also appeared on one of his hour long radio shows for FiveLive. In fact Michael was kind enough to give me a lift after his show. That's a measure of the guy; despite his high profile he is completely unpretentious. And I do see quite a lot of him away from work as he is also a member of Wentworth Tennis and Health club.

FA FAIL TO TAKE ACTION ON BUNG ENQUIRY

RICK PARRY
Former Chief Executive of the Premier League

Rick has been a very important ally in the war against corruption, as he was part of the three-man panel that took five years investigating transfer bungs in the wake of the George Graham affair. Rick knew that there was plenty of circumstantial evidence pointing an accusing finger at some high profile managers apart from Graham, but the Premier League dossier, of which I still have a copy, had to be passed onto the FA, who took another five months before opting out of 'prosecuting' Brian Clough because the then Chief Executive Graham Kelly felt he was too ill and it was a fruitless exercise because he was no longer in the game. But there were others that Kelly once told me he thought should be brought to justice, but the FA, back then, had no stomach for the long-winded legal battles that would have entailed.

PELÉ
Simply the world's greatest ever footballer

Heroes can often be disappointing, bland even, faultless; villains much more intriguing. However, Pelé is different. His very presence is inspiring, and to be in his company is a unique experience, almost cosmic.

Despite his image of being almost too good to be true, there is nothing bland about Pelé. I have been fortunate enough to have met him on numerous occasions, and even more privileged to be in a position to detail some of those meetings. It has also been an honour to have penned the Great One's biography, which I hope has lived up to my expectations in becoming the definitive work on Pelé's career. The book *Pelé: His Life and Times* became a bestseller in both England and the States, and continues to sell to this day.

Yet, there is a story within the Pelé story of how the book about his life came about.

Relaxing on the terrace of the holiday villas in La Manga one summer with my then girlfriend Linda, I was reading with great relish a book called *How They Stole The Game*, which incorporated much about the corruption of the Brazilian former President of FIFA Jose Havelange. In passing there were a number of intriguing references to Pelé. Not only did that bring back wonderful vivid memories of Pelé's contribution as a glorious footballing artist, but the book left me craving for more, much more, about his exploits on the pitch as well as his connections to the dubious Havelange.

I rang my convivial literary agent at that time Robert Kirby from the highly respected London agency Peter/Fraser/Dunlop to seek his advice and opinion about the possibility of writing Pelé's life story. Robert laughed. "There must be hundreds of books written about Pelé", he ventured. "Well", I responded, "that surely must be the case, yet I can't recall them". In fact I had only hazy recollections of once reading a very sub-standard translation from Portuguese of a Pelé autobiography published in the early 70s. Robert assured me that he was convinced he had seen many more Pelé books on the shelves, and went off to research the Pelé library of books to prove me wrong.

The next day Robert called. He couldn't quite believe it, but he couldn't even find the book I had been telling him about!

La Manga is the favoured haunt of many football coaches who bring their players for relaxation and training. England teams have long been associated with the Spanish retreat. I am pretty sure that Pelé has never visited La Manga, but for me it will always be associated with my desire to write Pelé's life story. Once my La Manga stay was complete, I returned eager to begin my research into Pelé's life, but I decided that I wouldn't write his life story unless I had his complete agreement and cooperation.

I contacted a long standing contact, Tony Signore, who handles the MasterCard account from New York, and who has become a close friend over the years. Tony is an endearing New Yorker who shares my passion for all things Pelé. As a result of my on-going relationship with Tony, first the *Mirror*, and then the *Express*, have been the beneficiaries of the Pelé World Cup column, which is syndicated globally and the papers for which I have worked have been afforded the UK rights. With Pelé's commercial contracts with MasterCard the company have access to the great man for media days, press calls and conferences, and Tony suggested that I tagged along at one of his events and would be granted an audience with Pelé, someone who I had interviewed on numerous occasions in the past, either through MasterCard or via another of Pelé's main commercial partners of the past, Umbro.

At the time I was the Chief Football Writer for the *Daily Mirror* and was covering a World Cup event in Tokyo. I waited patiently for my chance to meet Pelé and interview him on World Cup matters for my newspaper and when he saw me he had recognised me from previous interviews and greeted me warmly. When the interview was concluded, I approached the subject of my desire to write a book about his life.

The reaction took me totally by surprise.

He leaped from his seat to hug me, saying "I cannot believe anyone would still be interested enough to write a book about me."

My amazement must have outshone Pelé's!

I spent the best part of a year collating facts, opinions, from every country I visited, including Brazil, where I had great pleasure in meeting and talking to some of Pelé's contemporaries in that wonderful 1970 World Cup winning side.

I had been to Rio before, to meet Pelé when he was working for an afternoon for Umbro engaged for a photo shoot, and during brief rest periods he signed a number of shirts including a personal one to me which hangs proudly in my office at home.

I interviewed him about the declining fortunes of the England team, and during the discussion took a message from my office that Graham Taylor had been sacked!

My interviews with Pelé included a snatched five minutes that turned into 30 minutes over breakfast in a Frankfurt hotel before Pelé was whisked off to represent Umbro at a trade fair in the City. At the fair there were giant photos of England players, Paul Gascoigne and John Barnes and it was a photo opportunity that I couldn't let go to waste as Pelé had been discussing the virtues of both players. In fact my old sports editor at the *Mirror*, Keith Fisher, liked the Pelé interviews so much he ran them over two days across three pages on the first day, and a two page spread the second day, on Monday and Tuesday, 9 and 10 September 1991.

The article about Barnes was not very complimentary, as Pelé had indicated that the reason for Barnes' lack of consistency for his country compared to his superlative displays for Liverpool might have something to do with his broadening backside!

The unflattering headline read: "Pelé: Barnes is fat slow and lazy".

One night sometime later I was dining with several football reporter colleagues at a Chinese restaurant in the centre of Merseyside, winding down after covering a Liverpool match that evening. Halfway through our meal, John and several of his friends, including a number of young ladies, entered the restaurant. John spotted us and come over for a quick, pleasant chat. He returned to his table, and then after a few minutes, came back to us again.

John had remembered what had appeared in the *Mirror* a few weeks earlier. His mood changed. He complained bitterly that I should write something like that about him.

Of course, I pointed out that I had merely quoted the great Pelé, and John was, for the first time that I had known him, lost for words!

Some of my colleagues, or rather rivals from other national daily and Sunday newspapers, who had become friends over the years, distrusted the accuracy of my short hand note of what precisely Pelé had actually told me! Surely, they thought Pelé could not have been so provocative about Barnes. Well, I could understand their scepticism. In fact when Pelé was actually answering my questions about Barnes, Paul Gascoigne and other big name England stars of that generation, the guys from Umbro who had facilitated the interview could hardly believe it either. Top Umbro executives Martin Prothoro and Simon March looked at each other, knowing just how controversial Pelé's remarks would be in the hands of a red-top football journalist. They could see the size of the back page headlines as Pelé was talking! They looked at each other and looked at me, and privately said to me afterwards that they thought I had a fabulous scoop on my hands. They weren't wrong.

Pelé's other main marketing partner has been MasterCard, and I have been invited to a number of their media get togethers with the Brazilian legend. Once I was privileged to be selected along with a handful of global football media to have lunch with Pelé and Sir Bobby Charlton at one of the big central London hotels. Pelé was running behind schedule as usual, but no one complained because we were all looking forward to dining with him. Pelé and Sir Bobby signed a football for me, which is still one of my proudest possessions.

My meetings with Pelé went full circle as I interviewed him on a number of occasions for the biography, once taking my now wife Linda to Amsterdam. There, in one of the world's plushest hotels, Pelé was holding court to the world's media. Dozens of TV crews awaited their turn for an audience with him, and among them was Gabby Yorath for ITV. My wife, who is an avid Chelsea fan, accompanied me into the room where Pelé had been switching with relative ease from one language to another. Prior to my slot, he had just conducted an interview in German. After a few minutes he got into the English groove, and our usual five minute 'slot' turned into 30 minutes, with, eventually, his aides virtually dragging him out of the door as he would have missed his flight. Such is the generosity of spirit of this amazing man. Before he left, he posed for pictures with my wife and I, taken by the book's editor who was thrilled to tag along to be in the presence of Pelé.

Pelé must have enjoyed the book as he ordered quite a few, and even signed a number of copies of my biography and I have now managed to collect quite a sizable stock of Pelé memorabilia, which might be worth something in today's mushrooming interest in such items. But they are simply – not for sale.

To me they are priceless, along with my many memories of Pelé. I have been fortunate enough to get as close to the man as any journalist on the planet over the years. He trusts me and, I'm delighted to say, recognises that fact by spending more time with me than other, less scrupulous journalists.

Everyone expects Pelé to be an expert on every country's national football team, or events in world football. Of course he tries to keep up with global events, and he is also well briefed by his advisors. But I have heard him struggle with the names of some of the more obscure newcomers. Generally, though, he is well clued up on global the game, which enables him to move relatively smoothly from one interview to another across continents.

Pelé always strikes me that he is passionate still about the game, and he enjoys talking about the sport. He is a warm character, always approachable, particularly to people he has met before, he never seems to forget a face even though it must be difficult to remember all the names considering the volume of people he meets virtually on a daily basis.

Pelé is always immaculately turned out, wearing the MasterCard logo on his blazer whenever he is on duty for the sponsor. He is fully tuned in to how important people's perception of him is, and that image is so important in the modern game. Equally he is always well received, and I'm sure it's because of this respect he has for the fans and media that keep him on the pedastel his remarkable skills placed him on over 30 years ago. It is an honour and privilege to meet him, and experience this magnetism that draws people to him, happy merely to touch him, even see him.

HOW I SHOCKED PERRYMAN BY NEGOTIATING HIS WAGES

STEVE PERRYMAN
Legendary Tottenham captain of the 1970s and early 1980s

Club record appearance holder Steve was the shop steward of the Tottenham team in the 80s that produced arguable the best Spurs team since the Double side of the 60s. He enjoyed a firm grip of events inside the dressing room as captain of the team and I was a regular at White Hart Lane in my then job as football reporter on the north London Weekly Herald, so we knew each other well.

When he moved on from Spurs in March 1986, Steve and I became involved in one of the most bizarre incidents of my career when Robert Maxwell, then proprietor of the *Mirror* and, as it so happened, Chairman of Oxford United FC, rang down to request my presence in his private apartment above the *Mirror's* Holborn editorial offices.

He didn't give any reason for wanting my presence and when I arrived, Maxwell was sitting in a big comfortable chair in the office, and he beckoned me to join him in an equally relaxed seat. He told me that Oxford's newest and biggest signing was about to come through another door any minute now and, as he was unfamiliar with the terms expected by top First Division stars, he wanted me to help him negotiate the player's salary.

Wow. I'd never heard anything like this before. And, before I could gather my thoughts, in strode Steve Perryman.

I am not sure who was the more shocked – him or me. It was hard to keep a straight face. I just kept thinking that Stevie P would be absolutely mortified to see me there with his new chairman, with the subject of the meeting being his contract.

Fortunately I didn't think his wage demands were particularly excessive, just right in fact, par for the course, a top player taking a step down, not making undue demands. That is what I told Maxwell, and he agreed the terms on the spot. Time, then, I thought, for a quick interview. Given the circumstances, how could Steve refuse?

There was never a dull moment when Maxwell made that call to my number on the editorial floor.

MARTIN PETERS
England World Cup winning striker

One of the old-school footballers, who still turns up at White Hart Lane as one of the club's hosts, immaculately turned out in a suit and tie. Spurs seem to employ their former players more than most clubs on match days, and it was great to be a guest of the North London club in an executive box to mark my son Simon's 30th birthday. As a Spurs fan Simon was busy gathering autographs, and the first man he made a beeline for was Peters.

DAVID PLATT
The most complete English player of his generation

It's not strange to see the former Arsenal and Aston Villa midfielder in a TV studio. When he was still a player and moved out to Italy, one of his passions was to acquire as much knowledge as he could about the media. Like Gary Lineker during the latter stages of his career, Platt was clearly looking ahead to a future in our branch of the industry once his playing career was over. His great friend was Neil Harman, then the chief football writer on the *Daily Mail*, and Neil organised a number of get-togethers with David in Italy as he got to know the press and how they worked, paving the way for the England midfielder and captain to bring his tactical knowledge to supporters through his column in monthly magazine *FourFourTwo* and his many appearances on Sky Sports.

PLEAT SACKED BY SPURS

DAVID PLEAT
Former Luton, Spurs and Sheffield Wednesday manager, turned pundit

David was late for an hour long FiveLive radio show, and listened to the beginning of the show on his car radio. He eventually arrived half way through, and was intrigued to know how I knew, for sure, that Harry Redknapp would, indeed, be appointed the new Southampton manager. David had been acting as a consultant with Pompey, so I would imagine he had a fair idea himself about what was going on behind the scenes.

"Where do you get your information from?" David asked me on air.

"You, of all people, should know where I get it from, David," I replied.

David and I go back a long way. And, if anyone knows where I get my information from it should be David. I broke the story in the *Mirror* in 1986 that David would be the new Spurs manager following Peter Shreeves. He knew I was very close with the then Spurs chairman Irving Scholar. In fact, he never asked me how I knew for sure he would be named Spurs manager, so I can only assume he had a fair idea.

What's more, I also knew that he was getting the sack from Spurs, something that hurt him very deeply because it was for non-footballing issues, as he had been discovered kerb-crawling and dismissed because of it. It's funny how quickly events can turn. Not long before that, I was putting him forward as an outsider coming through rapidly on the rails as a contender to become England manager once Bobby Robson retired.

As they say, in football a week's a long time.

I wouldn't be surprised if David felt a touch bitter a times because he never quite fulfilled all of his potential. I'm glad to see that he has reinvented himself as an expert tactical analyst on TV and radio and starred for ITV during their limp coverage of the 2006 World Cup.

R

GORDON RAMSAY, SIR ALF RAMSEY, JEFF RANDALL, CLAUDIO RANIERI, HARRY REDKNAPP, JAMIE REDKNAPP, RICHARD & JUDY, KIERON RICHARDSON, PETER RIDSDALE, DENNIS ROACH, SIR BOBBY ROBSON, BRYAN ROBSON, DAVID ROCASTLE, WAYNE ROONEY

THE F*** WORD

GORDON RAMSAY
Channel 4's foul-mouthed chef!

Ken Bates took me to an upmarket restaurant in Chelsea, not too far from the Bridge, for a business meeting and was keen to introduce me to the head chef, who, at the time, was far from being one of the most famous TV personalities in the country. However, in the restaurant industry he had already gained a reputation for being a perfectionist and a fiery character. When told Ken Bates was in his restaurant, Gordon Ramsay came out to greet him, and he was introduced to me, saying he knew me from my articles.

Ken had been telling me that Gordon had played half a dozen first team games for Glasgow Rangers before his career was prematurely curtailed through injury. Gordon certainly had the appearance of a tough Scottish centre-forward, more than a cook, but it just shows you how appearances can be deceptive. Mind you, when I watch the *F Word* or *Ramsay's Kitchen Nightmares* on Channel 4 now, it's pretty clear that the kind of language learnt at Ibrox and on the Rangers training pitch stood Gordon in good stead for a life as the most demanding man in the restaurant business!

RAMSEY V ROBSON

SIR ALF RAMSEY
England's World Cup winning manager

Sir Alf had been long forgotten when *Mirror* Sports Editor Keith Fisher decided he wanted the World Cup winner to pen a regular column. I wasn't convinced, but Keith put up a sound argument, as simply no-one had Sir Alf's credentials. But it spoke volumes to me that none of the other newspapers or media outlets were interested in him because he had a reputation for being a dour personality living in the past. You have to hand it to Fisher, though, he called this one right. Sir Alf was absolutely brilliant for the *Mirror*, authoritative, eager, and willing to be controversial in a series of articles examining the 1986 crop of England footballers and their relative merits.

My *Mirror* colleague at that time Nigel Clarke 'ghosted' Alf's column, and the paper took him to Wembley in style, hiring a stretched limo. Once, when Nigel was unavailable, I took on the duty of writing the column, and accompanied Alf to Wembley in the limo, where there was plenty of time and opportunity to get to know him much better. That day we sat in the stands running the rule over a number of England players being given their chance in a friendly before the 1986 World Cup and his assessment of each player was illuminating. Ramsey went through each player detailing his strengths and weaknesses and it caused an uproar from then manager Bobby Robson, who responded by telling Alf to mind his own business. Robson took great exception to a former England manager being so critical of his tactics, team selections and formations, and also his damning comments about some of the players limitations.

Of course Sir Bobby now has no compunction against offering up his advice, as a former England manager, in his Sunday newspaper column!

Perhaps Alan Shearer was wise not to take up the offer to join Steve McClaren's coaching staff, having sat in the BBC's Brandenburg Gate TV studios during the World Cup criticising the England players.

But McClaren has hired Terry Venables and both the new England coach and the FA somehow tolerate El Tel writing a Sunday newspaper column, often making pertinent references to what is going on behind the scenes inside the England camp. You couldn't make it up, really, could you?

JEFF RANDALL
BBC Business Correspondent and former Sports Editor of the Sunday Times

Jeff is a big Spurs fan who loves his football, and who, in his capacity as Sports Editor of the *Sunday Times*, almost once hired me as his star columnist. I was keen to produce an investigative insightful football column. Jeff liked the concept, and we had a meeting and I initially accepted his offer. However, he subsequently confessed to me that he didn't plan to stay at the paper for more than another year and wanted to move back to the business pages, or take up a post with the BBC as their Business correspondent, which he subsequently did. Because Jeff couldn't give me a long-term commitment, I told him that I would stay with The *Mirror*. No-one at the *Mirror* was aware of the approach – until now – as I did not want it to look as though I was using the *Sunday Times* offer to force the *Mirror* into a pay rise.

TINKERING WITH THE TINKERMAN

CLAUDIO RANIERI
Former Chelsea Manager

Claudio was honoured by the Variety Club of Great Brain as Man of the Year for the dignified way he handled his dismissal by Chelsea. For almost the entire year he had been dubbed a Dead Man Walking, and it was tough on the Italian with Sven-Göran Eriksson courted the moment Roman Abramovich took over. Then, prior to the Champions League semi-finals with Monaco, the Chelsea coach heard that Jose Mourniho had been interviewed for the job by Abramovich and Peter Kenyon. The inside track is that Ranieri's mind was affected and that might have been the reason for his bizarre second half approach to the tie in Monte Carlo when Chelsea were comfortably holding a 1-1 scoreline and were in a commanding position in the tie overall having scored an away goal.

At the awards ceremony I was also on the list of honours, for Contribution to Sports Journalism and have a picture of Claudio and myself with one of the highly prized Silver Hearts awarded by the Variety Club.

JAMIE REDKNAPP
Former Liverpool and Spurs midfielder, whose promising career was blighted by injury

When starring for Tottenham, Jamie and his wife, former Eternal chanteuse, Louise, regularly enjoyed a lunch at Scalini's, which just happened to be one my favourite Chelsea eateries when I lived in the Borough, so we bumped into each other quite often. Louise is a very approachable down to earth pop star, and they make a smashing couple. Since his playing career came to an end, Jamie has moved neatly into the world of media, becoming a star Sky TV pundit, and branching out into magazine publishing with Icon, a magazine aimed at professional footballers, in which he has kindly asked me to pen a column.

PREMIER LEAGUE DROP
REDKNAPP TAPPING UP CASE

HARRY REDKNAPP
West Ham, Southampton and Portsmouth manager, never far from tabloid controversy

While I have an excellent relationship with Jamie, it's not quite the same with his dad. Harry is a football writer's dream, talkative, witty and always good for a headline or two. Unfortunately people keep pointing the finger at his association with agents such as Willie McKay, who had his bank accounts frozen in Monaco as part of a police investigation into a number of transfers in France. McKay also owns a racehorse or two with Harry, and knew all the intimate details of his move back from Southampton to Portsmouth when there was a great deal of heavy betting.

In the *Express* I exposed the potential tapping up of Harry by Pompey chairman Milan Mandaric and, although the Premier League issued charges, for some strange reason they then, a month later, dropped the entire case. Really, the explanation has not been very convincing. It was suggested that there was no longer a case to answer. So, why charge Portsmouth in the first place? To my mind this is one of the most curious cases I have come across. Simultaneously the FA had been investigating the client list of BetFair, with suspicions there had been a betting coup. Nothing came of that investigation either, although I will not let potential allegations of corruption drop.

Little wonder that I am not Harry's favourite journalist.

RICHARD & JUDY
Britain's best loved TV couple

Richard & Judy have a column in my paper, the Daily *Express*, each Saturday, and I have appeared once on their TV show (see Max Clifford). I found both of them charming and Richard reasonably knowledgeable on football. They are particularly good at communicating things to their audience, whose first interest is realistically not all things football, so it was a pleasure to help them understand the finer points of the game.

KIERON RICHARDSON
Manchester United and England midfielder

After Kieron's impressive displays for England during the 2005 summer tour of America, I suggested he might be one of the potential solutions to the problematic left side, which has caused headaches for England supporters and manager alike for over a decade. Then, after watching him dip in form and lose his place for Manchester United, I was a guest of the Old Trafford club for a feature on the prawn sandwich brigade and why they are not so bad after all, despite what Roy Keane had to say about them.

During my day at the club I picked up some interesting information about the attitudes of some of the young stars, and how Kieron was driving to training in a Bentley. I reported this in the *Express*, which provoked a response form Kieron's father, who contacted me to insist he had been driving his car, which looked like a Bentley. Fair enough, I am always willing to give someone the benefit of the doubt and did a follow up column item suggesting that the youngster won't be driving any more flash cars to training – until perhaps he has established himself in the side. Maybe then he would justify a recall into the England reckoning. I've no doubt that the article had an effect on Kieron, and I certainly hope it did bring him back down to earth. He is a promising talent, who needs to be focused on the football, not the trappings of such early big earnings. Otherwise he could go the way of other promising young talented players such as Kieron Dyer who have never got close to fulfilling their huge promise.

LEEDS TO SIGN RONALDO

PETER RIDSDALE
'Lived the Dream' as Leeds Chairman, just don't mention the goldfish...

Super agent Pini Zahavi arranged for me to meet Peter Ridsdale when he was chairman of Leeds United, at the Isreali's private club in Park Lane, so exclusive that our photographer was not allowed in to take any snaps and we all had to pose outside on the steps. The interview, in the relaxed surroundings of the plush restaurant, went exceedingly well, and the Sports Editor was delighted with the outcome, a special spread in the *Mirror*.

During my chat with Peter, it emerged that his manager David O'Leary was keen to take soundings about the feasibility of signing Ronaldo, then easily the world's greatest striker. Considering at the time Peter was authorising virtually unlimited sums on player acquisitions, it hardly seemed beyond the realms of possibility that Leeds might even bid for the Brazilian.

Peter was pliable to the idea that I floated the Ronaldo link, albeit with a touch of realms that it would almost be mission impossible to lure him to English football, but if anyone could try it would be Leeds. He was always open to talking the club up.

Given the fact that my Sports Editor knew precisely the source of the Ronaldo story, was fully briefed about the dinner and the interview that had already appeared in the paper, the validity of the source hardly needed to be checked out. But curiously he chose to confirm it by asking the freelance football writer in the region who covered Leeds to speak to Ridsdale to make sure he was happy with this story.

Ridsdale then rang me, confused, wondering why this was happening. He wasn't the only one to find the whole episode strange, but then again not everyone sings from the same song sheet in some newspaper offices where politics seem to play an integral role in a highly-strung environment.

For example, this was the same sports editor who 'stole' a story about Ruud van Nistelrooy signing for Manchester United on the pretext that neither he, nor anyone of his staff, could track me down when one of my contacts in Holland had rung with the tip. The story appeared the next morning with the Sports Editor's by-line on it.

At the *Express*, my present Sports Editor Bill Bradshaw, who has been a first rate on-the-road football writer in the past, would do exactly the opposite and at times helps with my research or pass on some tips of his own. That is a professional attitude. What the *Mirror's* Sports Editor was up to is open to conjecture.

DENNIS ROACH
Football's first super agent

Dennis once told me the story of how he first got involved in being a football agent. When his son was small, he played on the beach with the son of Johann Cruyff, as kids have no inhibitions about who they make friends with. Dennis and Johann got to know each other, and Dennis soon became one of the most powerful agents in the business.

Roach has been investigated by the FA, when their former compliance office Graham Bean brought charges against him, but the agent's lawyers proved that the FA did not have jurisdiction over him, because he was a FIFA licensed agent, and FIFA were holding no enquiry into his activities. Dennis thus caused a split within the industry. Some cruelly nicknamed him 'Cockroach', but others, such as Glenn Hoddle, who later became England manager, had Dennis as his one and only ever agent.

ROBSON MUST GO

SIR BOBBY ROBSON
The most successful English manager of the last 30 years

Everyone has their favourite Bobby Robson stories. The trouble is... it's so tough to pick the best one.

For example. I was sitting on a sun-lounger by the outdoor pool in the hotel in the centre of Mexico City where the England party and the media were staying in preparation for the 1986 World Cup Finals. I was relaxing after filing my copy, when Bobby lead the entire England squad down to the pool area, and they found themselves sun-loungers, as Bobby sat close by with a stopwatch in his hand. After every 15 minutes he blew a whistle and all the players simultaneously 'turned' from their backs to their sides. Again, after every 15 minutes Bobby blew and the players made one turn. Apparently Bobby had been told about the damage caused by the "ultra ray violets" because of the weak ozone layer in Mexico City and wanted to ensure that on the first few days that none of his players got sun burnt.

But this is perhaps the most popular of the Bobby Robson tales.....

Sir Bobby Robson is the England manager at the time, and Bryan Robson is his Captain Fantastic. Bryan is walking down the stairs of the England team hotel with his manager ready to greet him.

"Hi Bobby", says the England manager.

"No, I'm Bryan – you're Bobby", his captain replies.

Now, that is one of the classic moments, a true story, but not an uncommon occurrence, for Bobby Robson could hardly remember any player's name.

Sir Bobby, his knighthood fully justified for his services to English football, was somewhat of a comical character, but equally full of passion, pride and commitment, especially when he proudly wore the Three Lions on his England tracksuit. But his absent mindedness also got him into all sorts of trouble.

Unfortunately, on the eve of the World Cup finals in Mexico, his peculiar decision to substitute Glenn Hoddle during a friendly in Scotland because he had instructed the incorrect number on the substitutions board to be held aloft, brought Robson's frailties to the attention of the *Daily Mirror* proprietor Robert Maxwell.

Maxwell was flying back from an Eastern European summit with his usual entourage when he read about Robson's cock up in the *Sunday Express*. I was interviewing England striker Kerry Dixon for an exclusive prior to my departure the next day along with the rest of the media corps to prepare for the finals, when I received a rather strange call from the office. It was not from the usual sports desk staff, but from Maxwell's secretarial offices. Could I hastily arrange to meet Maxwell when his flight arrives at Heathrow?

I had not long been recruited to the *Mirror*, but calls out of the blue to see Maxwell on one football topic or another were becoming quite common place already. But with this coming on the eve of the World Cup the alarm bells began to sound, particularly as the message was pretty vague and no reason as yet was given for Maxwell's urgency in meeting me instantly his flight touched down.

I got to Heathrow as quickly as I could to await Maxwell's arrival. A private conference room had been hired by Maxwell's people in advance of his arrival, and he was escorted directly to the room, and as far as I could tell, had not gone through the usual passport control checks. In the room when I entered was Maxwell and around half a dozen of those he had travelled with, but within a blur most left the room. That left Captain Bob and myself and perhaps two flunkies remaining. Maxwell began to relate how he had read his *Sunday Express* and spotted a small item on the back page relating to the peculiar error in substituting Hoddle who was having an outstanding match when he really wanted to take off someone else. "This bumbling buffoon is not the man to manage our national team, we need someone who knows what he's doing to take us to the World Cup finals," announced Maxwell in those Churchillian tones, as if his pronouncement was indeed precisely what was going to happen.

My jaw must have dropped. But by the time I had composed myself, my first few words conveyed the stand I was about to take, I was clearly not in agreement. The last few of Maxwell's Men beat a hasty retreat. They had no doubt nodded their agreement all the way back from wherever he had been, but now found that someone with a smidgen of football knowledge was about to disagree.

Normally Maxwell would take on board my advice, knowing it was genuinely delivered and came with at least some expertise behind it. This time it was vastly different and I could detect in his tone that there was no way he was going to back down and I quickly discovered why not.

Maxwell had instructed his Editor and the Sports Editor to leave the front and back pages wide open for his blockbuster exclusive... Robson Must Go.

And, of course, yours truly would be writing it from an authoritative platform.

I had to find a way out of this.

First, of all I pointed out, I wasn't actually at the game, secondly from what I could tell, it was another of Bobby's blunders, but most people in the industry were fully conversant with his propensity to make such laughable mistakes.

However, he was a genuine man, and still the manager to lead the England team to Mexico. There wasn't a single football commentator who would say otherwise. The fans were backing Bobby and the Boys, there was no dissent among the supporters, or indeed, anyone else. We would be making a stand alone.

Maybe Robson would prove to be the wrong man for the job, but the timing was all wrong. The England team were leaving for Mexico and a couple of weeks of acclimatisation, and it wasn't feasible to find a replacement overnight. My argument must have hit home because Maxwell suggested that I wrote the article, but that he would put someone else's name to it. I said that would be a reasonable compromise, but I was still very uneasy about the whole thing, as the rest of the media and the England camp would want to know who actually wrote the article.

"What would make it eaSer for you?" asked Maxwell.

I replied, "I would like your permission to inform Bobby Robson about it".

Maxwell was never one to flinch from a face to face confrontation. Fine, he sad. And tell him that there would be more pages made available for his first hand response should he wish to make it.

It was a fait accompli. I had to go through with it or my job would have been under serious threat.

A typewriter miraculously appeared and I began to write the article that in essence Maxwell actually dictated to me. I then filed the 'copy' to the copy takers back at Holborn and left Maxwell to find the nearest telephone inside the airport and rang Bobby Robson.

I explained all the circumstances as accurately and as honestly as I could, plus my own recommendation about the campaign, which had not been accepted. The *Mirror* were going ahead with this front page "Robson Must Go", and my only advice was that whatever comments he made would counter balance the articles, and might even supersede some of the headlines.

Robson said he would go away and think about, but told me that he appreciated my honestly and felt that it might be good advice to respond, and he was made aware that whatever he said, it would be reported in its entirety.

I later discovered that he had rung one of his journalistic confidantes, of which he had quite a few, to seek their advice. He contacted the late Joe Melling who was on the Daily *Express* at the time, and Melling advised him to ignore it and not to respond. So when I called Robson back he told me that he had decided not to respond. He again thanked me for all of my effort, and I truly believe he accepted my version of events.

The next morning the headlines were shocking. ROBSON MUST GO in the biggest possible type on the front page. As for my name being left off the article, both the Editor and Sports Editor suggested that it needed the name of an authoritative football writer to hold any weight. My name therefore appeared on it. I had no choice.

I arrived at the England team hotel near Gatwick airport where the media were gathering to travel with the England squad, as they used to at that time.

It was Glenn Hoddle in the World Cup in France 98 who stopped the joint travel arrangements, Hoddle's sound logic was that the media were always last to leave the stadium waiting usually for the photographers to dispatch their pictures, or the last writer to file his copy. It meant the players sitting on the plane, which was held up on the tarmac until the media party was complete. Hoddle's view was that sitting in such cramped conditions unnecessarily added to players' fatigue, and he called a halt. The FA used to accept the inconvenience because the media paid a premium to travel with the party and stay at the same hotels, which greatly offset the FA's travelling budgets.

This was not to be a pleasant trip for me. One of Robson's back room staff spotted me arriving at the reception desk at the hotel, and launched into a tirade of abuse. I tried to explain the complete circumstances, of which I am sure he was aware, but he was not interested.

On the flight I sat alone. None of the other journalists felt it wise even to sit next to me. Inside the hotel in Mexico City the atmosphere was equally not a good one for me, so I asked to see Bobby to clear the air. He invited me into his hotel room.

This was my first opportunity to explain the circumstances face to face, although in truth the England manager simply got the same story. Thankfully Robson was not a man to hold a grudge, but this was extremely hurtful and might even have been the start of the kind of personal abuse that England mangers had to experience.

Back home the story escalated into a frenzy of activity as it was deemed to be a major tactical move in the Tabloid Wars; Maxwell's bid to gain sales on his main rival, Rupert Murdoch's Sun. To do so he had chosen to use the England team as a front line.

The truth is that, though it might well have evolved into one of the many facets of the cut-throat struggle for circulation supremacy, Maxwell actually simply kicked it all off on the whim of reading about one of Bobby's bizarre substitutions.

Whether Robson was a capable England coach came more pertinently and properly into question after an abysmal European Championship in Germany in 1988, and in particular the final humiliating game against Russia, which was to prove to be Glenn Hoddle's final England appearance, and a shambles of a culmination to a humiliating tournament. This time there was a justification for the vitriol that came poor Bobby's way, and by now it had turned highly personal and almost vindictive with the tabloids trying to outdo each other in the perceived humorous way of attempting to bring down the England boss.

Before a game in Albania, the *Mirror's* sports editor Keith Fisher, fed up with a series of headlines that had no effect on the FA, from ROBSON MUST GO to GO IN THE NAME OF GOD, GO, for this game he discovered that King Zog was the last monarch of Albania, and his headline was GO IN THE NAME OF ZOG, GO.

But the FA chairman Sir Bert Millichip was a tough cookie and the harder the tabloids tried to unseat Robson, the firmer his resolve to back his manager.

Robson stayed on at the European Championships as one of TV's panel of top analysts, which again attracted adverse publicity as a contradiction considering how inept his England team had been. A small select group of chief football writers from the main newspapers remained behind with him to cover the rest of the tournament and to interview the England coach on his summing up once the Final was over.

It was probably more of a dare than anything else, but that group suggested that I should seek out Robson to invite him to chat about the tournament. I took up the challenge, went to Robson's room, knocked on the door, and he was charming at first as he usually is, then realised that I had been one of the media at the forefront of feeling that it was time for a change in the England coach. Suddenly his mood swung to violent. He pinned me up against the wall by my collar, but quickly calmed down and let me go and it wasn't long before he apologised and took me into his room and gave me the interview I wanted, which, as prearranged, I shared with a few of my colleagues.

Robson has been wonderfully entertaining on the numerous occasions I have shared the same table with him along with my chief football writer colleagues.

I have also seen him blow his top and launch into a furious row with the then *Daily Express* chief football writer Steve Curry. It was strange to see Robson and Curry shouting at each other in front of all the other writers, considering how close they had been over so many years. But Steve's long association and friendship with Robson came in handy during his final tournament Italia 90. The tension and pressure always intensify the closer a tournament gets, and there is usually an uneasy peace between the England camp and the media. With little to write about on the long preparation days, the wilder and more extreme the headlines can become, often for no particular reason other than to drum up a bit of interest and controversy.

During the long hot evenings in Sardinia, the media had a night off because Robson was attending a local league match and none of the journalists were invited. The England team were encamped in a golf village complex about three miles from the media corps, who were billeted in the luxurious Forte Village, where a group of the chief football writers had the best rooms with massive balconies overlooking the shore. After watching the day's training session, then going through the usual press conferences with manager and a couple of players, all the day's work was finished, articles filed, and us media were enjoying a relaxing night in some of the Forte Village's large selection of restaurants.

Just after the main course, I received a message from the hotel. My office wanted to speak to me urgently. Michael Bowen, the deputy sports editor, informed me that the paper were going to carry a back page story about how Robson had been booed by local fans when he was paraded on the pitch before the game. The FA's charm offensive exercise to woo the local support had gone horribly wrong and Robson was clearly the butt of the fans' reactions to seeing the England coach.

I inquired the source of the information, and was told that it was a photographer who was present and had filed some pictures. I was asked to check out the story. I did so and was told by the FA's public relations guys present, that photographers were indeed at the game, but the story they had returned with was bogus. The fans had showed their appreciation of Robson, not booed him. The whistling when Robson came onto the pitch had been wrongly interpreted, as it was custom on Sardinia for whistling to show appreciation, and so was pro Robson, not against him.

I told Michael that I doubted the validity of the story, but was told that they were too late and were committed to running it. Worse still, my name was on it. "Here we go again!" I thought.

Being so far away from home on this type of drawn out tournament assignment it is helpful not to see the papers sometimes, but unfortunately the England camp had a habit of shipping over the English papers to keep the players and staff amused. Robson was far from amused next morning when he was told of the *Mirror's* back page story, long before the delivery of the newspapers to the south coast region of the island.

As usual we headed off to the England training camp, but it was far from a sunny day, in fact it started to rain quite heavily and the storm clouds were most definitely gathering over Robson. But Curry, being a close friend of mine at the time, knew the ins and outs of the entire episode, and knew that Robson was not in command of all the facts. The England manager was about to blame me for all of his current ills and I was about to get the old-fashioned managerial 'hair dryer' from Robson.

Give Curry his due, he boldly marched out to the centre circle before training began, and stood toe to toe with Robson, knowing he was fuming about that day's coverage, and explained to him what had happened and that I shared his feeling of being let down and had tried my damnedest to stop the article being published.

Robson's anger toward me cooled, but his fury in general at the way the media had been covering the England preparations with sordid Sunday newspaper headlines about scandals involving one or two of the players and the gorgeous young, Italian hostesses assigned to look after the squad, meant that Robson would probably have exploded in any case. This latest incident just about guaranteed an impending Robson rocket for someone. Thankfully it turned out not to be me!

Mike Langley was an award winning sports writer for the *Sunday People* at this time, later to become my colleague on the *Mirror*, who'd probably been oblivious to all these ramifications with the media rattling around behind the scenes, being a weekly journalist, and who had also brought his wife along to the training ground.

As the World Cup grew ever closer, so the world's media began to descend on each of the major nations participating, and the England camp had also begun to attract large quantities of foreign press, TV and radio.

Before any media conferences, Robson invited solely the English press, into the England dressing room.

It had just started to rain, so Mike Langley brought his wife into the changing rooms. Just as Robson was about to round on the gathered writers and lay into us all, he spotted a lady in his midst.

"Mike, is that your wife in here with you?" inquired Robson knowing full will that it was.

"Yes, it is Bobby," said Mike

"Why is she in here, Mike?" continued the England boss.

""Well, Bobby, because it's raining outside," explained the intrepid writer.

"Give her your f****** umbrella and get her out of here, Mike. I've got a few things to say and I don't think a lady should be present – and oh pardon my language,' said Robson.

Needless to say there was a touch more swearing going on.

Robson refrained from turning his venom on me, in fact he never mentioned the *Mirror* article, in fact I think he was more livid about lurid Sunday paper stories which had named John Barnes in some compromising sexual position or other.

Robson said that the players had no more wish to give press interviews.

When a handful of reporters tried to talk to the players, they discovered that they were already aboard the coach and were about to leave the ground. A couple chased after them, and Paul Gascoigne spat at them from the window of the coach. They got the message, and every day from then on in after training, the players got straight on the coach and refused to give any press interviews. It has become known as a watershed in relations between footballers and the press, the beginning of so much distrust and antagonism between the two parties.

You have to understand the reporters' frustrations in situations like that. Covering a World Cup might seem a doddle to the outsider, being paid to travel first class and stay in five star hotels alongside the players. The reality is far from that image, particularly when the tournament is being hosted somewhere like Mexico in 1986. It wasn't an easy job getting to the training ground. In fact it was dangerous. To travel from the team hotel, which was in an isolated location up the mountains to Mexico City, was a hazardous journey. The region was infested with kidnappers, mostly a group of renowned desperados. The team coach set off with all the journalists rushing to drive off at the same time, as many as they could packed into each car. It was a convoy. In front of the team bus and behind it was a rickety old vehicle each packed with locals riding shotgun, perched out of the lorries with their guns ready and trained on the surrounding desert!

As the 1990 World Cup progressed, and England began to fancy their chances of reaching the final and perhaps even winning it, the cold war with the media began to defrost and some players opted to resume interview duty.

Unfortunately, the booing of Robson story that appeared in my newspaper also had a rather nasty side-affect; a monumental internal office row that nearly led to my early exit from the World Cup. After Robson's rant, the England manager had got his anger off his chest, and as usual he calmed down and was always wiling to find a conciliatory way forward with his media adversaries. But the row lingered on when I confronted Michael Bowen when we all returned to the Forte Village. I told Michael, a man I had always got on well with, that I had suggested to the FA that the least we could do was to put it right, either to apologise, something that a national newspaper will never do willingly or make some kind of reference that Robson had not in fact been booed. I relayed all the squabbling and recriminations that had gone on that day and how the *Mirror* had been singled out for special rebuke by the FA, and that I, on the paper's behalf, had pledged that we would do all we could to rectify it.

Again, in a twist of circumstances, the sports editor, Keith Fisher, was on a day off and so too was the Editor, Roy Greenslade, who has now reinvented himself as an expert columnist on media affairs. Fisher had always been a Sports Editor who supported his men in the field and I had never found Greenslade anything other than highly professional in the way he edited the paper. Michael promised to contact Fisher, who in turn, under the chain of command, would liaise with the Editor if need be.

Several hours later, when I checked in after the day's work, Michael had not been able to track down Fisher, and the news desk had not been in touch with the Editor, whether they tried or not, or had even been asked to, I had no way of really knowing.

The frustration was building up, as the longer it went toward deadline, the less likely there would be of fulfilling my obligations to the FA, although that was of little concern to Michael, who pointed out, quite correctly, although I didn't really need it underlined, that my sole obligation was to the *Mirror*.

It was at this point, I made the biggest single monumental error of my entire career. One that I have regretted ever since.

With the ability to have direct access to Robert Maxwell, I informed Michael that if he continued to fail to contact his superiors and continued to refuse to make any editorial executive decision of his own, I would be forced to take the issue straight to Maxwell.

Even if everyone on the paper knew I had that facility, it was something that I should never have even contemplated using, let alone threatening to do so. But I did.

I waited another couple of hours and, knowing this was the last chance, phoned Bowen again. Was there going to be a small item even to redress the balance and point out our error?

No there wasn't.

I placed a call to Maxwell's office.

I explained the situation very briefly and he suggested that the man in charge that day, Michael Bowen, should be fired for his incompetence.

Blimey, I never thought that would be Maxwell's reaction.

I begged Maxwell not to take such an extreme view and that he should let me speak to him one last time.

I told Michael the proprietor's view, but he stood by his guns and reiterated that he was not in a position to take such action unilaterally and still could not contact either the Sports Editor or the Editor, and that I should wait another 24 hours and sort it out when they were back.

Maxwell was in no mood to back down, however, and Michael Bowen was sacked on the spot. The next day all hell broke loose. Fisher was angry with me, although, as he knew me so well, could appreciate my frustrations, but nonetheless was highly critical of my actions.

I too, was appalled. I realised I had overstepped the mark, and I was shocked by the repercussions of what I had done. My thoughts were with Michael and I rang Maxwell again and made every attempt to get him to change his mind. OK, agreed Maxwell, "I am only doing this because you feel so strongly about it," he hung up. I could tell Maxwell was not happy with me, making him back down in such a big way.

The Editor, though, was on the warpath. Roy Greenslade was so appalled by my actions in going direct to Maxwell he ordered me home from the World Cup immediately. I explained to Roy that I had spoken to Maxwell and that he will rescind his earlier orders. Not good enough, argued Greenslade, it was something that he would not tolerate and that I was to catch the first available flight back.

Of course, being in the field, I had a major advantage over any journalist caught in this position. If the editor orders you home, home you should go. But I knew that if I just sat tight and ignored the order then somehow it would be resolved.

Keith Fisher did not want me to come back from Sardinia and told the Editor so, making the point that it would severely diminish the *Mirror's* ability to compete with their rivals and Greenslade took that argument on board. After a while he had calmed down, and was no longer making it an issue.

I personally apologised to Bowen on the phone, and personally apologised to him when I returned when the Finals were over. I feel as though I have been apologising to him ever since. I have the utmost respect for Michael, especially seeing that, although my actions caused great grievance to him and his family, albeit only over night, he had the good grace to forgive me.

CAPTAIN MARVEL IS OUT OF THE WORLD CUP

BRYAN ROBSON
England and Manchester United's Captain Marvel

On a remote football field in Canada, Bobby Robson gave a less than revealing assessment of England's injury worries ahead of the 1986 World Cup Finals. While everyone was focusing on an update on Gary Lineker's broken hand, Robson avoided any comment about the real problem that was about to develop, captain Bryan Robson's shoulder.

Lineker looked like he would make it just in time, fortuitously for England as he went on to become the top scorer in the tournament, but the skipper's shoulder would become an ever bigger saga, eventually giving way completely in Monterrey in the same game against Morocco that Ray Wilkins was red carded. The blow effectively ruled him out of the tournament, although, had England reached the semi-finals and Final, he might have made a recovery by then.

Robson hung around the camp in the hope of a recovery, but was still swimming in the pool when the England squad had their final training session prior to the quarter-final clash with Diego Maradona and Argentina. I watched the final England training session, which took place inside a bull ring. In those days the press were allowed much closer to the players and as I strode toward the periphery of the field, Don Howe, who I had got to know over a long period of time, confided in me that if Robson had shown sufficient improvement he would have been the man his manager would have chosen to man mark Maradona and maybe could have changed the course of history. Instead Bobby Robson persevered with Peter Reid. Without Bryan, Bobby opted not to go for a man for man marker on Maradona, feeling that no-one other than Bryan would have been equipped to have pulled it off, and later, as he assessed England's tournament, was honest enough to admit that, in retrospect, it was the wrong decision and had he been a touch braver he should have selected Robson despite his suspect shoulder.

After all of Bryan Robson's problems in Mexico, England needed a fully fit Robbo for Italia 90 and they got him, until it all went pear shaped, or fizzled out at the bottom of a lager glass.

Fast forward to the day of the German World Cup draw in Leipzig. A good friend and associate of mine Andy Sutherden of Public Relations company Hill & Knowlton invited me to join David Platt and Martin Peters to provide media content to TV, radio and internet via Marketieers' central London studios, ostensibly to discuss England's prospective opponents, but also to promote Gillette's newly sponsored official FIFA inaugural Young Player of the World Cup. At one stage David Platt and I were sharing a radio booth doing back-to-back local radio shows. One of the discussion points was about retrospective best young players of the tournament and, talking about Maradona, Robson's name cropped up and I kind of cheekily asked David if he knew the real reason why Robbo was forced to fly home disconsolately from Italia 90, and how his broken toe had come about? I knew David did know because he, like me, was there, of course, but he wasn't saying. Live on air Platt challenged me to divulge all, but I brushed that aside.

A few minutes earlier, off air, we had both been talking about Robbo's injury – and we both knew the truth.

Back to Sardinia 1990, and the England camp were in relaxed mood on a rare day off as the team were looking forward to qualifying from their Sardinian based group by defeating minnows Egypt having drawn their opening two matches.

The England HQ was a lavish resort off limits to the English media. But in one of the many five star hotels inside the Forte Village, where the Press were billeted, Gary Lineker's lovely wife Michelle was staying with some friends to be as close as she could to Gary. After several weeks away from home, and no doubt bored even with the gizmos, gadgets and games the FA had laid on for the players, and even fed up with endless rounds of golf and games of tennis or cards, the players opted to spend some time at the Forte Village on one of their rare days off.

I was one of the infamous Morris Men, the small group of football writers who enjoyed each other's company and who travelled everywhere together. It comprised Colin Gibson, Stuart Jones, Steve Curry and myself. We spent the morning working and filing our copy to our respective offices, then planned lunch at the beach-side restaurant, followed by a spot of sun bathing before watching one of the late after-noon World Cup ties in my hotel room which was the nearest to the beach.

Stuart and I enjoyed hours in the sun, but the larger-sized gentleman in our group, Colin and Steve, soon got restless and opted for a stroll along the water's edge to cool down before deciding on one of the numerous beach side bars to have a beer in the shade.

We waited for so long we thought they must have got lost, or drunk, so Stuart and I went out in search of our colleagues, who were so late by now we had missed the first half of that evening's match. We had only strolled 150 yards when we caught sight of half a dozen England stars with Steve and Colin, so we wisely made a hasty U-turn. Knocking back the beers were the likes of Bryan Robson, Chris Waddle, Trevor Steven, Terry Butcher and Paul Gascoigne. We decamped to my room to watch the second half. Afterwards Stuart made his way back to his room and got ready for dinner. It was dusk by the time I received a knock on my door. There stood Colin and Steve, hardly able to utter a word, still in their shorts and covered in sand. They looked like synchronised divers as they simultaneously belly-flopped each onto one of my two twin beds, snoring before they hit the sheets.

I left them spark out and went out to dinner. They were still asleep when I returned. It seemed like a sensible solution for us all to enjoy an early night.

The next day was the last at the Forte Village before moving on to a new venue. It was a rather dead final evening, as we had all got used to the sheer luxury of the Forte Village, having spent six weeks there, using it as a base, with a media centre stocked up with the sponsor's booze and food and all the amenities to help you put up with such a lengthy time away from home; although some of us quite liked the time away.

At around midnight, as we were making our way outside of the Village in search of a local bar, Steve received a message to call Bryan Robson.

Although the England squad and entourage were decamping at around 9.30am, Bryan would be heading off to the Cagliari airport to catch a 6.30am flight to Rome, where he would then make the connection to London and then the shuttle home to Manchester.

He would be making the journey alone.

We had heard that Robson had an injury, indeed he had come off after an hour of the goalless draw against Holland, but no-one had said just how serious it had become, nor had anyone known that he was on his way home. Robson told Steve that it was strictly confidential, although an announcement was being planned for the next morning, but too late for anyone to be able to catch up with him on his way home, but he didn't have any objection if the four of us just happened to turn up early at the airport.

We decided to cut short our last night out and went back to our rooms around 1.30m to finish off our packing and get all our paperwork in order. We all booked a 5am early morning call, as we had to return the hire car, arrive in good time to change our tickets and make sure we were on the same flight as Robbo for what would be a major story with only the four of us having the inside track. Cracking.

Robbo confessed in confidence to Steve that when he and the other England players had returned back from that boozy evening from the Forte Village, Bobby Robson was none too pleased. Gazza was still riding the bike he had taken from the Village and the manager rightly suspected that Gazza wasn't alone in the high jinks.

Robbo told Steve he had gone back to his room for a shower to sober up, but cracked his toe getting into the shower. I have also subsequently heard that he was actually in his room with Gazza larking around and lifting up the bed which then fell on his toe. Whichever version is correct, Robbo confessed that it was a self-inflicted accident and not an authentic training ground injury.

The four of us respected the confidentiality of this episode. We were from the old school of journalism where we would always protect the sources of our information. And, in this case, we were the source.

Attitudes toward the press had changed around this time. At past World Cups there was usually just one writer per paper, the football correspondent, who had a relationship with players and managers built on years of trust. We shared the same hotels, travelled on the same flights, and generally got to know each other much better, even drinking together after the games.

As the media mushroomed, the No. 1 football writer was accompanied by a No. 2 who concentrated on the quotes and the news stories, then there was a columnist who wrote the colour pieces, and also came the news hounds, such as 'Dead Dog' Jackson, who used to work with me on the *Mirror*, and who once dragged a dead dog hundreds of yards to plant it outside an England team hotel to embellish his report about the dodgy surroundings for the England superstars.

But with only one writer it was much easier to keep some slight indiscretions 'in-house', and that built up the trust and made for good contacts and usually good stories further down the line.

Although the Morris Men had no intention of telling the tale of the drinking session and how Robbo smashed his toe, we were all very keen to be involved in the journey back to Rome from Cagliari, and although still blurry-eyed from the night before, we dashed away from the Forte Village long before all of our colleagues were awake.

Colin, who organised all of our travel arrangements, was in charge of returning the hired car. I was put in charge of the tickets and passport. I put my own in my top pocket, and the three others on the car dashboard.

When we arrived at the airport, with all our luggage to contend with, I made the dash to the check in counter to book us on the same flight as Robbo. When I got there, I could only find my own passport and tickets. Oh no, I'd left the others on the dashboard. They all rushed back to the parking lot, while I was the only one able to switch tickets and get on board the flight. Needless to say the other three were livid. If they hadn't known better they might have thought I had done it intentionally. But we had been together far too long and there was a unique bond and trust between us, they knew it was not a deliberate act.

In fact they knew how disorganised I could be. They also knew that I would fall asleep the moment I got into a car, and this morning was no different. They knew I was a non-driver with no sense of direction. This was a typical act of incompetence of which there had been many. Good at my job, maybe, but a disaster when it came to things like this.

But it was frustrating for them, having got up so early to be part of the day's big news, with all the colour that would have gone with it. But, of course, I promised I would be on the phone with all the quotes and share everything with them as soon as I could.

Robbo was worried that the real reason for the injury would emerge, but I reassured him that none of us would break a confidence, which would undoubtedly have seen him ridiculed across the entire nation's front pages if the truth had got out. That made him feel just a touch better. But he knew that it was a self-inflicted injury and that made the pain of his World Cup exit even harder to bear.

In his recently published autobiography *Robbo*, Robson referred to the contentious issues, "The gaffer was less impressed with his players – and this one in particular – after a bit of messing around left me with a bloody big toe. This was an incident that Gazza claimed in his book ended my World Cup, which he now accepts was a load of rubbish. We were at our training camp in Sardinia, and our first match was still several days away. A few of us fancied a last drink before the tournament started, so we went to a local bar. Gazza says that Bobby found out we were missing and sent the police after us. Well, we did hear police sirens as we walked back to the hotel, but that was nothing to do with us. There must have been some trouble in the town.

When we got back, we went to Gazza's room and started larking about. I tried to tip Gazza off his bed and caught my big toenail on the corner. I had no shoes on and it ripped the top of my toenail. It was bleeding badly, so I went into the bathroom to try to staunch the flow. I had to have an injection in it to kill the pain to play in the first game. Bobby went mad at me and rightly so. He comes over as nice Uncle Bobby, but he could be tough if he felt he had to be and he had a right go at me for pratting about that night.

Gazza says in his book that we were absolutely legless, which isn't right. He also says I broke my toe, which I didn't. Worst of all, he says that it was after the second match and was the real reason why I went home from the World Cup. It happened, so I've said, before our first match and I had to pull out of the tournament because of an Achilles injury, which I got in our second match. I have told Gazza he got it totally wrong about that night and he was distraught. He said, 'I just didn't know what was going on then, Bryan. If I got the story wrong. I'm sorry.'

As we all know, Gazza has had his problems. He has been in such a mess at certain stages of his life that there was a lot he couldn't remember clearly. We've not fallen out. We've managed to stay pals even though he's given me a few headaches over the years."

It's not how I remember it, though, Bryan – and I was sober.

He may now have publicly made clear his version of his World Cup exit, but Robson didn't tell anyone about how the Morris Men kept his confidence for over 16 years over what happened. Now Robbo has had his say, we can at least claim our part of one of the biggest stories to emerge from that 1990 World Cup.

ROCKY'S TEARS

DAVID ROCASTLE
Arsenal and England midfielder whose life was sadly cut short by cancer

Rocky, I am proud to say, was one of my close friends in football. I invited him to the Football Writers' award dinners and was always available for him if he ever needed help in his career, and there were times when he was struggling that I helped all I could.

At his peak, he played for England as a winger or even a wing-back and seemed to have enormous potential, but strangely it didn't last as long as some good judges thought it might. He was left out of Bobby Robson's 1990 World Cup squad, after being part of the 26 man training camp and did not take the news well. As his room-mate Paul Parker revealed in his autobiography, *Tackles Like A Ferret*, "Rocastle was crying his eyes out, his World Cup dream over in the space of one short sharp 30 second conversation. What should have been the pinnacle of his career had been snatched away from him." He never did recover from that shock and a knee injury the following season reduced his effectivenes.

In March 2002 Rocky Rocastle died of cancer and it is pleasing that his club, Arsenal, still remember him and have a Rocky Day in honour of his memory. I have rarely come across a nicer guy in football.

ROONEY'S BOOKED

WAYNE ROONEY
Football's modern day Wonderkid

Danny Fullbrook and I co-wrote a biography of Rooney when he was still only 18. Sounds absurd, preposterous even to write a life story of an 18-year-old, but he had packed an awful lot into it. In fact we were commissioned to write an updated version after his exploits in the European Championships.

There is no doubt in my mind that Wayne is an extraordinary talent, and he has a fascinating background. But Danny and I did not need to interview Wayne to acquire the full picture. He isn't one of life's most eloquent speakers. Nor is he even very articulate. Now Rooney has signed a five book contract with Harper Collins over 12 years worth £5m, so his ghost writer will have to earn his undoubtedly large fee.

Let's hope Wayne has read his new book, *My Story So Far*, because there are many footballers who have found themselves in big trouble for not carefully checking the manuscript. Roy Keane ended up on an FA charge for not looking closely enough at 'his' version of the tackle of Alf Inge Haarland, while Jimmy Floyd Hasselbaink more recently made an extraordinary claim in his book that Roman Abramovich had paid him a £50,000 illegal payment for beating Arsenal, as the Russian owner of Chelsea had done with all the players after that epic Champions League quarter-final triumph. But Hasselbaink failed to provide any proof of the payment and was charged with improper conduct by the FA, who cleared Chelsea of any wrong doing.

S

IRVING SCHOLAR, 'BIG PHIL' SCOLARI, RICHARD SCUDAMORE, DAVID SEAMAN, HANS SEGERS, ALAN SHEARER, DAVID SHEEPSHANKS, FREDDIE SHEPHERD, RICHARD SHEPHERD, TEDDY SHERINGHAM, PETER SHREEVES, PETER SHILTON, BARRY SILKMAN, ALAN SMITH, BOBBY SMITH, JON SMITH, GRAEME SOUNESS, MEL STEIN, TONY STEPHENS, ATHOL STILL, PAUL STRETFORD, SIR ALAN SUGAR, SUGGS

SCHOLAR DEATH THREAT

IRVING SCHOLAR
Former Chairman of Tottenham Hotspur FC

In his autobiography *Behind Closed Doors*, this is what the former Spurs chairman Irving Scholar had to say about me....

"The only journalist I was close to was Harry Harris. He had been on the local paper in Tottenham and shared my deep love for the club. Almost from the beginning we got on very well. Harry, by this time, was the Chief Football Writer of the *Daily Mirror*, which meant that, like all Maxwell employees, he was at the beck and call of Captain Bob. How Harry balanced Maxwell's dictats with his own journalistic need is a story that he must tell one day himself, but all I can say is that, despite everything I went through with Maxwell and others, my friendship with Harry remained unimpaired. If anything, I came away appreciating how well he understood my own, and Tottenham's predicament."

Well, Irving, I am finally telling a few stories about Maxwell. And, of course, I've got quite a few about you.

The predicament to which Irving referred in his eulogy toward me in his book was the complexity of the takeover bid when he relinquished control of the football club, with Alan Sugar and Robert Maxwell battling it out to the bitter end.

I sat with Irving in the intimate surroundings of the up-market Bleeding Heart wine bar-restaurant in Holborn close to the *Mirror* building the night before he sold out his shares to Alan Sugar and Terry Venables, telling him over and over again, that, although HE felt the time was right to go, it wasn't and that he would always regret it. Irving will never concede that I was right. What he didn't know at the time, was that his associate Paul Bobroff, the former Chairman of Tottenham Hotspur plc, was under financial pressure to sell his shares. Bobroff was made personally bankrupt in 2006, having failed in a number of subsequent ventures.

But when he tried his hand at football club ownership again with Nottingham Forest, I knew that he was missing his day-to-day involvement with Spurs, and Forest would always be a second best scenario for a man who had, and still does have, Spurs in his blood.

He had his moments at Forest, appointing Dave Bassett who got the relegated club straight back into the Premiership, and then appointing Paul Hart to revamp the youth policy. Ironically Spurs have now bought three players from Forest, Michael Dawson, Andy Reid and Jermaine Jenas who benefited from that policy.

Irving had also revitalised the Spurs' youth system in his time at the club, bringing through Sol Campbell and Nicky Barmby, by giving Keith Burkinshaw a totally unexpected £250,000 a year budget.

Irving could have left straight away with an offer to buy him out, but having appointed Harry Bassett he didn't want to let him down, and stayed. The enjoyment went out of it for him, and it was purgatory working alongside certain individuals, as they went straight back down and Irving left at the end of a nightmare season.

I also knew very well just how much he was suffering in the final days, weeks and months of his reign at Spurs. Only now do the Spurs fans appreciate what he did for the club, but at the time he lost popularity with mounting financial problems. Although the level of debt (£10 million), which today would be described as peanuts, created then an incredible amount of media hype, to put it into perspective, in September 2006 Arsenal announced to a silent audience that their debt in the next 12 months will reach £385m. At the time he left, just after having been one of the chief architects of the Premier League, Irving knew what was coming just around the corner. But he always put the club first. He was deeply hurt by the lies that the club could go bust. It was sheer nonsense. The facts didn't support the spin put about by his enemies. What a shame that such a genuine football man was hounded out. Many people who get involved in football, from afar, think that is easy; it isn't. But it proved fairly straightforward for Irving. He understood a manager's mind set and their problems.

The will-he-won't-he sell Paul Gascoigne scenario alienated his basic support, but the fans didn't know the truth. Irving, more than anyone, battled to keep him. His enemies tried to portray him as the culprit for selling Gazza and that had almost catastrophic results. I was covering a Spurs game one night in the press box, when, after the match was over, I was passed a message not to leave, but to wait in the foyer for Irving. When White Hart Lane was virtually deserted, he emerged from the private directors' landing lift, and was glad to see I had hung around for him. He was surrounded by three policeman, who escorted us to Irving's car. Two police cars followed us out of the ground and shadowed him all the way home. Irving had received a death threat that evening and the police had been treating it seriously.

So, who could blame Irving for wanting out?

But it had been such a battle to win control of his beloved Spurs that he was reluctant to give it up. Irving was also one of the game's great innovators, but has got only small change in terms of the recognition he deserves. He was the first to take a football club to the Stock Exchange, he was the first to have TV advertising for his games, he was the first to look at more global merchandising, and appointed the architect Bill Jenkins to prepare the master plan of the modern White Hart Lane. And on a Saturday you would even find him in the Spurs Shop selling the products himself in an effort to make his ideas work.

He was a real Football Man, who put his beloved Spurs before himself. His encyclopaedic knowledge of the game is legendary and he always loved a quiz because invariably he would win it.

On a more global scale he was also a leading light in the development of the modern game. Along with his close friend David Dein at Arsenal, he helped to smash the TV cartel which had artificially held back revenues to the game, and was one of the architects of the formation of the Premier League, having been party to an earlier threatened break away from the Football League.

Wrongly accused of wanting to cash in on players like Gazza and Waddle, Irving Scholar should long be remembered as the chairman who fought passionately to bring the best players to Tottenham like Gary Lineker, Gazza and Waddle to White Hart Lane in one of the most entertaining eras in the club's history and persuaded Glenn Hoddle to sign the longest contract of his professional career – four years.

In many ways he was a traditionalist. He loved to reminisce, especially with his idol Bill Nicholson, the man he called the Greatest Spur of all after leading his team to the twentieth century's first League and Cup double in 1961. Bill had an empathy with the chairman, who loved to talk about the old days. Just before Bill passed away in 2004, he would occasionally pop into the Board Room on a matchday and, if Irving was there, he would always seek him out and sit next to him for a good old chin wag, something Bill wasn't noted for.

After emerging from the world of property, Irving was shocked to discover that in football a handshake means little; sometimes that the word of an agent, manager and fellow chairman, meant even less.

He once shook hands with Alex Ferguson, yes when he was still plain Alex, to become his Spurs manager, only to discover it didn't mean anything when the Scot changed his mind and left Aberdeen for Manchester Untied instead. Irving was deeply upset. He wanted to take his club back to the top and, when he left, Spurs were still rated as one of the Big Five.

From fan to owner, he discovered the murky world of football; and bungs.

His first Tottenham manager Keith Burkinshaw is credited with labelling agents as 'leaches'. But Irving soon discovered how managers were on the take as the game began to be taken over by greed and crooks. The game was awash with agents spreading around the money in illegal payments to smooth deals, but only Arsenal's George Graham got caught red-handed with his fingers in the till – and then it was the Inland Revenue and not the football authorities who closed the net.

With the Lord Stevens Quest team pawing over 362 transfers from January 2004 until 2006, and *Panorama* desperately trying to snare Sam Allardyce and Harry Redknapp, the issue of bungs lead the national news bulletins in the early part of the 2006/07 season. For Irving, it is amusing to see so many within the industry shrugging their shoulders and suggesting that it doesn't happen now and it has never really happened.

Irving knows the truth after seven years as Spurs chairman. He knows of two unbelievably big name superstars and equally major managerial legends who have asked him directly for bungs – Irving flatly refused without a moment's hesitation.

Bung One. Irving's manager went to see him with a transfer target in mind, but with a problem: "I can't deal with this manager. He is so difficult. Can you speak to his chairman, but I really want the player."

Irving approached the chairman of the club concerned and, after a few conversations, thrashed out a price of £500,000 for the player, a lot of money at that time.

A couple of weeks later, Irving's Tottenham manager came back into his office, "I've just had a call from the manager's assistant with £30,000 in cash." A furious Scholar told him, "There is no way I will put the club or myself in that position."

Irving explained how he wouldn't have minded if the club had asked for an extra £30,000 for the player and what the club did with it after that would be their business. "I will not contemplate getting involved in anything illegal," Scholar told his Spurs manager. Everything has to be done in the normal way. The manager left with a flea in his ear, but totally accepted and understood and the matter was never ever raised again. The transfer did not go through.

Bung Two. This time Irving wanted to sign one of the best young strikers in Britain, one destined to become one of his country's greatest ever strikers. But the deal fell through because he refused to pay a bung.

Now here's the twist. Usually an agent, or the manager himself through his assistant, would ask for the cash in such situations. On this occasion Irving received a call from a Director/Chief Executive of another club NOT involved in the purchase of the player. Mr X, a well known figure in board rooms, suggested that if a £50,000 cash payment was made to the manager of the player's club, the star striker would be on his way to Spurs.

It's interesting to note the rationale behind this particular demand for an illegal payment. The striker was on his way out because he was just too good for this club and was on the move to bigger and better things. His manager feared that without this striker his club would be relegated, and he would get the sack. He was seeking some 'insurance' for the inevitable consequence of selling the striker. The proposed deal was a £750,000 fee plus £50,000 for the manager – and this proposition came from the senior figure of a rival club! Quite what it had to do with him is a mystery to this day.

However when Irving started negotiations with the club actually selling the player, the price suddenly rose to £1m and the deal was dead.

This snapshot of how major transfer deals regularly occurred a few years ago is the backdrop against which the current Lord Stephens' Quest 'bung' enquiry is set. The problem has been endemic for a long time. The question is how do you prove things when there are no records and while managers, players and agents keep their lips tightly shut?

Of course Irving did once fall foul of the football authorities himself when it emerged that Spurs had paid interest free loans to induce players to sign for the club. But Irving has always told me that if he had known he was breaking the rules he would never have done it. He had been told by the professionals inside White Hart Lane that this practice was perfectly acceptable. The club notified the Revenue and actually paid the tax due, which was how the problem came to light.

Irving insists he never intended to break the rules, and once he discovered that the loans contravened the rules, ordered them to cease immediately.

Irving was regularly accused of selling Spurs' stars, but actually his only interest was buying them. He never interfered to the extent that people thought he did. He did not sell Chris Waddle in 1989, for example. Spurs had been approached with an unbelievable offer from Marseilles, who had established themselves as a major European force at that time, and he felt it was an obligation to a player he particularly admired to at least inform him of this unique opportunity. Irving hoped Waddle would turn it down and made it absolutely clear that he didn't want the England left-winger to go.

To help put Marseilles off, his manager Terry Venables put a ludicrously high valuation of £4.5m on 29-year-old Waddle's head, and no-one expected Marseille to come up with that kind of money, then the third highest fee of all time. It's like Real Madrid offering Manchester United £100m for Wayne Rooney now; they might want him, but surely they wouldn't pay that much.

Spurs had to accept the money on offer for Waddle. It would have been madness not to. Don't forget Spurs actually paid a mere £600,000 for Waddle to Newcastle. The funny thing is that, following the sale, Spurs then came third in the league the following season and won the FA Cup the year after. The banning of English clubs from European competitions for five years from 1985 proved a real setback for a club with such a fine European pedigree and geared for success, having qualified more often than not. It is ironic that in the 15 years since Irving left they have only qualified twice, the second time in 2006.

Irving also fancied himself as a footballer, and to be fair he wasn't bad. Eighteen months before he bought the club, Irving played in a Tottenham shirt on the White Hart Lane pitch and scored two goals in a charity match. That, no doubt, persuaded him to go off and buy the club!

Just two weeks before the 1984 UEFA Cup Final, he played in the same team as Ossie Ardiles at Leyton Orient in another charity game. But it didn't end happily for Irving, he snapped his Achilles and ended up on crutches. In fact when Spurs lifted the trophy after a thrilling penalty shoot out at White Hart Lane, he had to be wheeled around the stadium in a wheelchair and was determined to be in the dressing room to celebrate despite his handicap.

Despite all the problems I inflicted on Irving with my probing questions during this period of great personal pressure, the former Spurs chairman has remained a true friend and confidante many years after his break from any business involvement in football.

His biographer, Mihir Bose, called him "the Martin Peters of the Boardroom", reflecting Alf Ramsey's comment about his midfielder being 10 years ahead of his time. Couldn't agree more.

SCOLARI IN AS ENGLAND'S NEW COACH

LUIS 'BIG PHIL' SCOLARI
Future England Manager?

BBC News began their sports coverage on Friday 21st April 2006 by announcing the Battle of the Tabloids, with their presenter Sue Thurle announcing that four tabloids had set the agenda with their back pages focussing on the recruitment of the new England coach to replace Sven-Göran Eriksson after the 2006 World Cup.

Two boldly went for Steve McClaren, with the *Mirror* declaring "The Truth" – that the FA had sought from Boro a compensation quote to suggest their boss was The Chosen One.

Then the BBC turned to the back page of the *Daily Mail*, which declared "The Split," that the FA were sitting on the fence and hadn't made up their mind.

Then the BBC showed the back page of the *Express*, and Sue said, "a Harry Harris exclusive reveals that the FA will choose Portugal coach Luiz Felipe Scolari." "Well," I thought, "that's it. I had better have got it right!"

That Friday, the *Express* set the agenda with its back page headline, "Scolari Goes To The Front".

This is what happened next... Saturday 22nd April, *The Times* said, "Scolari set to make a late surge in race to succeed Eriksson." *The Independent* declared, "Scolari back in the race to take England reigns." *The Mail* back-tracked, "Don't make it McClaren... Dein's late bid to railroad FA into new foreign boss."

Then, in the Sundays, it was the *Mail on Sunday* changing their tune, "Forget McClaren, Big Phil is the man for England says Juninho" and the *Sunday Mirror* following suit, "Big Phil in the hunt."

Finally, on Monday morning came the latest *Express* exclusive, "FA Have Their Phil – Scolari in as England's new coach. Scolari Gets Nod.... Big Phil is talked up by Dein."

Tuesday, it was more of the same as the FA fought against the tide, "Phil: The Heat is On – Kingmaker Dein rages over claim he blabbed. FA chasing Scolari."

And, what about the dear old Beeb. They spent three whole days reporting religiously the misconception emanating from a misunderstanding during a Radio Five interview with Scolari that he had not been interviewed for the job – when, Scolari thought he was being asked for an interview with their man in Portugal.

But at the *Express* we continued on our agenda that Scolari was the man being offered the post to succeed Sven. We even published an article that the FA were actively seeking the mole who had leaked this explosive news that they had chosen to go for another non-English coach against all the clamour emanating from certain journalistic quarters, to me.

So who did give the game away?

Every member of the five man Selection Group were ordered to take their phones off the hook. They were instructed not to speak to the media, in particular to me! In the past this order has been ignored, but on this occasion the stakes were far too high.

The finger was pointed at David Dein, because, in my article, I had given the Arsenal vice-chairman the credit for persuading the sub-committee to move for Scolari. But in a conversation with Adrian Bevington, the head of communications at Soho Square, I explained to him that, while I was not in a position to name my source, and never would be, I could confirm that it wasn't actually one of the five men entrusted with the 'state secrets'.

Now, for the first time anywhere, I can reveal that this is how it came about.

A Premiership chairman sounded out the agent of one of the managers on the FA shortlist of five, Scolari, Steve McClaren, Martin O'Neill, Sam Allardyce and Alan Curbishley. The chairman wanted to know the manager's availability if he hadn't landed the England job, which by now seemed most unlikely.

The chairman in question already knew who was the No. 1 choice because he had already spoken to a number of the selection group, possibly two of them, and had discovered that it was Scolari.

The agent of one of the other four candidates told the chairman that his client would be interested and during the course of the conversation asked who was likely to be the new England coach. He was then shocked to be told it would be Scolari.

During the course of my working days I speak to so many people within the industry that I wouldn't possibly tell you how many. So, by chance, I had a conversation with this agent, and because of my sound relationship with so many people who trust me, he simply causally passed on the 'gossip'.

I then made a few calls and discovered that the agent was on the ball, and explained the process of how I obtained Scolari's name to my Sports Editor Bill Bradshaw, who then felt confident enough to run with the story.

That Sunday evening, I attended the PFA awards night at the Grosvenor House, where Wayne Rooney picked up the Young Player of the Year and Steven Gerrard the senior award. One of the first people I bumped into in the VIP room at the Grosvenor was Garth Crooks, who I know well and think is vastly under-rated.

"Who will be the new England coach?" I asked Garth, provocatively?

"It's going to be an English coach, I'm sure, probably McClaren," Garth replied.

"Oh no it isn't," I told him. "It's going to be Scolari."

A few days later FA Chief Executive Brian Barwick was caught out travelling to Lisbon to see Scolari to formally offer him the job and return with a declaration of intent that he would take it. It seemed all agreed, and I received a call from Garth. He wanted to interview me for *Football Focus*. I agreed, and he made arrangements to come to my home to conduct the interview on the morning of Friday 28th April.

While he was sitting in my kitchen with the crew sipping tea, courtesy of my wife Linda, I took a call from BBC on-line and was interviewed by Simon Austin, who put a story out early afternoon.

The item referred to how the Football Association announced on 24 January that Sven-Göran Eriksson would be stepping down after the World Cup, Sam Allardyce was the early favourite to replace him, with Alan Curbishley, Steve McClaren and Martin O'Neill close behind, and Scolari was a 20-1 outsider. The Brazilian's odds slipped even further on 9th February, when Premier League chairman Dave Richards, one member of the then three-man selection panel, announced, "It's time for a British manager."

The article went on that on 27th April, Barwick was in Lisbon trying to persuade Scolari to become England's new coach.

It continued: "So what happened in between? The major factor seems to be a change in the composition of the selection panel. On 2nd February, Richards, Barwick and Noel White, head of the FA's international committee, were chosen to find the new manager, with Trevor Brooking, the FA's director of football development, acting as an advisor. Arsenal vice-chairman David Dein was notable by his absence. After all, the FA director had been instrumental in securing Eriksson's services in 2000."

The reason for the omission was not entirely clear.

"Harry Harris, chief football writer for the *Express* newspaper, says the FA board wanted to consider Arsenal manager Arsène Wenger for the England job and thought there could be a conflict of interests if Dein were involved in the selection process. And there have been suggestions that Dein's influence at the FA had waned after he reportedly drove through Eriksson's contract extension and £4m salary."

Whatever the reasons, Dein had been added to the selection panel by the time the FA board met on 27th February.

"Harris says Dein convinced the board Wenger had given undertakings he would not take the England job. Former England manager Graham Taylor questioned Dein's right to be on the panel in an interview with BBC Sport."

"Could he be objective if asked about the credentials of his current club manager?" asked Taylor. "Now, maybe it is that Dein has asked Wenger and he doesn't want to do it. But if that's the case, why not say so publicly?"

Dein's preferred choice as England manager is believed to have always been Scolari. The duo had had dealings "two or three years ago," in Dein's capacity as Arsenal vice-chairman, according to Scolari. And earlier this week the Brazilian told BBC Sport, "he is my friend only".

Yet Dein was still out-numbered by the members on the panel who wanted a British manager. Richards was outspoken in this desire and White and Brooking are believed to have agreed that England should not have another foreign manager. Yet Richards was seriously undermined during the period of the selection process. Barwick was reportedly infuriated when Richards told the media he wanted a British boss and the former Sheffield Wednesday chairman was forced to write to FA chairman Geoff Thompson denying Sunday newspaper allegations. On 16th April, the *Sunday Times* newspaper reported that Middlesbrough were so sure McClaren would become England's new manager that they were looking for his successor.

"Harris admits that at this stage McClaren was 'nailed on' for the job."

But on 21st April, he exclusively reported that the selection panel had decided Scolari should be Eriksson's successor. "Dein had convinced the other members of the panel that they could not compromise," Harris told BBC Sport. "McClaren was not anyone's first choice – he was their compromise choice. Barwick wanted O'Neill,

Brooking wanted Curbishley, Richards favoured Allardyce, White's first choice was Pearce and Dein wanted Scolari. At this point Barwick agreed he would go for Scolari if he was the best man for the job and the tide had turned."

"On 24th April, Harris revealed that Scolari was set to become the first Brazilian coach in English football. Barwick travelled to Lisbon on 27th April to begin negotiations with the Portugal coach and the rest of the selection panel updated the FA board. The FA is currently conducting an investigation to try and find out how Harris got his scoop. 'No-one will ever find out exactly how I got the story, because only I and the *Express* sports editor know,' Harris said."

It had been well-documented that Barwick had travelled to Lisbon to meet Scolari's agent Gilmar Veloz and clearly there were 'negotiations' so advanced that the media speculation had hardened into fact. Scolari had said 'yes' in principle to a four year contract at £2.5m gross, just over half of Eriksson's current salary, but with massive bonuses.

On his return, Barwick told reporters the selection process was continuing 'apace' which contradicted Scolari's assessment that nothing concrete had occurred. In reality Scolari had shaken hands on a verbal declaration of intent which the FA then pressurised him into putting into writing which they considered to be binding, even though Scolari refused to go the next stage and actually sign a contract.

Just to add to the confusion and the intrigue, in an interview published on the website of Portuguese newspaper *Diario de Noticias,* again just hours before his shock 'resignation' from a job he had yet to be officially unveiled for, Scolari said no decision had been made about the England manager's job. "There are four or five names and only within seven or 15 days will it be settled. My situation with Portugal remains the same until July 31." It was an indicator of events about to unfold.

Garth and his crew set up in my upstairs office, spending around an hour on the interview, before Garth dashed off to attend a Football Foundation launch at Soho Square.

Linda and I were preparing that evening to leave, along with my publisher Simon Lowe from Know The Score Books, for a Chelsea-related charity function chaired by Ron Harris at the Gatwick Hotel, when word spread that Scolari would be making a statement when he arrived in Germany at the base of the Portuguese national team to check out the facilities there.

My departure was put back as I hastily rewrote the *Express* back page lead. Scolari had been scared off by the English media. What a load of bull!

Apparently the FA had turned his life upside down. Scolari gave a telling insight into his mindset before he boarded the plane to Germany where he called a press conference to make his shock statement that he wanted nothing to do with the poisoned chalice of managing England. He confessed that he had already felt like a 'devil' in Portugal for daring to even discuss the FA post, where, just days before his links with England, he had been a sporting hero in that 'foreign' land. Scolari also knew that Real Madrid were about to come calling and maybe even Barcelona if Frank Rijkaard failed to beat Arsenal in the Champions League final. It wasn't the money; the FA had offered him an Eriksson-sized wage packet, but half of his basic salary and more than double his bonuses, to lift his £900,000 year salary in Portugal to a guaranteed £2.5m a year in England.

No, it was that the FA had placed him in an intolerable position by their tortuous selection process being exposed when Barwick raced off to Lisbon to capture the FA's No. 1 choice. Within days Scolari had been depicted as a traitor across Portugal with the World Cup finals just weeks away. Scolari, before flying off to Germany, said that it had turned into a 'clown show' after the *Express* first broke the story at the beginning of the week.

Back in England, the majority of the industry were almost treating Scolari as a leper for not being English. As a result Big Phil was suffering the 'Impossible Job' syndrome of English managers – before he was even formally signed up as the next coach! The media attention was so intense that he was forced to defend his contacts with the FA publicly and Scolari admitted that the reason for meeting Barwick in Lisbon was because he was looking to secure his future once his Portuguese contract ran out on July 31st, after the World Cup in Germany. "At this time of the season coaches change clubs and listen to other clubs. Your coaches negotiate, am I any different?" Scolari told reporters at Lisbon's airport before flying to Germany to open Portugal's training camp at Bielefeld.

"That hypocrisy that someone who's born here is a saint and someone born on the other side of the Atlantic is a devil, that doesn't exist. It's time to stop that clown show. I'm just like anybody else, I've got two legs, two arms and a head."

Big Phil was in such a hole that the more he tried to dig himself out, the deeper he got. He added: "I'm not negotiating with anyone, I've heard 200 offers and the one who has to decide yes or no is me. That's it. It's over. Until July 31, I'm the Portugal coach."

In Bielefeld his speech was beamed live across the world, and into British homes by Sky TV. Scolari suggested that the FA meeting was "a simple talk, informal and with the consent of the Portuguese Football Federation, since I am still a Federation professional, with a contract until the 31st of July, and up until then no-one knows what is going to happen," he said. Scolari said he would only talk after the World Cup was over. Then, tellingly, he added: "And you ask, what if we lost in the (World Cup's) first round? Would there be anyone that would like it if I stayed in Portugal? No."

Whatever his true reasons, Scolari was not going to be signing the FA's proffered contract. And, as their declared intent was to have their man in place before the World Cup finals to ensure a smooth succession, that ruled Scolari out of the running.

The recriminations inside Soho Square started immediately. Who was to blame. Barwick? Dein? The FA usually seek out a scapegoat.

When Barwick 'took the bull by the horns' and dashed off to meet Scolari, he had returned with a 'declaration of intent', but the FA's desire for Scolari to firm up his handshake and verbal agreement on a deal that would come into affect after the World Cup meant they applied even more pressure than the media. Barwick had suggested that a legally binding commitment would be good enough and Scolari could stop short of signing a contract, which would mean he could keep the essence of his word to the Portuguese FA to stay with them until July 31st. However, the intensity of the media interest stunned Scolari and he reeled from it. He knew he wouldn't be left in peace for a second. He either had to pacify the FA, who were eager to announce his arrival, or satisfy his present employers by showing them respect and loyalty. It was a no-win situation, and he had been put into that corner by the FA's incompetence, both in terms of the contract negotiations, the public manner of their pursuit of Scolari and the blabbering of the committee to their mates.

However, all those who bitterly opposed a second foreign coach would have got their way – a positive the FA can work on. If they could spin that around, then their internal spin doctors would have earned their money.

But the truth was that the FA suffered the massive embarrassment of 'Big Phil' publicly bottling out of taking the England job because of the intolerable levels of media intrusion.

Sir Bobby Robson, Terry Venables, Glenn Hoddle and Graham Taylor have all been on the receiving end of media investigations or scrutiny into their activities. Sir Bobby lasted eight years, but left after he and his players fell out with the media at the 1990 World Cup. Hoddle was the victim of non-footballing issues about his personal beliefs, and Taylor cracked with The Do I Not Like That Channel 4 documentary exposé into his paranoia and stress levels. Big Phil might have had a reputation of dealing with the media in Brazil and Portugal, but it was nothing compared to what awaited him in England.

The back-biting, recriminations, and internal turmoil created by the botched bid for Big Phil, though, was swept under the very substantial FA carpet for fear of dragging down virtually all the Soho Square hierarchy. However much the FA mandarins would love to seek out a scapegoat and sack him, much as they have done in the past, the reality was they only had themselves to blame – and even FA incompetence doesn't stretch to conducting a witch hunt against themselves!

Usually it is the Chief Executive who gets it in the neck by the Machiavellian plotters in the corridors of power. The previous three incumberants have all fallen on their swords as a result of FA cock-ups. Barwick's predecessor as Chief Executive, Mark Palios, was embroiled in the Eriksson sex scandal inside Soho Square and paid the price for his indiscretion, despite being a single man. The one before him, Adam Crozier, was given the boot for becoming too dictatorial and derailing the power and influence of the committees by taking unilateral decisions. Some may think that a good thing, of course, but the FA moved him on before he could devolve too much power away from them. Before Crozier, it was Graham Kelly and his chairman Keith Wiseman, who were shown the door in the cash-for-votes World Cup scandal.

So, why isn't there a Scolari Scandal that will bring down Barwick? Or, why isn't Dein in the frame for the role as scapegoat, considering how much he pushed for the job to go to the Brazilian with the most impressive CV? Internally, the selection process has been described to be 'stupid', with unnecessary 'cloak and dagger' interviews. One of my very well informed FA sources told me about the ridiculous lengths the FA went to in order to keep the names of the interviewees away from the press, "We were left in the dark about where we were going and who we were seeing until we got there. It was a like a James Bond movie. But what did we have to hide? I don't know. All those being interviewed should have turned up at Soho Square and let everyone know what was going on. This game calls for transparency in so many areas and yet here we are, the FA, hiding in dark cars, and trying to avoid the media. We created a monster after Sven and all this cloak and dagger stuff is just sheer stupidity."

However, Barwick is seen as an administrator who has fouled up, but unwittingly and for all the right reasons! My source explains, "If nothing else the process has been methodical, and that has never happened in the past. So when Scolari said no after saying yes, we were all in possession of all our notes on the other candidates and it just took the weekend to come to a conclusion." As for Dein, that is a vastly different matter. Dein's 'intervention' had 'derailed' the seemingly smooth path to McClaren's door.

However, as the clubs are wallowing in the FA's most humiliating botched attempts to sign up Scolari, they are hardly likely to worry themselves about events inside Soho Square. But a prominent chairman close to those on the FA tells me, "Dein's colleagues are laughing at him behind his back. They are secretly pleased that he has got his come-uppence. Many resent his influence. This has only come about because Brain Barwick has listened to Dein. More fool him. I am sure David will keep a low profile for a while. Although we feel he lacks credibility right now, he is one of the game's great diplomats. He is smooth and charming. He will need all of that charm to get over this one."

RICHARD SCUDAMORE
Chief Executive of the Premier League

The Premier League Chief Executive is one of several members of the Barclays panel of judges to decide the Manager of the Month and the Player of the Month and then eventually the annual awards. I am also a member of the panel, which consists of around 25 people representing every constituent part of the football industry. Barclays organise a lunch every three months at Homes House in central London, a very old fashioned and upmarket club, bar, restaurant, and hotel, that used to be frequented by Madonna. No-one receives a fee for being on the panel, but the lunches, plus Barclays' exceedingly popular pre-season three-day trips abroad, more than make up for the lack of any cash.

SHEARER AXED BY GULLIT

ALAN SHEARER
Newcastle legend and former England captain

As a confidante of Ruud Gullit's, I knew the intimate details of the falling out between the No. 9 icon of St. James's Park, and his manager at the time, the former World Footballer of the Year. You couldn't possibly get any more high profile a bust up. I phoned Ruud a few days before the north-east derby game with Sunderland in September 1999 and he confided in me that he was thinking of dropping Shearer to the bench and playing Kenny Dalglish's son, Paul. Ruud felt that Shearer had become a liability to the team, because they relied too much on him, and he had become a touch slower and a little more predictable, as he wasn't making those trademark penetrating runs into the channels that was such a dynamic aspect of his play in his prime. It was a problem that Glenn Hoddle also confided in me about Shearer's role within the England team. Hoddle couldn't find a way round his dilemma, but Ruud loved such a challenge and was ready to ditch Shearer. I warned Ruud of the consequences.

"Look, lovely boy", he said, "I am not worried about Alan Shearer, I will only do what is best for the team."

With Ruud's permission I ran a speculative story suggesting that Shearer might be axed. The morning the *Mirror* story broke, it was ridiculed in the north-east. In fact right up until kick-off time, journalists were convinced that it wouldn't happen. Of course, to the horror of the Newcastle public, Shearer was on the bench, next to Ruud, and it was interpreted as Gullit signing his own exit papers if it failed to come off. As Newcastle lost to their local rivals, it was the signal for Ruud to go.

For many years I have seen Shearer in action as England captain, and in the modern game there haven't been many more influential figures inside a dressing room for both club and country. Alan is now carving a career in television, which might take precedence over the risk factor in the dug out if his performances as a BBC pundit at the 2006 World Cup are anything to go by.

DAVID SHEEPSHANKS
Ipswich Town Chairman

Ipswich Town was the most hospitable club in football in terms of the media relationships dating back to the Cobbold family, and their current chairman David Sheepshanks certainly measures up on that score.

When I was on the *Daily Mail* it was my pleasure to cover Ipswich in Europe when Bobby Robson was the manager, and one of the best matches I have ever witnessed took place in St. Etienne, when the French club, with Tigana, Giresse and Platini in their midfield, were outplayed by a courageous Ipswich side in a thriller, which finished 4-1 to the East Anglian side.

ERIKSSON FOR NEWCASTLE?

FREDDIE SHEPHERD
Newcastle Chairman

Freddie has been one of the high profile victims of the *News of the World*'s Fake Sheik, so he would have known how Sven-Göran Eriksson felt when he was caught out prior to the 2006 World Cup. Ironically, Freddie was seeking a new manager at the time that Sven and the FA decided to part company after the World Cup finals, and Freddie was most definitely keen on the Swede. I know for a fact there had been contact between the two, through intermediaries. Freddie was also keen on Martin O'Neill and Sam Allardyce, both on the FA's final short list of five candidates.

While Freddie was looking at his options for a successor to Graeme Souness, I received a fascinating email from a contact in TV-PR circles who informed me that Inter Milan's coach Roberto Mancini, who had played for part of a season with Leicester City, had bought a £3m home in Newcastle. Now, my Sports Editor Bill Bradshaw, who hails from the north east, knew that you could probably buy the whole of Newcastle for that amount. However, when I checked it out it did appear that Mancini was showing a keen interest in leaving Italy again and returning to the Premiership as a manager, and would not be adverse to listening to Newcastle. However, with Freddie's priorities elsewhere, Mancini was not high on the wanted list and the much less glamorous, but quite possibly equally talented Glenn Roeder was appointed to much fan acclaim.

RICHARD SHEPHERD
Co-owner, along with Sir Michael Caine, of Langan's Brasserie

Langan's Brasserie in Stratton Street, Piccadilly has been a favourite haunt of the footballing fraternity for years. Since being run by Richard Shepherd, as Head Chef, the place has become very classy. Yet, it is also a place for journalists to pick up a descent story by catching managers and occasionally players in a social environment. On one occasion I was lunching at Langan's when the then FA Chief Executive Adam Crozier came in with a well known Sunday paper journalist. Adam was so up tight about being spotted talking to this journalist by me, that he broke a glass on his table not long after sitting down, and made a hasty exit.

While researching my book with Paul Merson about his drug and gambling addiction, there was a large group of us dining at Langan's, so that I could get to know him better and ask a few questions in a more relaxed atmosphere than an empty room with a tape recorder running. Because of Paul's need to be discreet, we were seated at the top table, right in the corner. We were all very conscious of Paul's drinking problems so we stayed off the booze and ran a dry ship instead that night!

TEDDY SHERINGHAM
Oh Teddy, Teddy; a top performer in the top flight well into his forties

Teddy Sheringham's £1.1m transfer from Nottingham Forest to Spurs in 1993 was the catalyst for the famous £50,000 bung heading off to Brian Clough and his pals at Nottingham Forest, which brought Tottenham into so much trouble with the FA, resulting from my investigation into the then Chief Executive Terry Venables' actions. The story went that Forest's Assistant Coach Ronnie Fenton's part of the payment funded his daughter's wedding reception. Mind you that wasn't the strangest part of Fenton's involvement in questionable practices during transfers. For his part in the deal which brought Toddy Orlygsson from the Icelandic club

Akureyrar to the City Ground, the Premier League inquiry was told by Forest's Allan Clarke that "it was his understanding that Mr Fenton had collected £45,000 in a fishing box off a trawler in Hull".

My favourite part of the entire sordid Sheringham episode was that VAT was added to the bung and had to be hastily returned to White Hart Lane when the 'error' was detected. It was hidden away in the club safe and forgotten about until it was spotted about a year later. Teddy gave evidence to the Premier League enquiry at the time of the report into bungs in 1997, but there were so many conflicting statements that, although the three-man panel consisting of Rick Parry, then Chief Executive of the Premier League, Robert Reid QC and Steve Coppell were sure that the £50,000 was intended as a bung to ensure Sheringham's move to Spurs went through smoothly, nothing could be proven conclusively and anyway, the likes of Clough and Fenton had retired from active involvement in the game.

BARRY SILKMAN
Former Orient and QPR midfielder turned football agent

"Silky", as he is known, lived in the same street as a kid as me and I enjoyed kicking a football about with him. We grew up in one of the more 'ungentrified' parts of the East End, round the corner from the Krays, and we would play outside until the light faded or our mums bellowed that our tea was ready. I only dreamed about being a footballer, but Barry, a silky winger, went on to star for Crystal Palace and Manchester City, where he was signed by Malcolm Allison.

JON SMITH
Football superagent

Jon and Phil Smith head up the agency First Artist Corporation whose offices are just opposite Wembley. They also happen to both be very good friends of mine as well as contacts. It is an indication of the direction of such large agencies that they are diversifying. FIFA's introduction of transfer windows has seriously curtailed the workload of agents and restricted cashflow. I have visited Jon at his home, and was surprised to discover that he keeps Lemurs.

MEL STEIN
Solicitor, author and agent

Mel was Gazza's friend, minder, agent and virtually babysitter along with his friend and accountant Len Lazarus. Mel has been a wonderful source of information on Gazza over the years, and while the *Mirror's* rivals might have wondered how we knew so much, a great deal was down to my friendship with Mel and Len; a relationship that has not deteriorated since Gazza and the pair fell out.

PAUL STRETFORD
One of the new breed of agents

As agents go there are few more controversial than Paul Stretford, who represents Wayne Rooney. For some time a number of managers had shares in his agency business, but so too did a freelance journalist who worked for a range of national titles.

Certain agents are renowned for 'feeding' stories to chosen reporters in an effort to create a market for their clients, or agitate a move. One Sports Editor became highly suspicious of stories being planted which seemed to be solely for the benefit of the agent and his client. Newspapers love transfer gossip, and will lap up the speculation, but there is always a danger of conflict of interest, if football writers have shares in a football agency.

VOICE OF AN ANGEL

ATHOL STILL
Athlete, Opera singer and football agent

Athol Still is a football agent who used to be an opera singer and is one of the most dedicated gamblers I've come across, with every bet calculated down to the most minute detail. Once, over lunch, Athol gave me a few notes to show me the range of his operatic voice, and I was most impressed. He is most definitely the biggest showman-agent I have ever come across; very likable and extrovert.

He also fronted one of the consortia interested in buying 'Deadly' Doug Ellis out of Aston Villa during the summer of 2006, although his group lost out to American Randy Lerner in the end.

As well as high-profile sportsmen such as Sir Steve Redgrave, Athol represents former England coach Sven-Göran Eriksson and was present when caught out with the England coach by the infamous Fake Shiekh. Naturally livid, he and Sven have been trying to take legal action, and I've even been told there could be criminal action in the Middle East. But most victims of the *News of the World* sting have rarely been successful in stinging back.

SUGAR CANED BY VENABLES

SIR ALAN SUGAR
Owner of Amstrad, star of TV show The Apprentice and former owner of Spurs

Sir Alan was still plain old Alan when he invited me and my *Mirror* Sports Editor Keith Fisher to his Chigwell home accompanied by his public relations expert Nick Hewer. I had been nagging Nick for some time that I thought it would be in Alan's best interests to comment on Terry Venables, after his enforced exit from Spurs for financial dodgy dealings. In the midst of the storm caused by my revelations that Venables had cheated Spurs out of £400,000, the club was threatened with having 12 League points deducted and being banned from the following season's FA Cup, although in the end most penalties were merely suspended. As the supporters' ire grew, Alan, as Chairman, took enormous flak as Venables had been hugely popular with the fans due to his style of play on the pitch.

Of course it was also in my best interests to pull off such an exclusive, but there was no point in trying it on with someone as astute as Alan Sugar or his vastly experienced media advisor, Nick. So, it was a genuinely mutually beneficial exercise.

Alan took us into his vast office at his home and the interview was terrific. Keith could hardly contain himself as we left for the nearest pub to plan the day's paper. Keith contacted the office and instructed his back room team to clear the decks for the back three pages.

The inside spread was "I feel like the man who killed Bambi" as Alan explained why he had no choice other than to rid the club of Venables, and why he was painted as the ogre, even though he knew he was taking the correct course of action. The back page was an even bigger exclusive about how he planned to hire the popular Ossie Ardiles as the new Spurs manager, even though he privately asked me to sound out whether Glenn Hoddle could be persuaded, at the last minute, not to go to Chelsea, but to come home to Spurs.

Alan's Chigwell mansion was pretty impressive. But I was stunned when, for the first time, he invited me on to his yacht for a follow up interview. The instructions were to turn up outside the restaurant La Cantina on Butler's Wharf, near the Tower of London, where someone would greet me and take me to the yacht. I turned up on time, I was at the right venue, but where was this boat? I walked round to the opposite side of the dock, still no damn boat. I wandered about for half an hour and couldn't make it out. I knew Alan liked punctuality, and this wasn't going to make a good impression. Suddenly I heard this guy yelling at me. I looked down and there was a very smart looking young man all decked out in a perfectly white uniform. "Where have you been?" he inquired politely.

I wasn't quite sure where I had been. I hadn't been anywhere. "I've been here all the time".

"Couldn't you see Mr Sugar's yacht?" he asked, pointing towards a huge boat I'd given hardly a moment's thought to.

"That's not a yacht," I thought. "That's a ship!" When I looked closer I saw it was the biggest floating vessel I had ever seen. It looked more like the QE2.

On board I explained to Alan I hadn't imagined it would be that big. He gave me a guided tour, the dinning room had a ballroom annex, and each of the bedrooms were en suite, the master bedroom was bigger than my entire Chelsea flat.

When Alan first hooked up with Venables, he had been told that I was a journalist to avoid. I had no contact whatsoever with the Spurs chairman. Whatever Venables had been telling him, Alan found out the truth for himself.

However we became good friends and dined out together regularly with our wives, often getting lifts home from his driver in Alan's top of the range Rolls Royce.

Linda and I were guests at Alan's 50th birthday bash at the Reform Club where Michael Aspel had been drafted into to do a live *This Is Your Life* presentation to Alan complete with the big red book. Apparently Michael got a ticking off from his TV employers for taking part in the stunt, but it went down well that evening.

There were no other journalists at the party, which is a measure of the trust that had developed between us.

SUGGS
Lead singer of Madness, TV Presenter, DJ and ardent Chelsea fan

Suggs is good company and highly knowledgeable about his football, and of course recorded what has become a classic song for all Chelsea fans, *Blue Day*. Ken Bates can be a hard task master, but it's indicative of the affection that Suggs has generated among Chelsea fans, that even Ken welcomed him into his private chairman's Supper Club which became a feature of his later years as the Bridge chairman.

T

GORDON TAYLOR, GRAHAM TAYLOR, PETER TAYLOR, JOHN TERRY, GEOFF THOMPSON

GORDON TAYLOR
Chairman of the Professional Footballers Association

Gordon has a love-hate relationship with the media. There is one faction, led by Charlie Sale at the *Daily Mail*, who is forever finding ways of criticising the Players' Union leader. Personally I am supportive of the stand he makes on behalf of his players and the role that he assumes to act for the good of the game. Clearly his priorities lie with protecting the interest of his union members, that's what he is paid for, but there are times that he expresses views that are beneficial for the sport as a whole, and I applaud him for that.

SWEDES 2 TURNIPS 1

GRAHAM TAYLOR
Former England manager, who managed to turn his career around after being likened to a turnip to become a widely respected radio pundit

Graham's father was a journalist, so he had a rather different perspective to the way he was treated by the media. However, nothing protected him from the depth of personal abuse he suffered at the height of the media campaign to get him out of the England job. To be depicted as a Turnip was over-stepping the mark. *The Sun's* Sports Editor at the time was actually on a day off and his deputy was in control when one of the sub-editors came up with the concept of planting Taylor's face on a turnip. Such is the way Fleet Street history unfolds.

Graham did not deserve the sort of attacks he had to endure, as he was a genuinely nice guy, who had created a family atmosphere at Watford, a club where he had fulfilled the dreams of his chairman Elton John in taking them to Wembley, but more importantly right through the divisions to join the elite. It was a remarkable managerial success story that, via success at Aston Villa, culminated in the England job. But it brought Taylor nothing but misery. It took him many years to overcome the scars of his treatment at the hands of the media. Ironically Taylor is now a media star, writing a column on the tactical intricacies of the game and using his broad knowledge to pontificate on the important issues in the *Daily Telegraph*.

PETER TAYLOR
Manager of Crystal Palace and coach to the England Under-21s

Peter was the England coach, albeit for one game, who made David Beckham captain before handing over the reigns to Sven-Göran Eriksson. Peter was in charge for a friendly in Italy and picked an extremely young side, which was to become the basis for the next few year's international line-ups with the likes of Jamie Carragher, Kieron Dyer, David James, Emile Heskey and Gareth Batty given starts in place of more senior stars. A highly capable coach, Peter would have been a candidate for the vacant position as England head coach in 2006 had he been at more fashionable clubs than Brighton and Hull in the interim.

JOHN TERRY
Inspirational Chelsea championship winning skipper

Ken Bates always told me that he had enormous faith in John's potential to emerge as an influential captain of his club and eventually his country. Ken was on the point at one stage of reading the riot act to John, who was going off the rails as a young professional just breaking into the big time. But Ken gave him one last chance, and John responded to it.

He had blotted his copybook by being one of a trio of Chelsea players... Known as the Nightclub Three, Terry, Jody Morris and Wimbledon's Des Byrne were charged with assault, possessing an offensive weapon and affray following an incident at a London nightclub in 2002. It was alleged Terry had used a broken beer bottle to threaten a man who had become involved in a drunken argument with the three young players. In the event, Terry and Morris were cleared, while Byrne was found guilty, but fined rather than jailed.

During the affair Terry received a temporary ban from the national side, which cost him a place in England's 2002 World Cup squad. However, the court case acted as a wake up call to John and he mended his ways to the point that he is now praised as a model professional, has lifted the Premiership trophy as Jose Mourinho's captain for the last two seasons and succeeded David Beckham as England skipper.

I'm sure Ken will claim that's all due to the opportunity to start again he gave John Terry back in 2002.

GEOFF THOMPSON
Chairman of the Football Association

Geoff is often depicted as the invisible man of the FA. In the past the FA have had high-profile, dominating chairmen, but Geoff chose to blend into the background. That is not to say he doesn't have strong views, and he is also a man of high principles. His detractors simply don't know him, and give him stick for failing to take an overt lead, irrespective of their limited knowledge of how much Geoff does quietly behind the scenes.

TERRY VENABLES

TERRY VENABLES

VENABLES CHEATED SPURS OUT OF £400,000

TERRY VENABLES
Former England and Spurs supremo, disgraced by my enquiry into Spurs' finances

Terry was strolling along in the sunshine, outside the five star La Manga hotel, oblivious to all around him as he concentrated on the business deal he was hatching on his mobile phone. El Tel was back on his Spanish beat putting into place the final part of his master plan to construct a La Manga-style resort, that specialised in coaching young players. My sources had told me that Tel wanted to import poor African kids with outstanding footballing promise and develop them into future stars, and then have part-ownership in them to sell onto the elite European clubs. Naturally, my chances of discussing this grand scheme with Venables were zero considering our history.

Although I knew in advance of Venables' mission in Spain, it was sheer coincidence that I just happened to be spending some time in the resort also. Suddenly our paths crossed outside the hotel, Venables' jaw dropped, he cut short his mobile phone conversation.

"Don't worry Terry, I'm not stalking you." I said.

Venables smiled, unable even to speak.

Hours later he had checked out of the hotel and vanished from the resort. Clearly, he could take no chances.

But it seems our paths are fated to cross. We dined at the same Indian restaurant early in 2006, the Bombay Brasserie near Gloucester Road tube station. Yes, I can forgive Venables for thinking I was stalking him. But again as I walked past his table, his jaw dropped open and all he could manage was one of his usual cheeky smiles. "Still, not stalking you, Terry," I said cheerily as I walked on.

Paranoia impregnates itself into those who spend a very long time at the top of the modern game. For example I received a phone call from Harry Redknapp, who was travelling back from a game in early March 2006. Harry wanted to know whether I had some sort of vendetta against him. I had been writing about the suspected betting scam when there was a flurry of money placed on Redknapp switching back as manager to Portsmouth from Southampton, and just a few days before his call I had revealed how the Premier League investigation into bungs, sparked by Luton manager Mike Newell's revelations that he had been offered inducements by rival club directors, would take in 26 clubs, including four from the Championship, and that Redknapp's deals at Saints would come under scrutiny.

I told Harry there had been no vendetta, and there never will be.

I would tell Terry Venables the same, but he has not called me recently. In fact I haven't even heard from his lawyers. Despite the fact he has always threatened to sue me, he has never quite pulled that one off either.

Yet, at the height of my *Daily Mirror* investigations into his financial dealings involving Spurs, there was constant media speculation that Venables had issued legal proceedings or was about to take me to the High court.

Once, I even received a call from a young lady working for the Press Association asking me to comment about the fact that I had been reported to the Press Complaints Commission. The call was a huge surprise, because I hadn't been reported at all. At least, as I discovered later, Venables' lawyers had written to the Press Complaints Commission seeking guidance about the procedures they would have to follow IF they were going to report me. A couple of Terry's 'pet' journalists were briefed that he had taken legal action, and one of them even taunted me that Terry would see me in court to prove his innocence.

Terry had a media gang of four who idolised him, drank with him regularly when he part-owned a Kensington wine bar-restaurant Scribes West, and fell for his every word. One or two have consistently pushed for a Venables return to the England job. And now, of course, El Tel IS back as part of Steve McClaren's backroom team , as the FA have shoved all thoughts of his previous misdemeanours aside.

Despite items neatly placed in the media that I had been sued, I hadn't.

But to keep up appearances, Venables did try a couple of legal tricks. Libel actions can be brought up to three years after the event but no longer, or at least that was the law at the time, and Venables waited until the very last possible day inside the three year limit. His lawyers dispatched a messenger to deliver the writ, which had to be handed over personally on that final day within three years. Off the messenger went to the *Mirror* buildings, conned his way passed security, reached the third floor and found his way to my desk.

Now, came the crunch, he had to find me and hand it over.

So where was I?

Well, I was at home on a day off. We football writers, and indeed journalists in general, do not work nine to five and certainly don't keep 'normal' office hours or even work weekdays only.

During the height of my investigations into Venables' nefarious financial dealings at Spurs, I was attending a football press conference at the Landmark Hotel in London, and Venables, by chance, happened to be there. He had no idea the media were going to turn up, let alone see me there. But this time he did talk to me. I explained to him it was nothing personal and armed with the evidence I had in my possession any journalist worth his salt would publish it. He warned me off. He made veiled threats and that it would not be in my best interests to pursue my enquiries.

That put El Tel on his guard, though, and he devised a canny way to try to deal with the threat I posed. He got his lawyers to try to get me into the witness box in a case that had been brought by a company who claimed El Tel owed them money, which Venables was contesting. In reality I had no evidence to provide or opinion to give on the central issue of this court action and so did not need to appear. But I did get to hear a judge brand him an "unreliable" witness and "wanton" in his evidence. It made for yet another hard hitting back page *Mirror* headline: 'You Are Unreliable and Wanton.'

The subpeona I received from Venables' lawyers was an hilarious pretext to cross examine me in court, under oath about the sources of my information in my pursuit of Venables' dodgy dealings at Spurs, and if I refused, as they knew I might, then to seek more legal moves to cause trouble for me for obstructing the case – and ultimately try to get me jailed.

It didn't work. The *Mirror* lawyers correctly argued it was all a front for another purpose, and the judge declined the application to subpeona me to appear in the case.

It was always smoke and mirrors with Tel, there was always a hidden agenda.

But whatever intimidatory tactics were used, I persevered with producing damning documents that eventually led to two TV documentaries, and 11 charges for criminal activity by the DTI.

To this day, it must remain a mystery to Terry where all the documents and information came from. Of course, he has his suspicions. In fact I am sure he would immediately point an accusing finger at Alan Sugar.

But, I am not telling.

However, I will give Terry a clue.

The very first incriminating piece of evidence arrived at my home address via the post. Whoever sent it had written the address left handed. The post mark was London, but not from an area that I recognised from any of my close contracts.

I knew of three people who had hard evidence in their possession of Terry's misdemeanours at Spurs. I asked all three if they would supply it to me anonymously, posting it from a destination that would not be traceable back to them.

And so the truth is that I do not actually know which one of those three sent the first document that set the wheels in motion. I might hazard an educated guess. But a guess it would be.

So, even if I had been forced into the witness stand, under oath, I would have sworn that I do not really know to this day who sent me the first piece of documentary evidence.

The fact that the Department of Trade and Industry declined to pursue the matter of Venables' financial affairs in the criminal courts was a fear of losing yet another high profile action. A number of cases against celebrities had failed in front of star struck juries, so the DTI opted for a civil action against Venables instead. However, when the charges were made in court, they referred to criminal activities. Terry was lucky not to go to prison, as he would have done if he had been found guilty in a criminal action. Instead he was found guilty in the civil court and banned by the DTI for seven years from serving as a company director. That ban expired in January 2005.

Now, after all this it may be a huge surprise that my declared opinion about Venables is not clouded or prejudiced – I believe he is an outstanding coach.

This is where Patrick Collins of the *Mail on Sunday* and I part company on our views regarding Venables. Patrick has never been convinced about Venables' success rating and abilities as a coach.

However, I have never doubted his abilities.

And, in fact, I recommended him to be England coach. Graham Kelly, as FA Chief Executive at the time, made a decision that it was time the FA came down from its Ivory Tower and consulted some of the constituent parts of the footballing industry about the selection of the new England manager, and as such asked a group of three respected football No. 1 writers to give him our opinions. We were invited into Graham's room when we were all together covering an England game. Unanimously we agreed that Venables was the right choice. However, I told Graham, that in my opinion, he ought to sort out the Venables 'baggage' in advance of any appointment.

If the FA thought he should face charges of disrepute for his financial dealings at Spurs, they should be proactive and not use the tired and old excuse of waiting for legal proceedings to run their course before they could consider any intervention.

Of course the FA have a legitimate policy, as any FA charges might well be seen as prejudicing up and coming court action. But I felt it was imperative in this instance to make an exception, charge Venables, hear a disciplinary case, ban him from the touchline for a month if that was the judgment of the commission, and then he would be clear of these issues and free to concentrate on the England job.

Venables was, indeed, appointed England coach and had a good tournament when England hosted the European Championships in 1996, but it wasn't long before the legal actions caught up with him and side-tracked him. However, contrary to the public perception that half a dozen potential legal actions derailed Venables to the extent that he felt concentrating on protecting his reputation was more important than continuing as England coach, the reality was that Kelly offered him only a one year extension prior to Euro 96 and Venables wanted a much longer commitment from the FA, at least up to the France World Cup in 1998, which they were not prepared to give him.

CHRIS WADDLE, VIC WAKELING, NEIL WARNOCK, DAVE WHELAN, HOWARD WILKINSON, RAY WINSTONE, DENNIS WISE, PETER HILL-WOOD, IAN WRIGHT

WADDLE SIGNS FOR SPURS

CHRIS WADDLE
Flying Geordie winger, former Footballer of the Year and Pop star

Chris inscribed his autobiography "To Harry. Thanks for being around".

Perhaps, this was a reference to the time that I helped recruit Waddle for Spurs after a personal plea from the then chairman Irving Scholar. Irving had been telling me that he wanted to sign Waddle from Newcastle, despite all the competition for his signature. Irving came to realise that Chris was a shy young man from the North East who, like many Geordies, would be very nervous at coming down to The Smoke. So, Irving asked a favour. Would I go to Wembley and sit with Chris's wife, who was travelling down after work to watch her husband play for his country, but hadn't told him she was going? Irving had organised the tickets and I sat with her, and tried my best to make her feel at home, and persuade her to use her influence to make sure he signed for Spurs.

My reward? The exclusive story of Waddle signing for Spurs.

VIC WAKELING
Head of Rupert Murdoch's Sports TV Empire

Vic is head of Sky Sports, but it's a little known fact that he was also one of my first Fleet Street Sports Editors and as such was a big influence in my developing years as a football reporter. Vic is an ever present at the Sky pre-season media lunches and there are a few of us left who were there from the inaugral get together at Shepherd's restaurant.

It was at that lunch that *Hold The Back* Page was formulated after the lunch time drinks were downed and the inhibitions loosened. Almost straight away the arguments began, and it was soon suggested that a journalists' forum would make compelling TV. Credit to Vic for spotting its potential. *Hold The Back Page*, to which I was a regular contributor, has since metamorphosed into the popular Sunday morning show *Jimmy Hill's Football Supplement*.

BRINGING TRAINING TO A HALT

NEIL WARNOCK
Abrasive Manager of Sheffield United, no stranger to controversy and touchline bans

My *Daily Express* Sports Editor Bill Bradshaw knows Neil very well and recommended that I should call him as someone who was ideally positioned to discuss the merits or otherwise of some club chairmen's proposal to issue a set of automatic fines for managers who fail to adhere to a new code of conduct. Neil had been in hot water several times with some outspoken after-match comments and the club chairmen were knocking around ideas to curb such managerial excesses. Neil is most definitely a larger than life character who stands for no nonsense and is willing to speak his mind. I contacted Sheffield United's press officer, who informed Neil that I wanted to speak to him. I expected that I might get some cooperation, but not until after training. Not a bit of it. Neil came to the phone immediately.

He told me, "'I have just stopped training and told the players that it shows how far Sheffield United have come that someone like you wants to speak to this club's manager. I told the boys that it must be important and that they would have to wait for me."

Well, that was definitely a first.

DAVE WHELAN
Multi-millionaire Chairman of Wigan Athletic and founder of the JJB Sports Empire

Wigan's PR contacted me out of the blue to say how much the club's chairman enjoys my column and, as I had been supportive to Wigan's cause during their rise through the divisions to the top flight, would I like to interview Mr Whelan before the 2006 League Cup Final, the club's first major cup final? Dave made himself available for a phone call even though he was on holiday at his Barbados home the week before the Final at the Millennium stadium. He gave an illuminating interview that appeared in the *Daily* and *Sunday Express*.

THE WORST EVER ENGLAND TEAM?

HOWARD WILKINSON
Former Sheffield Wednesday and Leeds manager

When Wilkinson was in temporary charge of the England team for a friendly against World and European Champions France in the wake of Kevin Keegan's shock departure after the defeat at Wembley in October 2000 by Germany, the theme of my article on the day of the match was to ask our readers whether this was the worst England team ever fielded. The performance that evening just about justified its billing. Needless to say Wilkinson was not the man destined to be appointed full-time England coach no matter how much he desired it.

WHO'S THE DADDY?

RAY WINSTONE
The Daddy of British film actors

The last time I met Ray was at a charity football match at Stamford Bridge in 2000 and after some hospitality we started reminiscing about the old East End days and how a group of us used to go on holiday together in caravans down by the coast. I phoned Ray a while after to see if he wanted to come along to a black tie football dinner, but the message he left for me said he was in Spain, putting on weight and getting a sun tan, so he couldn't make it. Turns out he was out there for months filming the highly acclaimed *Sexy Beast,* also starring Ben Kingsley and Amanda Redman.

DENNIS THE MENACE

DENNIS WISE
Former Wimbledon and Chelsea midfielder, now beginning his career in management

Dennis is a Rotweiller on the field and, although he can be charming off it, he can still be quite aggressive if the mood takes him, particularly if you've rubbed him up the wrong way. I received an angry call from Dennis when, after playing a blinder for England, the *Mirror's* marks out of ten gave him a four. He was livid. And he let me know just how he felt with a volley of abuse. However, as I tried to explain to him, as a match reporter, you don't always award the marks out of ten. Sometimes it is done for you by another journalist inside the office watching on TV. Deadlines are very tight on match nights, especially the big England games, when the report and analysis often takes up five of the back pages. Purely on the issue of speed, it is more practical for someone watching on the telly to do the marks. However, more often than not, the sub-editor inside the office can be distracted, answer the phone, or goes off to get a cup of tea, and might end up with a distorted view of the performances. Had I been marking Dennis in that game I would have given him an eight, maybe even a nine.

Unfortunately I don't think he accepted my explanation, nor did he ever forgive me.

Nonetheless, as a close friend of the Chelsea chairman Ken Bates, and because Ken interceded on my behalf, Dennis was willing to put his grievances to one side and agreed to be interviewed by me ahead of the victorious last FA Cup Final at Wembley in 2000.

PETER HILL-WOOD
Chairman of Arsenal FC

I knew Peter's father Denis very well and will always be grateful for the Old Etonian in helping me out with a story or two in my formulative years. Denis was arguably the last of football's great traditionalists. He despised the sponsors and advertisers he saw creeping into the game and the Gunners were among the last bastions opposed to the corporate financing of football. Peter, who succeeded his father on his death in 1982, is also very much of the old school, and because of that you know you will get the truth from him, which is more that can be said of many club directors and chairman these days.

IAN WRIGHT
Arsenal's record goalscorer until Thierry Henry came along, now a TV presenter

In his autobiography entitled *Mr Wright*, the vivacious striker inscribed the book... "To Harry & Linda. I love Linda. Harry, I don't know". Typically mischievous of Ian.

Of course, in my time I have given him some stick for some of his over the top antics, but that was mainly in his youth when he was as much a fighter as a footballer, making his way from Crystal Palace to Arsenal. But he developed into a lethal goalscorer whose record has only just been surpassed by Thierry Henry. There have been times when Ian has sought my advice and help, and I have willingly given it. Other times he has supported my campaigns on tackling racism in football.

Y

DWIGHT YORKE

MAKING THE DWIGHT CALL

DWIGHT YORKE
Former Manchester United and Aston Villa striker and father of Jordan's first born

When he was a big star with England and Arsenal, David 'Rocky' Rocastle signed one of his England shirts for me to take to Trinidad & Tobago with a good luck message inscribed on the shirt. I was bound for the Caribbean to watch a vital World Cup qualifier and Rocky, having family which hailed from the islands, wanted to show his support.

This was November 1989 and Trinidad & Tobago had to beat the USA to qualify for the first time for the World Cup, to be held in Italy. Football fever had truly taken hold of this tiny cricket mad nation. There were thousands queuing up to get into the stadium on the morning of the match, a snake-like queue standing in the baking hot all day to get in. There was a carnival atmosphere before the game, it looked like a scene from Rio, and the fans made quite a din. It was the first time I saw an 18-year-old they had all been raving about – Dwight Yorke. The kid was in tears as the USA scored the only goal of the game, and it was a long wait until Germany in 2006 for Trinidad & Tobago to qualify for the finals, and Dwight made a comeback to skipper his country to a famous goalless draw with Sweden.

When I returned from Trinidad. I recommended Dwight to a couple of clubs, but they didn't seem to want to take the word of a journalist. When he ended up at Aston Villa and then Manchester United paid a sizable fee, I just about resisted the temptation to say "I told you so".

Z

PINI ZAHAVI, GIANFRANCO ZOLA

PINI ZAHAVI
The World's most powerful Football Agent

Pini Zahavi has been called a 'Super Agent' or 'Mr Fix It', but he is also Mr Untouchable.

Pini had a hand in the infamous tapping up of Ashley Cole, which ultimately led to the Arsenal and England left-back agitating for a move to Chelsea through the media and via his autobiography, brought out after the 2006 World Cup. But it was Zahavi's friend and fellow agent Jonathan Barnett who was charged by the FA over the incident. Pini is a registered agent with the Isreali FA, therefore outside of the FA's jurisdiction. Any charges would be a FIFA matter.

But the fallout from Cole's infamous meeting with Chelsea officials continued to fester more than 14 months after it took place, with Barnett, the player's agent, having his licence suspended by the FA for his role in setting it up. Barnett was hit with three separate charges by the FA for his part in a meeting that led to Cole, José Mourinho and Chelsea being fined by the FA Premier League in June 2005, one for breaching FA rules, one for breaking FIFA rules and a further catch-all charge of improper conduct. "The charges relate to his alleged involvement in a meeting involving his client Ashley Cole and representatives of Chelsea FC at the Royal Park Hotel on 27 January 2005," an FA statement read. "This meeting led to Premier League disciplinary action against Cole, José Mourinho and Chelsea FC. Mr Barnett has been charged by the FA with a breach of FA Rule E1(e) which covers breaches of the rules of leagues affiliated to The FA. It is alleged that he brought about a breach by Ashley Cole of Premier League Rule K5 which relates to illegal approaches to clubs by players under contract. He has also been charged with a breach of the FIFA Players' Agents Code of Conduct, which requires agents to respect the rights of third parties, in this case Arsenal FC. Mr Barnett has been charged as an alternative with improper conduct (breach of FA Rule E3) for the above matters."

Barnett requested a personal hearing in front of the FA's three-man disciplinary commission. He was angry at being charged, believing himself to have been made a scapegoat for the activities of many agents and is determined to fight to clear his name. "We will deal with the charges appropriately," Barnett's lawyer, Graham Shear, of Teacher Stern Selby, said.

But just as pivotal, and far less widely reported, was the role played by Zahavi. "The meeting at the Royal Park Hotel was initiated by Pini Zahavi and Jonathan Barnett," the Premier League's commission's report read. "Barnett was acting as Cole's agent and on his behalf. Cole knew that the meeting was being held. He attended the meeting. This constituted an 'approach'. At the meeting he was present throughout. Barnett was acting on his behalf and Cole himself contributed in some part to the discussion with the officials of Chelsea, endorsing what Barnett had said regarding his discontent with Arsenal and his interest in joining Chelsea. This was 'with a view to negotiating a contract' for his transfer from Arsenal to Chelsea.'"

When the News of the World first reported that Mourinho and Peter Kenyon, the Chelsea Chief Executive, had met with Cole, Barnett declined to confirm the meeting had even taken place, which was taken as a denial by him. Cole was fined £100,000 but lodged an appeal, which he lost, although the fine was reduced to £75,000. Further appeal to Court of Arbitration for Sport was also dismissed. But while all of these legal actions were going on, Pini escaped it all under the cloak of protection afforded him in Israel.

Pini has, though, been forced to take legal advice over the constant sniping from David Mellor in his *Evening Standard* column. Pini is sure that has been inspired by Mellor's close association with Ken Bates.

Pini's row with Ken is well documented. Pini introduced Roman Abramovich to the possibilities of buying Chelsea and as such believed he was entitled to a commission. As Bates had not dealt directly with Pini, but through Chelsea's Chief Executive, he argued that he had not instructed him to arrange the sale, and so refused all demands for payment of a commission. The fall out between them was cataclysmic.

However, all is well in the land of milk and honey; Pini has since been well-rewarded for bringing Roman to the Bridge with a string of commissions earned due to numerous player purchases.

Mind you I hear that when Bates and Zahavi met up at a west London club there was a fairly frosty and feisty atmosphere. Football will always throw up conflict, controversy and an abundance of stories to whet the appetite of the millions of lovers of the game who devour newspapers every day. It's been my job for the last 30-odd years to unearth them and it's been interesting, challenging, moving, entertaining, hard work and ultimately a pleasure to do so.

LA, LA, LA, LA, ZOLA!

GIANFRANCO ZOLA
Chelsea and Italy's Mighty Midget

On my office wall is Zola's Chelsea shirt that he wore on his final appearance from the club. My wife Linda and her entire family are avid Chelsea fans, and Linda wanted Zola's shirt as a memento of his stay at the Bridge, where he was the fans' all-time most popular player, and probably still is, despite so many wonderful, world famous stars who have arrived since the little Italian. His shirt hangs alongside two personally signed by Pelé and George Best's European Cup winning shirt signed by El Beatle just before he died in recognition of the work I did on his last ever book. I also am proud to own a World Cup 1966 shirt signed by Geoff Hurst and Martin Peters, and a David Beckham England shirt. Then there is Ally McCoist's Glasgow Rangers shirt signed to Linda; a special present from another of her particular favourite players.

I had great pleasure in penning Zola's biography, one of 40 books I have now written, but the life story of the superbly gifted Italian forward ranks as one of the more enjoyable works I have undertaken. Franco was not only one of English footballs greatest talents, but he always played with a smile on his face and off the field he was such a lovely bloke. The majority of my books are ones initiated by myself from personal choice rather than merely commissioned by a publisher and this was most certainly one of them.

When he first arrived in English football, Franco was famous for his Sardinian style and homely-knitted pullovers, but he didn't seem to mind the inevitable Mickey-taking of his team-mates. His generosity is legendary and his welcoming attitude was a refreshing change from most modern day footballers' insular approach to life. A true gentleman.

HARRY HARRIS

Harry Harris is the Group Chief Football Writer for *Express* Newspapers, writing the most influential daily football column in the country.

He appears regularly as an analyst on football related matters on all major TV news and sports programmes and channels, including Richard & Judy and Newsnight, BBC Radio One, Four, and FiveLive. Amongst his 35 football books are the best-selling *Pelé – His Life and Times, All The Way Jose, Chelsea Century* and *Wayne Rooney – The Story of Football's Wonder Kid,* plus a series of autobiographies for Ruud Gullit, Paul Merson, and Glenn Hoddle. He has twice won British Sports Journalist of the Year at the British Press Awards, the Oscars of Journalism.

PRAISE FOR HARRY HARRIS

"Harris treats the back pages in just the same way that news reporters treat the front page – as a place to surprise, shock, amuse and enthuse." *Press Gazette*

"Harris's series on the Bung and Betting stories were examples of popular sports journalism at its best." *John Humphrys*

KNOW THE SCORE BOOKS

Know The Score Books is the UK's most exciting and innovative sports publishing house. It was set up in 2005 with the mission to provide readers with the opportunity to delve behind the 21st century hype and rediscover the passionate and often astonishingly crazy world of football and re-evaluate the reasons why we all love this great game so dearly.

www.knowthescorebooks.com

KNOW THE SCORE BOOKS PUBLICATIONS

CULT HEROES	Author	ISBN
CHELSEA	Leo Moynihan	1-905449-00-3
NEWCASTLE	Dylan Younger	1-905449-03-8
SOUTHAMPTON	Jeremy Wilson	1-905449-01-1
WEST BROM	Simon Wright	1-905449-02-X

MATCH OF MY LIFE	Editor	ISBN
ENGLAND WORLD CUP	Louis Massarella & Leo Moynihan	1-905449-52-6
EUROPEAN CUP FINALS	Ben Lyttleton	1-905449-57-7
FA CUP FINALS (1953-1969)	David Saffer	1-905449-53-4
FULHAM	Michael Heatley	1-905449-51-8
LEEDS	David Saffer	1-905449-54-2
LIVERPOOL	Leo Moynihan	1-905449-50-X
SHEFFIELD UNITED	Nick Johnson	1-905449-62-3
STOKE CITY	Simon Lowe	1-905449-55-0
SUNDERLAND	Rob Mason	1-905449-60-7
SPURS	Matt Allen & Louis Massarella	1-905449-58-5
WOLVES	Simon Lowe	1-905449-56-9

HARRY HARRIS	Author	ISBN
HARRY HARRIS WORLD CUP DIARY	Harry Harris	1-905449-90-9
HOLD THE BACK PAGE	Harry Harris	1-905449-91-7

AUTOBIOGRAPHY	Author	ISBN
TACKLES LIKE A FERRET (England Cover)	Paul Parker	1-905449-47-X
TACKLES LIKE A FERRET (Manchester United Cover)	Paul Parker	1-905449-46-1

FOOTBALL FICTION	Author	ISBN
BURKSEY The Autobiography of a Football God	Peter Morfoot	1-905449-49-6

CRICKET	Author	ISBN
MOML: THE ASHES	Sam Pilger & Rob Wightman	1-905449-63-1
SMILE LIKE U MEAN IT	Paul Smith	1-905449-45-3

FORTHCOMING PUBLICATIONS IN 2007

CULT HEROES	Author	ISBN
DERBY	David McVay	978-1-905449-06-4
MANCHESTER CITY	David Clayton	978-1-905449-05-7
RANGERS	Paul Smith	978-1-905449-07-1

MATCH OF MY LIFE	Editor	ISBN
MANCHESTER UNITED	Sam Pilger	1-905449-59-3
BOLTON WANDERERS	David Saffer	978-1-905449-64-4
FA CUP FINALS (1970-1989)	David Saffer	978-1-905449-65-1
HULL	Grahame Lloyd	978-1-905449-66-8

GENERAL FOOTBALL	Editor	ISBN
OUTCASTS The Lands FIFA Forgot	Steve Menary	978-1-905449-31-6
PARISH TO PLANET A History of Football	Dr Eric Midwinter	978-1-905449-30-9
MY PREMIERSHIP DIARY Reading's Season in the Premiership	Marcus Hahnemann	978-1-905449-33-0

PUB BORE: 1001 incredible facts to bore your mates with		ISBN
MANCHESTER UNITED		978-1-905449-80-4
NEWCASTLE UNITED		978-1-905449-81-1
SUNDERLAND		978-1-905449-82-8

CRICKET	Author	ISBN
THE 2006/7 ASHES IN PICTURES	Andrew Searle	978-1-905449-44-6
GROVEL! The 1976 West Indies Tour of England	David Tossell	978-1-905449-43-9
MY AUTOBIOGRAPHY	Shaun Udal	978-1-905449-42-2